PAC

A SHORT HISTORY OF ITA

A
SHORT HISTORY OF
ITALIAN LITERATURE

BY

J. H. WHITFIELD

with a new chapter from 1922 to the present
by J. R. Woodhouse

Manchester University Press

© J. H. Whitfield 1960, 1962, 1976, 1980
Chapter 16 © J. R. Woodhouse 1980

First published by Penguin Books Ltd 1960; reprinted 1969
Cased edition by Cassell & Co. Ltd 1962
Reprinted by Greenwood Press Inc. 1976
This edition published 1980 by
Manchester University Press
Oxford Road, Manchester M13 9PL

British Library cataloguing-in-publication data

Whitfield, John Humphreys
    A short history of Italian literature.
    – 2nd ed.
    1. Italian literature – History and criticism
    I. Title
    850′.9   PQ4038
    ISBN 0–7190–0782–8

The publishers and printers regret that owing to unavoidable technical difficulties the quality of reproduction in this edition is not quite up to the usual standards.

Printed in Great Britain by
Redwood Burn Limited
Trowbridge & Esher

Contents

Introduction

TIRABOSCHI began the habit of writing the history of Italian literature, and had material for fourteen quarto volumes. His was a history of authors, more than an account of works; and for our purpose he might profitably have given to the consideration of these the space that went to Latin or Etruscan origins. Since Tiraboschi there have been two centuries and more of vigorous production, and the material grows embarrassingly. This is especially true for a *short* historian. For a short history may be only a long list, and we are familiar with those compilations with half a page of biography, half a page of synopsis, and for the major writers an occasional line of commendation. But as the boundaries of literature are uncertain all its histories subsist by omission. And a short history of Italian literature has good right to achieve viability by this means. For it is sixty years since Richard Garnett published the last one written by an Englishman in 1898. Since then much has changed, and other generations look to Italian literature as a new world. In such conditions it is natural to think in terms of clear outlines, and to look most hard at what is most significant.

But there are difficulties before beginning on the subject. At certain obvious points the history of Italian literature fuses with the history of Italy. You cannot read the *Divine Comedy* unless you have breathed the atmosphere of Florence and of Italy in Dante's times; you will misread Machiavelli if you leave out the context of the early sixteenth century; and who can divorce Mazzini and the rest from the political struggle of the Risorgimento – the main, sometimes the only, platform for their writings? And this is complicated by the fact that Italy has no unitarian history till 1860. Instead, a fragmentation, often with the bitterest of rivalries, left Italy divided politically, and culturally. In the sixteenth century that culture nearly became a national one, but then the political impotence of over two centuries prevented cultural unity from being sealed in nationhood.

In these conditions the lamp of literature burnt fitfully, with a regional brilliance which may find no comparable echo elsewhere; and districts, like Tuscany, which had borne the noblest part, lost their pre-eminence, having transmitted their vitality. It is in this

7

theme that the first outlines are best seen. The first flowering – and it is characteristically a poetic one – is that associated with the court of Frederick II, in the first half of the thirteenth century. Here was the focus for a native form of poetry based on the *amour courtois* of Provence. Frederick II's writ holds for the Kingdom of Naples (and Sicily), and it is by Dante's baptism that this becomes the 'Sicilian' School. And just as its prototype, in Provence, had been extinguished with the Albigensian Crusade, so with the death of Frederick in 1250, and the defeat of the Hohenstaufens finally with Manfred and Conradin, the contribution of the South ceases for two centuries. Central Italy takes up the torch, with Guittone d'Arezzo, and with the first undertones of Dante's poetic theme from Guido Guinizelli of Bologna. Then Florence assumes that cultural primacy of Italy, to which, so proud the moment, there was annexed as appanage the primacy of Europe also.

The architect of this ascendancy is Dante, and his vast achievement establishes the language which will become the inheritance of all Italy. Boccaccio then occupies the ground floor, Petrarch the *piano nobile*. But Petrarch, like Dante, is an exile from Florence; and unlike Dante, an exile from his birth. His poetry clings to the linguistic mould already set, his mind runs on to different attitudes, and his Latin correspondence revives the *studia humanitatis* for Italy and Europe. It is his heirs in Florence who set the seal upon this process. The moment is that of the threat from Giangaleazzo Visconti, the despot of Milan, and in this struggle Florentine scholars jettison the old legends on the foundation of their city at the hands of Caesar (ideas which fitted with Dante's respect for universal Roman monarchy), rediscovered its origins in the Roman Republic, and made of it the predestined champion of republican ideals. Giangaleazzo died conveniently, and at the beginning of the fifteenth century the civic pride of Florence in the ability of all her sons finds release, and in its impetus makes the new Athens of the modern world. The practical value of this new humanism, often denied by nineteenth-century scholarship, is written in the rich cultural scene of Florence.

Even so, the Quattrocento in Florence is not to one pattern. When Medici rule virtually supplants the republic the active life becomes less advertised. This is the moment of Ficino, and neo-Platonism, and what more suitable, from a new ruler's point of view, than the assertion of the contemplative ideal? The first half of the Quattrocento had seen humanism personified in men like

Leonardo Bruni, Chancellor of the Florentine Republic, and from such as he it is a downward step to a courtier-scholar like Ficino. Meanwhile the early Quattrocento had not denied the vernacular, though it had been understandably predominantly Latin in expression and enthusiasm. The second half of the fifteenth century is the heir to an enrichment from the classics in the revival of Italian writing. Then, after Lorenzo and Politian, comes the Florentine Republic, and the return to the guiding principles of Leonardo Bruni. It is the moment of Machiavelli and of Guicciardini, and the difference between the two is accentuated by the fact that one writes while the struggle is still unresolved, the other after the flood, and after the fall. Machiavelli dies in 1527, the Florentine Republic gives place finally to a principality in 1530. Florence has ceased to be the mainspring of Italian literature.

Her successor had been previously prepared. In Florence itself the wayward genius of Pulci had brought the old themes of Charlemagne out of the spoken into the written world. But independently of him the same process takes place in Ferrara, and it is Boiardo, with the *Orlando Innamorato*, who marks the first step to the establishment of Ferrara as the epicentre for the multifarious Cinquecento. His is still an overture, and there is an indefeasible northern, dialectal, tinge to Boiardo's writing. But the moment of Florence passing is also that of Florence triumphant, with the linguistic supremacy of Tuscany as the writ for Italy. The theorist is Venetian, Pietro Bembo, but his first and greatest pupil is Lodovico Ariosto, inheritor of the matter which Boiardo left unfinished, and to which Ariosto gave a Tuscan surface. The *Orlando Furioso* is the most immediately popular of the great works of the Cinquecento, and its revision, down to the definitive edition of 1532, upon the principles of Bembo hands to all Italy what might have been the language only of one part. That Italy was ready for this literary unification is shown by the fact that others who will exert strong influence, as Sannazaro or Castiglione (in spite of a polemical lombardism in outward attitude) move in the same direction, if at differing speeds. Boiardo and Ariosto are the glories of Ferrara; and the latter also, starting from the Este's enthusiasm for Latin comedy, brings an imitation of this formula into the Italian tradition. Molière is round the corner from that departure, and Ferrara becomes the centre for the literary theatre. With Ariosto, comedy; but soon, with Speroni and Giraldi, tragedy, and the theory of tragedy; then with Tasso and Guarini, tragicomedy. And Tasso completes the trilogy of the epic for Ferrara. His *Gerusalemme Liberata* is both a culmination, and a swan-song. Tasso dies in 1595, Ferrara ceases to be an independent duchy in 1597, absorbed by Clement VIII into the orbit of the Church. For Ferrara there remains a mouldering decline, and in poetry there are no echoes, no successors. Like the Sicilian School, the epic of Ferrara does not survive the moment of political defeat.

The banner-poem of the seventeenth century was written by a Neapolitan, and printed in Paris in 1623. The *Adonis* of Marino marks with a blaze of fireworks the eclipse of Italian poetry from the scene of Europe; and though he gives his name to a movement it has been, till modern efforts at reappraisal, attainted with the stigma of extravagance and decadence. Hereafter a lethargy, not in production, for the seventeenth century lets loose as large a flood as did the Cinquecento, but in vitality. Not for nothing is the great name of the Seicento the scientific one of Galileo. Arcadia is born to restore natural simplicity, only to slither and subside in petty conventionalism and pretty sound. The rescue comes from provinces that had contributed little to the literary sum. But when Austria replaces Spain as the dominant power in Lombardy the natural richness of the region is allowed to give the Milanese its obvious lead. But regeneration comes from dis-ease, and a Lombard peasant brings moral fibre to supplement the thinness of Arcadian verse. Alongside Parini are other northern voices: two Piedmontese, Baretti and Alfieri, bring into the circle of Italian literature a part of Italy so far almost unrepresented. But both take pains to *dispiedmontize* themselves, and Alfieri in particular, author of this verb, took refuge in the harsh and the unmusical in order to shun the insipidities of Arcadia.

We are on the threshold of the Risorgimento, and the nineteenth century, opening with the Lombard voice of Manzoni, will finally inaugurate the era of Italian literature, to take the place of the literature of the regions of Italy. But it is a noticeable phenomenon that when the regions merge in a united Italy the regional author and the regional novel comes into view. Verga is the foundation-member, and with his pictures of humble life in Sicily there returns, in different form, a voice that had been heard at the beginning. Florence, Ferrara, and Milan (to make a focus for the north), with Sicily as both *hors-d'œuvre* and epilogue: it will be apparent from this brief sketch how separatist the tradition has remained, and how much dependent on the hinterland of history. From the fall of the Roman Empire Italy knows no unity. In the Middle Ages, two aspirants to universal authority: the papacy and the revived imperial power of Charlemagne's successors; underneath, the rising vigour of city-states, elbowing their way to independence. When the Free Communes of Lombardy defeat the Emperor Barbarossa at Legnano in 1176 the destiny of Italy is cast. Venice, Pisa, Genoa, Florence – to look no further – spread their commerce, build their wealth. These cities begin as communes, end sometimes as *signorie* (principalities). In the south the one Kingdom, that of Naples (and Sicily), known from its uniqueness as the Regno, straddles a region. When its ruler is on the verge of adding northern Italy to his dominions the papacy appeals to some other power to prevent the trap closing, and the Patrimony of St Peter from being squeezed out of existence. Thus in the year after Dante's birth the Angevins were summoned to prevent Manfred from realizing the ambitions of his father, and the tombstone of Benevento (1266) replaces Hohenstaufens by Anjou. Contending dynasties, and there is Aragon to add, drain the resources of Naples, and explain the intermittence of its cultural achievement.

Elsewhere it is faction, and tyranny, which is its outcome, that is the danger. The greatness of Florence is bound up with its commercial strength: the staples, banking, wool, and silk. But its history is entangled with the feudal nobility who hold the castles of Tuscany, and who can cut the arteries of trade. Florence razes their strongholds, forces residence within the city walls. But this success presents two difficulties: a new circle of hostilities, of communes this time, as Pisa, Siena, or Arezzo; and within the city, a body of men with revenue from great estates, accustomed to respect, anxious for authority. The feuds which rack the Florence of Dante's time are internecine quarrels of the Grandi, ambitious of mastery against the rising power of the Popolo Grasso, the bourgeoisie enriched by commerce. The closing years of the thirteenth century see the clipping of the wings for the nobles, and the institutions which seal the supremacy of the other side. The Priors of the Arts, the *Ordinamenti di Giustizia*, are the twin symbols of this victory. In it lies a danger: these nobles had the military virtues, and after their abasement Florence will have to rely on mercenaries to fight her battles. *Hinc illae lachrymae*, and the bitter words of Machiavelli. But meanwhile, the bitter struggle of Blacks and Whites, and the exile among the latter of Dante Alighieri. The *Comedy* is linked ideally with the Jubilee of 1300, but its birthright is in the bitter year which follows, and Dante's hankering for an ideal whole solution must never be divorced from the fact that he never had a fractional one to hand.

Though Dante was sacrificed, Florence survived the crisis, and continued on the settled course which led, appropriately, to the principality of the Medici: merchant-princes before they were princes. And the basis broadened till the State of Florence comprised most of Tuscany. So the Italian scene crystallizes to that pattern of a few major States (Venice, Milan, Florence, the Papacy, and Naples), whose precarious balance just survives the fifteenth century. At the beginning that clash of Florence and Milan which served to set the course: if the Visconti had won, there might have been an Italian Kingdom, at the expense of Florence. But in a moment of inspiration Giangaleazzo died (1402), and Florence breathed freely in the new atmosphere of civic humanism. The galaxy of names, from Bruni and Alberti on, is an eloquent witness to the glories of the Quattrocento. And the policy of balance, often associated solely with Lorenzo, was implicit in the situation.

The nostalgic picture, painted by Guicciardini, of Italy just prior to 1494, may not correspond in every detail to reality. But seen in conjunction with the cultural scene it is right in its atmosphere. With the coming of Charles VIII the house collapses, not because it was built on rotten foundations, and deserved retribution (the old thesis of the splendid, and immoral, Renascence), but because none of its walls were jointed, and by dishesion all were equally undone. From 1494 to 1559 the struggle, of foreigners for dynastic succession in Naples and Milan, and then of Charles V against Francis I, shakes the peninsula. The epigraph of Michelangelo, in answer to an epigram on his statue *Night*, fits like a cap:

> Sleep is dear to me, and dearer yet
> My being stone, while loss and shame remain.
> Neither to see, nor hear, is fortunate,
> Speak softly that I may not wake again.

The beginning of the century had seen, with Machiavelli, Ariosto, Castiglione, the fruition of the Quattrocento; now Guicciardini is the historian of what was; Michelangelo is tortured by the present; Vasari chronicles the triumph of art, at the moment of decline. Ferrara keeps its independence, and its literary importance. Venice alone, in spite of cruel battering in 1508-9, recovers its territory, its trade, and its prosperity. But the fruits thereof are rather Titian, Veronese, Tintoretto, Palladio, than in prose or poetry. Venice is the great emporium of the new world of printed books – no less important than the New World we write in capitals – but not a literary centre in the same way as Florence. Yet, by this survival she is the protagonist of Italian liberty. Out of the clash between French and Habsburgs comes victory for the latter. Charles V is virtual master of Italy, but not of Venice. And though Venice has cruel moments to traverse in the next two centuries, and though she will survive in the eighteenth only at the expense of her initiative, yet this abiding independence accounts for the vitality of the Venetian Settecento. Piazzetta, Tiepolo, Canaletto, Guardi, Piranesi, or Canova: they are all Venetian, and this is the last flowering of the old Renascence in its last stronghold. That accounts for what is valid, and invalid, in the last art of Venice. And her authors, as Gozzi or Goldoni, though they do not compare in quality, are in like case.

Elsewhere, quiescence under despotism. Spanish viceroys at Milan, Naples, Palermo; little courts which had shone with a light unequal to their territory, as Urbino under the Montefeltro, Ferrara with the Estes, wither in the clutches of the Papal State; or like Mantua, sink with the sack of 1630, losing at one stroke the treasures of the centuries. Had not Rome also suffered cruelly, in 1527? And if she rose again, there was an irremediable *diminutio capitis* after the loss of the northern provinces of her spiritual empire. We are coming to the picture which beginners of Italian literature know from the background to the *Promessi Sposi*. The ink still runs as copiously upon the printed page, but the names make no impression in European literature. And when one rises to baptize an era, it is court poetry, in an alien clime. Metastasio is the poet, Vienna is the venue, just as Vienna has succeeded to Madrid as mistress of Lombardy. This is the moment for the *melodramma*, in its rightful sense. *Mere sound*, said De Sanctis scornfully, for both Metastasio and Arcadia. But from the Vienna of Joseph II came the new wind of reform, reviving especially the Milanese and Tuscany. Nevertheless, no major changes break the gentle sleep till the rude wind of 1796 blows unexpectedly. The French Revolution, like a tornado broken from its moorings, raged through Italy, shaking the breath from dying dynasties. That had its logic, if not its justice. The King of Naples was brother-in-law to Marie-Antoinette, and ready to protect the divine rights of sovereigns. The ruler of Savoy was more eager than avenging, hoping to add a slice or two to his boundaries. And since Austria held the Milanese, here was a French option against the arch-enemy. Once the way is open for the ragged armies the *via crucis* of the placid Italian scene begins. Republics rise, fall, rise, and are amalgamated; the magic formulas are brandished, and shown meaningless, and the oldest of republics – which had given a sister's welcome to the French one – is harried to destruction, handed over in a parcel to Austria at Campoformio. There is no unarmed neutrality of sheep in front of lions; or, at least, no profitable one. The Empire in France brings the Kingdom in Italy, the Papacy is humiliated, then expropriated. Soon the whole of continental Italy is arrayed in one way or another under the French, and the basis laid unconsciously for the future. Milan as a new capital knows glory, and receives embellishment, and the lifeblood is set flowing elsewhere.

In 1815 Napoleon, doomed since 1812, falls and takes his system with him. For a brief moment his henchmen, Beauharnais and Murat, manoeuvre for survival as independent kings. Then the Congress of Vienna calls back the past, and the obscurantist rulers emerge to reconstruct pathetically what was before, at the expense of all that had replaced it. And Austria, straddling now Lombardy and Venetia, stands at the ready to defeat all liberal aspirations. Even to Naples, in the first insurrection of 1820, her white-coats march to uphold the trade-union of kings. Into the struggle all the energies, literary and political, are poured. By various steps, through various rebuffs, the heights are climbed. The formulas of the Carbonari, of Mazzini, of the neo-Guelphs, vanish in the conflict. The pale Charles-Albert of Savoy redeems himself, but loses his throne, and it seems clear that Italy cannot do it by herself when Cavour and Garibaldi bring unification for the major part of Italy. 1860 is the crucial date: till then, success, even through failure. After that, failure, even through success. The missing parts, Venice and Rome, are added in humiliating circumstances. Cavour's death leaves the new Parliament of Italy to the place-seekers and the incompetent. The southern problem is shelved, not solved; and when the timorous new boy ventures on a foreign policy it is to end in the wrong camp, the *quantité négligeable* of the Triple Alliance, with Prussia and ... Austria as seniors. The appetite for colonies, when at last awakened, leads to the acquisition of deserts, and the disaster of Adowa. The nineteenth century ends on a depressing note, with parliamentary corruption, bank scandals, and socialistic ferment in the south. We may take as a symbol of the unheroic ending of the Risorgimento the assassination of Umberto I on 29 July 1900. What is left then, before events and movements that are in the minds of all, is a dozen years of parliamentary management, the age of Giolitti and of patient economic progress. But by then literature and history are separable entities.

CHAPTER I

Italian Lyric Poetry: from the Sicilian School to Petrarch

IN a legal document of 960 there is inserted the spoken testimony, *Sao ko kelle terre* ... and in its sharp differentiation from the contaminated Latin in which it is enshrined it makes clear that the vernacular exists as a new entity. But it will be long before it acquires a literary use. And when it does, it will be in curious circumstances of subordination. For when the poetry of Provence overflows into northern Italy at the beginning of the thirteenth century it finds no competition in themes or language. The feudal society of Provence had evolved a poetry of chivalrous love, with the troubadour as vassal to his lady, owing homage, and receiving only disdain and cruelty. Is she not, as *châtellaine*, out of reach? From her comes all worth, to her goes all praise; the rest is faithful suffering. In this exaltation there lies ready the promise of the ethereal poetry of Dante and his circle; but in its imitation also is the threat of artificiality. In north Italy this poetry circulates in its own guise, and is imitated by Italians without change of theme or tongue. The troubadours frequent Italian courts, Savoy, Monferrato, the Malaspina, the Estes, even the bloody tyrant, Ezzelino da Romano, Lord of Padua, smiled on occasion at their art. And Italians tried their skill with them: as Rambertino Buvalelli of Bologna (d. 1221), who left seven poems in Provençal; or Lanfranco Cigala, who chose not to imitate the *ric trobar*, but the simpler side, and who begins with the senses to end in idealism, and with poems to the Virgin. In notoriety Lanfranco is overshadowed by a name to which two poets have given prominence; and though few now may read with Browning Sordello's story none can escape the influence of Dante, or forget the mag-

nanimous spirit of Sordello in the early *Purgatorio*. At Genoa
Bonifacio Calvi, at Venice Bartolomeo Zorzi extend this
picture of Provençal imitation.

But in the South these themes can operate without the
language from which they came. Frederick II married in
1208 Costanza, sister to the Count of Provence, and before she
died in 1222 she had brought to the Magna Curia the graces
of Provençal poetry. And in the south another strand from
France was interwoven. Had not the Normans also conquered
Sicily? The poetry of northern France is echoed in the
Sicilian School, and may account there for that more popular
side which used to be thought autochthonous. Its favourite
themes (the *innamorata*, the woman abandoned, ill-mated, the
girl wanting a husband, the dawn-song, or the altercation) are
echoed, mainly in a courtly form. But the more vigorous and
more memorable poems of the Sicilian School, as *Giammai
non mi conforto* of Rinaldo d'Aquino, *Rosa fresca aulentissima*,
the solitary *contrasto* which forms a dramatic entity, by the
enigmatic Cielo, or Ciullo d'Alcamo, or *Donna di voi mi
lamento* of Giacomino Pugliese belong to this tradition.
Alongside it comes the tide of Provençal imitation in a
language which may have been dialectal to begin with, but
modified first by the exigencies of a court which drew on
much of Italy, and also by transcription. The most important
manuscript of the 'Sicilian' School (Dante's adjective for this
court phenomenon) is the work of Tuscan scribes who carried
out an unconscious transformation in language. Even Frederick and his sons (Re Enzo, Re Federigo), or his famous
chancellor, Pier della Vigna, are credited with compositions
in this manner: though it is clear that the relations of an
absolute monarch, in a semi-oriental court, were not really
those of liegeman to a sovereign lady. Though this may not
apply to the more substantial poets, as Jacopo da Lentino,
Jacopo Mostacci, Arrigo Testa, Percivalle Doria, or the two,
Giacomino Pugliese and Rinaldo d'Aquino, whom we have
seen as exponents of the other trend, it is symptomatic of a
discrepancy.

Where the matter matters least, the form receives the

emphasis. Not only does the *canzone* (with some Northern French, as well as Provençal, elements) derive from this connexion, but the technicalities tend to have importance at the expense of sentiment. Since it is a formula that is being prepared, rather than an achievement which needs appraisal, the invention of the sonnet form, credited with a little question-mark to Jacopo da Lentino (for it may have been a casual amalgamation of two *strambotti*) is as important as the inheritance of the *canzone*. Out of this prosody, and with this set of conventions and poetic capital, and with for good measure the tricks and faults of the troubadours, will come the European lyric; and after Petrarch it is, as petrarchism, largely the tricks which are most apparent. At the same time as the freshness and originality of the Provençal inspiration go, so does the manner become marked, the apparatus over-prominent.

In a celebrated passage of *Purgatorio* (XXIV, 55–7) Dante swept into the Sicilian School poets like Guittone d'Arezzo and Bonagiunta da Lucca, who form the Tuscan bridge to his own new departure. And it is Guittone (*c.* 1225–*c.* 1294) who is most often, and most harshly, damned for excessive imitation of Provence. Dante could not forgive him his uncouth dialect; and the modern critics have seen Guittone abounding in the artificial devices and the hermeticism of the *trobar clus*. Here all is alambicated, and the charm of Sicilian poetry lost in formal imitation and exaggeration. There are two parts to Guittone's poetry, since he became a convert in 1260 to the new Knights of the Virgin Mary, those who quickly won the nickname of *cavalieri gaudenti*. Guittone belongs to their better purpose, but switched the direction of his verse, using the same devices for moral and religious poems, usually assessed as being as tedious as before. But this is not quite just, and in spite of Dante's efforts to demolish Guittone's reputation, and of the gulf that divides the two, it is Dante who springs at times to mind. It may be from a detail, as with St Dominic the *agricola* of the Lord, anticipating Dante in *Paradiso* XII. But it may also be a question of mood, as in the lines

> Ogni cosa fu solo all'uom creata,
> E l'uom non a dormire né a mangiare,
> Ma solamente a dirittura fare.

In bulk Guittone is tedious and patchy, but there is no other who can rouse such comparisons, and he deserves more consideration than he gets.

Guittone is sometimes thought of as the poet of transition, but there are others having right to this title. First, Chiaro Davanzati (second half thirteenth c.), a Tuscan follower of Guittone, treating similar subjects in the same heavy and scholastic style, but graduating finally, under the influence of Guinizelli, to appear in his best poem, *La splendiente luce, quando appare*, as the gentle poet. Or allied to this in mood, Ciacco dell'Anguillaia in *O gemma leziosa*. With these Rustico di Filippi (*c.* 1230–40–*c.* 1291–5), close to them in love poetry, but beginning also an odd naturalistic style, burlesque and satirical, bourgeois not chivalrous in tone. But Rustico is overshadowed by Cecco Angiolieri of Siena (*c.* 1260–*c.* 1312–13), a gamester with few scruples, who led a noisy life of pleasure, frustrated by the avarice of a wealthy father, harried by an ugly, quarrelsome wife. Cecco has more wit, and spleen, than Rustico. He is the Rutebeuf, or the Villon, of Italy, though he lacks the importance of the latter. On money he is amusing:

> Cosí è l'uomo che non ha denari
> Come l'uccel quand'è vivo pelato;

and even more efficacious in the melancholy of poverty:

> I'ho tutte le cose ch'io non voglio
> e non ho punto di quel che mi piace.

And he is notoriously most memorable in his perverse sentiments against his parents (*Se fossi foco arderei il mondo*), and in biting satire against his wife, as in the sonnet on her morning air before her make-up's on.

Hidden in Guittone one can find the idea that nobility is not from descent, but an individual quality; but this, one of the strands of the new poetry, is usually credited to Guido

Guinizelli of Bologna (*c.* 1230–*c.* 1275). While Enzo Re, taken captive by the Bolognese in 1249, languishes as captive, typifying the slow death of the Sicilian School, a new poetry arises, with a more noble conception of love and woman, and a new idealism. And the *clef de voûte* of the new style of Dante may be thought to lie in this concept of nobility – best expressed in *Convivio* IV, in the canzone *Le dolci rime d'amor ch'io solia* and its commentary. Neither birth nor riches, but the gentle heart: and *gentle* looses itself from *gens* (from noble stock), to acquire the nuances we know. For this programme the best-known of Guinizelli's poems is the manifesto, *A cor gentil ripara sempre amore*, its lesson repeated by Dante himself in the *Vita Nuova, Amore e cor gentil sono una cosa*. We must not exaggerate for Guinizelli: his poems are few, some are decidedly in the manner of Guittone, to whom he dedicates a sonnet. The group that can be brought round his major *canzone* is slight indeed, and the old ideas of philosophical novelties are to be taken at some discount. The main novelty is in the penultimate stanza of *A cor gentil*, where the lady takes the place of the Angels which preside over the spheres. Through her as intermediary the lover will receive his good. That puts her on a lofty pedestal; and its relation to the poetry of Dante is apparent. Is not the name of Beatrice *she who blesses*? But in Guinizelli, what use of this innovation? He has the old psychology, anxiety for love to be requited, sorrow at indifference, hope or despair, entreaty for pity, grief at abandonment, and the desire to end with death the sufferings of love. Nor is he alone without much use for this ornamental novelty. The group so long held together by Dante's phrase of the *sweet new style* is for the most part also innocent of this attitude. It is Dante, and this in the austerer world of the *Commedia*, who is the heir and the proprietor of this conception of which Guinizelli happens to be author.

With the *Vita Nuova* we approach a major figure, in the minor key. Here reader and writer are at cross purposes. We cannot help ourselves from spying on the facts of Dante's life, and questioning the identity, even the reality, of Beatrice; and Dante wraps in mystery his love for her, giving an atmosphere

of dreams to what may have been reality. At nine years old
Dante Alighieri (1265–1321) sees, and loves, a Beatrice who
may have been Beatrice Portinari; nine years later she greets
him, but on the rumour of his love for the 'screen-lady' she
withdraws her salutation, and Dante is reduced to praise
alone; he foresees her death, it happens, and the city becomes
a peopled solitude; he forgets Beatrice in the consolation
offered by a *donna gentile*, seen first as recalling Beatrice, then
for her own sake; and ends with that intention to celebrate
the praise of Beatrice *by saying of her what had never been said of
any woman* which presupposes the apotheosis in the *Comedy*.
So slight the web, so shrouded all the outlines, as Dante a
short while after Beatrice's death looks back upon his youthful
life. And out of this how many problems rise! One thing
seems stable, the date of Beatrice's death is 1290, and the
Vita Nuova is written a few years after that. In form it is a
gathering of related poems, some of which antedate the book;
and these are set in a prose commentary which gives an
alternating pulse. For the verse tradition has its history, but
prose is still shy and awkward, and brings arid divisions of
the matter as well as analysis of the sentiments.

Let us look to the problems inherent in this brief synopsis.
With the reality of Beatrice there is bound up that of the
screen-lady (not one, but two), and of the *donna gentile*. The
first may seem mysterious now we have a different screen, with
other ladies to inhabit it; but she comes naturally in the
tradition of courtly love, where love must be concealed for
fear of evil tongues. So Dante gazes in church at Beatrice, and
in between sits one whom rumour makes the object of his
looking. And when he writes for her upon conventional
themes are his affections a pretence? And did Beatrice with-
draw her greeting just on rumour, or because Dante had
withdrawn his love? And is the love for the *donna gentile*
another interlude, or should we interpret her as Dante did later
in the *Convivio*, where she is made the symbol of philosophy?
And how does all this answer to the accusations which
Beatrice brings against Dante on the mount of Purgatory?
or to those of Cavalcanti in his sonnet on a shameful period in

Dante's life? or to the remarks of Boccaccio as biographer on the sensual temperament of Dante? and what of Dante's wife, Gemma Donati, once thought of as a consolation-prize for Beatrice lost, but married to him in the 1280s?

The last question can have the clearest answer. The tradition of courtly love is out of wedlock, and it is the process of idealization, parallel with mariolatry, that lifts it up and rescues it from mere adultery. St Bernard trembled like a lover before the Virgin, reproached himself with sins to expiate, saw her main quality as humility, and proclaimed his owing everything, ineffable joys and consolation in this wretched life, to her; and so also Dante can enter a new world of sentiments in his cult for Beatrice. Gemma, wife, mother of Dante's children, not sharer in his exile, remains a mute both in the period of youthful love, and afterwards, through all the *Comedy*. For the other questions, there are presumptions, and no safe answers; nor does this diminish the tantalizing quality of the *Vita Nuova*. And if this is the sweet new style, is it operative throughout the book, even in the commonplace opening sonnet, or in the Guittonian ones? For though the sonnet had started right in shape it had received improvement, intrusive lines, a tail. And the young Dante pays his entrance-fee to poetry in this archaic fashion. It has been customary, on what seems a reasonable interpretation of Bonagiunta's words in *Purgatorio* XXIV on the new verse beginning *Donne ch'avete intelletto d'Amore*, to see a break within the *Vita Nuova*, where Dante finds at last his way to Love as a beatific, not a torment. Even if those words may bear a simpler meaning, some special solemnity will still attach to this *canzone*, long thought of as crucial by Dante's own confession, and in whatever way we look at it, still a change in his direction.

After the questions, what of the content? Dante controls the widest range in Italian poetry: soon we shall find him wanting to be harsh, and meanwhile sweetness is his goal. He finds it in the elimination of the technical pirouetting of Guittone's style, and in the warm limpidity of some of his sonnets (*Tanto gentile e tanto onesta pare*, *Vede perfettamente onne salute*) he surpasses what has gone before. The *Vita Nuova* remains a feather-bed in which one sinks, but the feathers are often winged. Outside this unity of prose and verse there are the unincluded *rime*, sometimes, as with the *rime pietrose*, offering the same problems in a new context (for with the harshness there is a sensual note quite absent from the poems for Beatrice). And we may find occasionally a pointer forwards to the *Comedy*, or a line which lights graphically the figure of Dante himself, as that on exile counted honour,

l'esilio che m'è dato onor mi tegno.

We may legitimately glide past the minor members of the *dolce stil*, as Lapo Gianni, or Gianni Alfani. With them we have a superficial, decorative, treatment of the theme, and residues of the old manner. It is Guido Cavalcanti (*c.* 1259–1300), the first of Dante's friends, though he cannot quite be bent to Dante's way of thinking, who stands with him as the major representative of the new manner. He also set out a programme in a solemn *canzone*, the more notorious than celebrated *Donna me prega*; and it has left uncertainty on his philosophy of love. Once or twice he strikes a note that might be Dante's, as in the sonnet *Chi è questa che ven, ch'ogn'uom la mira*. But it is his grief which springs from unrequited love which fills his poems, and gives them poignancy. And when those torments temporarily cease it is the brief pleasure from her pity that he sings. Dante finds sweetness in the elimination of the senses, Guido in the kindness (would it were!) of his lady. Cavalcanti passes from a thoughtful youth (alone among the tombs, whence came those whisperings, echoed by Boccaccio, that he sought to prove *that God was not*) to early manhood in the first poetry of love and praise, to the turbulent period of political strife, to the last sighs of exile. Always there is with him a note that is his own: we feel the strength of his desires, rarely controlled, and of his will. He may be sweet as Cino da Pistoia, quarrelsome as the haughty Corso Donati, proud and disdainful as Farinata. There is no unity to his loves, except his grief: and he is most successful in his favourite form, the *ballata*. In 1300 his friend, maybe his former friend, Dante, is party to his exile with the heads of both the factions to malarial Sarzana. As he had written in illness from Toulouse *Perch'i'no spero di tornar giammai*, death closes his poetry, and is the most insistent of its chords. A tinge of atheism we may deduce from Dante's treatment of him in *Inferno* x; but an elder than Dante, who can speak sternly to him (as in that sonnet on *la vil tua vita*), and one not unworthy to stand as equal by the Dante of the *Vita Nuova*.

Following on the heels of Cavalcanti comes Cino da Pistoia (*c.* 1265–1336), significantly outliving his exact contemporary, Dante. For Cino forms the link between Dante and Petrarch. In him are manifold traces of the *dolce stil*, especially in that rejection of the Provençalisms and Guittonian complications whose disappearance counts for much of the refreshment which its readers feel. He comes near too at times to the daring novelty of Guinizelli in the elevation of the *donna angelicata*, and echoes that essential spiritual note of the sweet new style. And on the other side Cino inherits from Cavalcanti that opposite note which disturbs the unity of the *dolce stil*. For Guido, as we have seen, love was more often a torment than a beatific, his most personal note, one of anguish. Cino echoes this more plaintively, and with a gentle melancholy. It is only as a decorative theme for Cavalcanti and for Cino that love is a virtue which ennobles man. It is in reality a desire which calls for satisfaction in the sight of the lady, and, unsatisfied, leads to despair. Now in Cavalcanti's poetry these two dissonant elements are juxtaposed, but not resolved. In Cino there appears as an important novelty that these conflicting strands, hitherto unyielding to each other, are at a few points contaminated. Cino achieves a synthesis between two opposites, and opens a new field for poetry. Bittersweet, pleasure in melancholy: before Cino poetry was in the position of primitive painting. It could speak clearly, because it had the primitive's simplicity of colour and outline. Cino introduces a new tension between opposing elements, and offers a new horizon. After this the lyric may sin by sophistication, but it will not be limited by naïvety, or inexperience.

Cino puts off in part the awkwardness of the medieval lyric, and prepares a mood which will become an overtone with Petrarch. And there are other correspondences: thus his desire for solitude is a prelude to one of Petrarch's most splendid sonnets, *Solo e pensoso i piú deserti campi*. Cino is, of course, Cino, and Petrarch, Petrarch. This means that this prelude to a new poetry is in a minor key, and in a small number only of the unordered compositions given to him. But this fact does not prevent another phenomenon of some importance giving prominence to this pre-Petrarchan note. This is that Cino has learnt at times to end with a resonant line, closing the sonnet dramatically, and deliberately. Here one can only think that the process of ripening has led to a shift in the centre of gravity for the sonnet. For none before Cino builds a sonnet to a climax, and the memorable lines are to be found at the beginning, or in the body of the piece. This was true, naturally, of Jacopo da Lentino, who established a form, but filled it with nothing of importance. After him, as we have seen, came those who had other ideas of making poetry poetical. But even when Dante and his circle sweep away excrescences and restore simplicity they do not explore the potentialities of the sonnet-form. Even with Dante, and in the best sonnets of the *Vita Nuova*, the proud opening dwindles to an end which is, by comparison, haphazard and insignificant. And if we looked back to Guido Cavalcanti's *Chi è questa che ven, ch'ogn'uom la mira* we should find the downward slipping clearly instanced. The weakness of the whole last tercet leaves in our mind only the buoyancy of the opening. The close neither summates, nor does it add: it is the deadest member of the sonnet.

With Cino, then, we have for the first time a quiet opening which can lead to a triumphal close. In a composition of only 14 lines this is an innovation of the first importance; but so natural that Cino's successors will accept it almost without being aware that any innovation has made. Let us put once for all the prefatory sonnet of Petrarch's *Rime*,

> Che quanto piace al mondo è breve sogno,

All that pleases in the world as brief as is a dream. Just as Petrarch is fully conscious of the richer world of opposite, yet subtly blending, emotions (*les fleurs du mal*, though of a different sort of ill), so he realizes also the efficacy of the new sonnet which has dawned with Cino. And if we balance a first line of Dante, *Ne li occhi porta la mia donna Amore* against the line from Petrarch it will be clear enough, despite the attractiveness of Dante's, that the poetic weight rests with Petrarch. And indeed, that judgement puts in right relation the lyric poetry of Petrarch and his predecessors. The poetry of the *dolce stil* is this side of the senses, it comes with a first flush of enthusiasm, but it cannot help itself from being juvenile. It is lightweight because of its attractiveness, which is boyish and engaging, not enduring. Petrarch's line may represent a final mood, but it is one that has seasoned the *Rime*, and in that retrospect he weighs human experience as the preceding lyric had not done.

This is clear also from the relative positions of the *Vita Nuova* and the *Rime* in the life of their authors. The first was written when Dante was twenty-seven, and the gap that looms between this youthful work and the *Commedia* is immense. But though Petrarch affected to despise his *rime sparse*, and though Laura dies in 1348, yet Petrarch's care for his poetry continues till his death. This is not only the main monument of his activity in the vernacular: it is the only one. Here he is the culmination of the whole tradition of love poetry, and at the same time the fountain-head for the European lyric, which finds it hard to look past him, for the simple reason that he blocks the view. Francesco Petrarca (1304–74) claimed that his father had been banished from Florence the same day as Dante. That was an approximation, but he was born at Arezzo, and followed his family to Pisa, and to Avignon, starting his studies at Carpentras, under Convenevole da Prato. After the unwilling study of law at Montpellier and Bologna Petrarch returned to the papal court in 1326. He took minor orders (the foundation of his economic independence, but not the start of a clerical career), but his ideas remained still worldly. The 6th of April 1327 he saw Laura in the church of St Claire, and the 6th of April 1348 she dies. The guess of the Abbé de Sade, Petrarch's great biographer, that she was Laure de Noves, who married Hugues de Sade in 1325, remains the most credited hypothesis about her. More credited, certainly, than the idea that she is a figment of Petrarch's fancy. For if Laura is an invention, there is no obstacle to prevent Petrarch's imagination making what demands it likes upon her. The tenuousness of his connexion with her, as stated in the *Rime*, might be taken as an argument even for her existence. But even if the whole battle of fluctuating sentiments were fought out in Petrarch's mind, or in relationship to that personal drama within his life from which spring his two children, it need not lack vitality. For we shall find that it is Petrarch, more than Laura, who is the centre of the *Rime*.

This will serve to mark him off from Dante, and from the *Vita Nuova*. There Dante proposed 'only to take as matter ever afterwards the praise' of Beatrice: in whom, therefore, the *Vita Nuova* centres. So only can she be promoted to the rank and office that she will hold within the *Commedia*. But the centre of the *Rime* is the conflict generated within the mind of Petrarch. To it doubtless Laura is essential, but it is, to use a language Dante might have used, as accident to substance. We have seen already, in the last line of the first sonnet, where this conflict tends, and ends. For the beginning of the *Rime* is also an ending: part of that care for these 'trifles' in the vulgar tongue which gives a shape, almost a frame. The emergent theme is death, and, beyond death, the appeal to a higher court which should have disciplined the appetites of life. And it is for reasons such as this that the *Rime*, where they are genuine statement, are so much more substantial, and so much more adult, than the *dolce stil*.

Now in the sixteenth century du Bellay voiced a strong dislike for the whole tribe of love poets sprung from Petrarch's lineage:

> Ce n'est que feu de leurs froides chaleurs,
> Ce n'est qu'horreur de leurs feintes douleurs,
> De leurs amours, que flammes et glaçons ...

And when Petrarch sank from view with the end of the eighteenth century it was with this embarrassing taint of petrarchism that he was remembered. That is both natural, and unfortunate. It is natural, because Petrarch is the obvious heir of all the techniques of his predecessors. From them he takes the antitheses with which the Provençals endowed the lyric; though it is to be noted that he offers none of the old theorizations on the nature of Love. That marks him off from the thirteenth century. But what is called petrarchism (as seen in the *Rime*, not in the earlier, forgotten, poetry) is an abiding element rebaptized. And it is marginal to Petrarch, as we may see from the focus I have quoted from the first sonnet. For there is no mannerism, no frigid conceits, no ice or fire, even no puns on Laura's name. Is Petrarch then a petrarchist? Yes, and no. He was eclectic, open to the influences that lay within his view; and in this matter of techniques he put back into common circulation what else might have been buried with Guittone and the Provençals, something that was to remain an embarrassment until Marino (so much more successful than Petrarch in the matter of conceits, because they are for him the substance of poetic statement) sets the old frigidities alight in a baroque blaze of fireworks, thereby producing a new embarrassment. But Petrarch has paid a heavy price for his mistake, in that men have in their impatience with one ingredient of his poetry identified him with it, as if he only had begotten it, and it were all him.

Against that prejudice the remedy is to read the *Rime* with the first sonnet as a sounding-board: to sift out what is to be accounted *galimatias* or rigmarole, and to put on the credit side what communicates itself directly as straightforward and valid statement. And it will be well to remember that, in spite of the disproportion between the bulk of the *Rime* and the *Vita Nuova*, there are not more facts or episodes to be discovered. The data of the *Rime* hardly amount to more than can be read in the famous note to Petrarch's *Virgil*, the time and place of his enamourment, the coincidence in time of her death. Add to these data the repentance which forms the final mood, we have the beginning and the ending, and in between there is only

La lunga istoria delle pene mie,

29

with no path clearly indicated. True, there is one division: between poems in the life of Laura, and after her death, though that division is not hard and fast. The proportion is as 1 : ½, and there is less mannerism in the smaller second part. If the *Rime* open with enamourment they soon develop contradictory sentiments. With the praise for Laura's beauty, and the recognition that she points the way to heaven, there is also the confession of his desire as sensual, and this the path to hell. And if Laura's honesty blocks the path to his desire, her beauty and his temperament block the path to honesty. This is the conflict that gives strength to Petrarch's *Rime*. Here is the world of contrasting sentiments which Cino glimpsed, and they blend continually, with continually varying proportions, through the book. In the later compositions of the first Part there is a more sophisticated treatment, saved from being ludicrous by a genuine exasperation, and a consequent insistence on the sensual side of his love for Laura. It is no longer only a combat, it is one in which he fears to lose. And as an essential part of this exasperation there is the harping note of advancing age, as in *Di dì in dì vo cangiando il viso e'l pelo*. Then comes the first presentiment of Laura's death in an ambiguous note, soon caught up to become a vision and a prophecy. Look on her quickly for most beauty is most transient (*Chi vuol veder quantunque po natura*),

Cosa bella mortal, passa e non dura.

So we pass from the first part to the second, more impressive, if perhaps less attractive, than the first. Here there will be none of the colour or the warmth of the first part at its best (as in the celebrated *Chiare, fresche e dolci acque*), but there will be none of the metrical exercises. It opens on the note of pure lament, to which is soon added a desire for death for himself (*La vita fugge e non s'arresta un'ora*). Then comes the retrospective note, that Laura was right, her honesty his salvation. In her life, Petrarch had been uncertain: was Laura the object of a passion involving the senses, or the ideal capable of rescuing Petrarch from them? The ambiguity of the first part lies in the fact that Petrarch himself does not know, or, rather, knows only at a given moment. Now he becomes increasingly sure, and the praise of Laura emerges in dispraise of himself: his love for her sensual, her merit in combating it the greater (*Come va'l mondo! or mi diletta e piace*). But beyond this there is the abjuration of both love and Laura. It was an affection of the earth, and whatever the merit of Laura, a distraction as much as a guide to heaven. *Cover her face, mine eyes dazzle*. The close of the *Rime* is in the abandonment of the creature for the Creator: *I'vo piangendo i miei passati tempi*, where the last sonnets express the mood more satisfactorily than the last *canzone* to the Virgin.

It will be clear, I hope, what little relationship this bears to the earlier love-lyric, and how little relevance the shafts of du Bellay have to the *Rime*. There is a line which may summate his conflict,

> Fuggir la carne travagliata e l'ossa.

To flee the travail of his flesh and bones: it is a good clue to the nature of the *Rime*. This is a combat between desire and reason, something that admits of contradictions, which in their turn are not a proof of Petrarch's insincerity, rather the opposite. If that turmoil had not been there Petrarch might have stood clear on one side or the other of it. With the youthful Dante of the *Vita Nuova* he might have expressed a reverence untroubled by the senses. Or else he might have anticipated the Tasso of the *Aminta*, author of one of the fullest lines in Italian poetry,

> Mostrommi l'ombra d'una breve notte.

Nor will the Italian lyric achieve real greatness again till Tasso takes this further step, into the world of the senses, for the sake of the senses, and with no afterthoughts. But meanwhile Petrarch, *aeterno devinctus volnere amoris*, seeks escape outwards to either of those statements, and is held back in between them. Hence his desire for refuge, the one he tries, the one he finds. The first is solitude, *Solo e pensoso i più deserti campi.* But we can shun others, not ourselves; and Love goes with him, and his cares, and solitude is no escape. So Petrarch comes to that last mood, which I quoted first, proposing it as the touchstone for his best poetry. Nor will it fail the reader who holds it as a clew through the labyrinth of the *Rime.*

CHAPTER 2

From St Francis to Dante

ST FRANCIS OF ASSISI (1182–1226), son of a rich merchant, Pietro Bernardone, renounced the world in his early twenties, to embrace evangelic poverty and chastity. The Franciscan Order, approved by Honorius III in 1223, is a phenomenon of prime importance in the life of the Church; and in the history of literature it leaves one deposit, the poem which comes first in anthologies of Italian poetry, the *Laudes Creaturarum*, written after St Francis received the stigmata in 1224, and with the additional lines on 'our sister death' written only the month before his death. This is not all St Francis wrote, but it is a compensation for what is lost. Here an all-embracing charity wraps the appearances of the universe – all manifestations of God's power, so felt as 'brother' sun and wind and fire, or 'sister' moon and stars, or 'sister-mother' earth; while the qualities of St Francis reappear in the attributes of 'sister water',

> La quale è molto utile e humele e pretiosa e casta.

Here the province of man is suffering and praise, with no activity in his own right beyond thanksgiving for 'the different fruits and coloured flowers and plants'. And though suffering is given thanks for, the essential note is of the brightness of the sun – already, as it will be for Dante, symbol of the light of God. Essential also in the flavour of this praise-sequence is the absence of the note of sin. Day and night and mother earth and sister death, with no other note than praise for these, given and given thanks for.

To this there is a gloss, and though its compilation is later and its authorship uncertain, it is not unworthy in spirit to stand besides the *Laudes Creaturarum*. This is the *Fioretti di*

Sancto Franciescho, the little flowers which are the actions of his life. Over all an atmosphere of beguiling simplicity and humility, and the sense of stepping back out of the concerns of men into direct contact with the spiritual Unseen. Here is St Francis preaching to the birds, or adopting the wolf of Gubbio, with the same note of joy, in providence or providential suffering, as in the *Laudes*. It is, of course, a limited world, for one must have nothing to have everything.

And St Francis answered him: – When we reach St Mary of the Angels, soaked by the rain and numbed with the cold, covered in mud and afflicted with hunger, and we knock at the door of the place, and the porter comes angrily and says: – Who are you? – and we say: – We are two of your friars; – and he will say: – It is not true, you are two rogues who go cheating the world and stealing the alms of the poor; go away; – and will not open for us, but makes us stay outside in the snow and the rain with cold and hunger until nightfall; then, if we bear patiently such wrongs such cruelty and such dismissal without vexation and without murmuring against him; and think humbly and charitably that the porter really knows us and that God makes him speak against us: o brother Lione, write that here is perfect happiness.

It is an inflexible message, uttered in the gentlest tones, as in the simplest language. And we must not discount its influence, for it may well be that the Dante who gives such eloquent praise to St Francis in *Paradiso* XI would in the last resort tame his proud spirit to Franciscan humbleness.

We shall find this gospel set in a violent key when we turn to Jacopone da Todi (1236–1306). Of noble origins, a lawyer by profession, Jacopone was shocked from his normal life when a floor collapsing at a wedding brought one casualty, his wife, found to be wearing a hair-shirt under her party-clothes. For ten years he lived on his own a life devoted only to contempt for the world and for himself. So mad were his ways that he was not a welcome applicant for admission to the Franciscan Order, though his 'holy humility', his cheerfulness in doing chores won favour. Even so, he was a difficult companion. Once he subdued gulosity by buying some lights, hanging them in his cell, but only sniffing them. This he continued long after they were verminous, and stank through all the dormitory. When the cause at last was found the friars threw him in the privy, where he composed a *lauda*, *O jubilo de core che fai cantare damore*. As he sang Christ appeared to him, offering the sweetest odours in compensation, but Jacopone asked only for another deeper and more horrible hell in which to purge his sins. And after there remained with him a perpetual light, he seeming 'drunk with sweetness, so that he suffered afterwards much persecution'. This included imprisonment at the hands of Boniface VIII when at the century's end the Franciscan movement had split into the Spirituals and those relaxed. Making party with the Colonna the Spirituals came to grief when the fortress of Palestrina was razed in 1298; and from then Fra Jacopone remained in his dungeon till the death of Boniface in 1303.

Jacopone gives an acrid tinge to the *lauda*, or hymn of praise. We might think of his action on that genre as parallel to that of Ranieri Fasani on its users. After disciplining himself in private for many years the latter received a miraculous letter which the Bishop of Perugia read in public. When he came to the words of the psalm, *Apprehendite disciplinam nequando irascatur Dominus*, Fasani stripped his back, began to flagellate himself. The bystanders followed his example, and all Perugia followed suit. So attractive a movement spread through the peninsula except where (as Milan or Naples) the gallows were erected to keep it out; and whole towns marched in a body to flagellate themselves for the edification of their neighbours, as the Bolognese to Modena. All these communities had used the *lauda*, ejaculatory and repetitive in its first guise; and just as Fasani brings a note of violence to the communities, so does Jacopone to the composition itself. He is the most forceful, though not necessarily the most likeable, of the poets of the Duecento. The way to peace is now through expropriation of the love of all creatures and of self. It is only in this new poverty of the spirit that divine love can fill the mind. And after that, patience and tranquillity in all afflictions, or more than patience, willingness in suffering. St Francis had been ready to embrace the world in honour of its

Maker: Fra Jacopone must reject it for fear it gets in the way, preventing self-annihilation. His prayer is for the ills of life,

O Signor, per cortesia, – mandame la malsania!

and the catalogue continues, from dropsy down to passage through the digestion of a wolf as a last exercise in self-obliteration. With this, the recipe for man:

Quando t'alegri, omo de altura,
va', pone mente a la sepoltura.

Here the consequence of divine love is the engenderment of hate for all that is else: and in this the theological lore of Paris, as destructive to the message of Assisi as any other element. Nor is anything stronger in his poetry than the satirical attacks on Boniface VIII, with an attendant picture of the abuses of the Church. Where he turns to doctrinal presentation Jacopone is less effective than in expressing feeling; and naturally the ecstasy of divine love in its exclusiveness (*Già non posso vedere creatura*) or in the desire for dissolution (*Amor, cui tanto bramo, – famme morir d'amore!*) is one of the most insistent notes. In the poem on Christ as the husband of the soul, with its reiterations of *amore*, we find a vibration of the senses, their revenge over the spirit which was to oust them. Jacopone rejected the physical world as a bar between his soul and God, but the final expression of his love for Christ turns out to be other than a spiritual one. Perhaps for this reason his readers will prefer, as the highlight of his poetry, that dramatization of the Passion into which he poured a flood of tenderness without us feeling these more dubious bases of his poetry. But all in all, Jacopone will remain, as poet, the strongest individual voice of his own century.

This is, of course, apparent on his own side, a large field, with some prominent northern representatives. Gerardo Pateg, or Patecchio (fl. early thirteenth c.) is first in time, author of two surviving works, the *Splanamento de li Proverbi di Salomone* and a *Frotula noie moralis*: the latter with a first line which may sum him up, *Noioso sun, e canto di noio*. Then of uncertain date, and equally uncertain naming, Uguccione da Lodi, whose *Libro* admonishes the reader to save himself from Hell and win the joys of Paradise. No nearer poetry is the mid-thirteenth-century Giacomino da Verona, who wrote such poems as *De Jerusalem Celesti, De Babilonia Infernali*, with that comprehensive simplicity of choice which Savonarola will sum up for his hearers: *O quassú, o quaggiú!* Up, or down; not sideways, into the world of men. Slight also is Pietro da Barsegapé, who seems to have written his long *Sermone* in 1274, with a variety of metres for the Creation, the Life of Christ, the Last Judgement. More copious is Fra Bonvesin da la Riva (before 1250–*c.* 1313–15), but always with a religious or didactic aim. He is the first to write on table-manners (*De Quinquaginta Curialitatibus*), but it is to the *Libro delle Tre Scritture* that his reputation is particularly attached, and for this first trilogy the name of Dante has been troubled. The Writings are Black, Red, and Golden, with the twelve joys of Heaven meant to balance the twelve pains of Hell, but Bonvesin finds one easier to write than the other. Hammers which fall more heavily than mountains, rivers of molten bronze, harrows to drag the body over thorns and hills back to the burning streams, with Bonvesin piously hoping that he will be spared, for every little pain distresses him, a nettle-sting, an ant-bite.... In Heaven his resources are much fewer, often eked out with negative delights, as with the circumstance that none of one's neighbours smell. And, in between, the Scrigiura Rossa, the drama of the Passion, has none of the qualities of Jacopone, but the poor iteration of lament. Moreover, the accent in the first part falls on attrition, rather than contrition, and Bonvesin returns to this note at the end, with the clear principle, Pay in suffering and poverty, to receive the due reward:

> Lo avere e la grandeza e lo mondano onore
> Non è se non uno sogno, che se sogna el peccatore;
> E quand'el se desvegia, perduto ha lo so lavoro,
> In mano niente se trova, se non pena e dolore.

That is only a bargain, but even so it might have been better for the poetic reputation of Bonvesin if he had written only the close to his trilogy.

It was an editor of Bonvesin who wrote enthusiastically of the correspondences between his poem and Dante's. But those resemblances end before they quite begin, and we may turn with relief to the figure which eclipses all the predecessors: that of Dante. We left him rich in promise and in such native culture as belonged to the tradition of courtly love, and author of that solemn promise to write of Beatrice what had not been written of any woman; and now must take him through the minor works to the poem which puts him among the world's first poets. For Petrarch, or Boccaccio, we have a cloud of autographs, for Dante not a scrap in his own hand; and for his life a few, scattered, data. The ideal half-way of his life – 1300 – sees him confessedly astray, and points us to the years 1290–1300 as a period of *traviamento*. But apart from our deductions the resources of the biographer are few. In 1289 Dante took part in the battle of Campaldino, against the forces of Arezzo. In 1300, as one of the Priors, he was participant to the exile of Guido Cavalcanti; and when Charles of Valois comes to Florence in 1301 Dante was absent as envoy to Boniface VIII, and was exiled himself. From now on Dante is a wanderer hoping for the return which never comes. Till 1304 he makes common cause with the company of White Exiles; then draws aloof to make a party of himself, around a theory of his own. His wanderings increase, the going up and down others' stairs irks Dante's spirit. This is the period of the treatises, *De Vulgari Eloquentia* and *Convivio* (1304–7), both left uncompleted, as being perhaps both superseded by the *Comedy*, which must absorb all Dante's energies. One other work accompanies it, and is the fruit of Dante's hopes in Henry of Luxemburg, and in his coming to receive the imperial crown and pacify the garden of the empire. Here Dante finds the general solution of all problems in the fulfilment of Universal Empire, and demonstrates the necessity of one Roman Monarch for the whole world, as also of the independence of the Emperor in his own sphere of the Papacy. But Italy had little stomach for this lesson, and Florence was the kernel of resistance to this threat to her own liberties. From the first Henry found ˙faction springing beneath his feet, and ended in casual death at Buonconvento in 1313. From now on Dante is doomed to exile without other end than the death which overtakes him at Ravenna in 1321, whence Florence in later days will often strive to wrest his bones, and where, in the temple built by Bernardo Bembo in the fifteenth century, they still repose.

In 1329 John XXII condemned the *Monarchia* to the flames, in 1554 it figures on the Index of Prohibited Books; nor is it till the end of the nineteenth century that a pope will be prepared to endorse the *Divine Comedy* as a supplementary gospel. Now, after Gilson, the accent has shifted to the originality and heterodoxy of Dante, if no longer in an unwelcome way. Nowhere is this truer than with the *Convivio* and the *Monarchia*. The first echoes in form the *Vita Nuova*, with the meat of the banquet in the *canzoni*, and the bread the accompanying prose: and the relationship will always be remembered in Dante's words, the *Vita Nuova* 'fervid and passionate', the *Convivio* 'temperate and virile'. The purpose of the banquet is to offer knowledge to those who stand outside its portals: hence the vernacular, and the need to defend it against Latin and against French. The warmth of this advocacy is amongst the most attractive elements of the introductory treatise; as is also Dante's picture of himself in exile, 'a ship without a rudder or a sail, carried to different ports and estuaries and shores by the dry wind that blows from grievous poverty'. But here the *donna gentile* turns into the symbol of philosophy, and arbitrary allegorization dulls the doctrinal *canzoni*, causing less regret that Dante broke his treatise off. Here, or in the views upon nobility (of individual merit, not of blood or wealth), or in the providential role of Roman monarchy, with the Emperor as the necessary 'rider of the human will', are to be seen the traditional highlights of the *Convivio*. But a new emphasis has grown up, and we may see the pointer to Dante's allegiances in all the many deferential references to Aristotle ('most worthy of faith and of obedience', 'e puotesi appellare quasi cattolica oppinione'). Allied to one casual reference to the 'good friar Thomas of Aquino' they show Dante as avowedly aristotelian, not thomistic. Aristotelian, not averroistic, because he sees no opposition boding between philosophy and faith. The first for St Thomas was subordinated to the second, Dante makes them independent of each other. Philosophy can give us in this world the beatitude of which here we are capable. The truths of Aristotle are neither contradictory to revealed religion, nor replaced by it. Once stated they legislate for all men, only needing the presence of the Emperor, to compel men on the right paths. Here in the *Convivio* the authority of the Pope is obliterated from the natural life of men, to be concentrated only in the supernatural sphere. And on the other side, Cato can become God's major representative, and Virgil speak with God's authority when he writes of an empire given to the Romans without bounds of space and time. So Dante looks – it is a feature of the medieval mind – to authorities which legislate for the whole activity of man: but these are not the sole authority on which the Church had insisted.

In the *Convivio* Dante announced his intention to write on the *volgare*, so that the *De Vulgari Eloquentia* is slightly later. The *Vita Nuova* had been in the vernacular to be intelligible to women because it dealt with love. But now his claims for the *volgare* rise, and his desire is to give full account, starting from the beginning. Though the debate whether the angels spoke, and how, or if Eve could have spoken before Adam, or the unity of the human race in Hebrew speech down to the Tower of Babel, may all seem unpromising as a beginning, Dante is the first philologist, and his analysis of the languages of Europe, and of the one language most within his ken, is fundamental. On the one side, the stability of the universal language, Latin; on the other the inescapable mutations of the spoken speech. And for the first time an attempt to classify the dialects of Italy, and in their deficiencies, an option for a *volgare* to transcend them all, one which will be *illustre, aulico, cardinale, curiale*: all this for the benefit of the noblest form of poetry, for the *canzone*, dealing with the loftiest themes. Then, abruptly, Dante breaks off in the middle of a chapter: he does not come back to theorize on the nature of the vernacular, but proceeds to consecrate it in his major work.

In Frederick Barbarossa's time the jurists of Bologna had propounded the dogma, 'What has pleased the Prince, that has the force of law'; and opposite there was the other extreme, with the picture of Boniface VIII sitting at the Jubilee of 1300, crowned with the crown of Constantine and sword in hand, exclaiming, 'I am the Pontiff, I am the Emperor'. To these problems we have seen in the *Convivio* the first draft of Dante's answers. In the *Monarchia* also he starts from the beginning: three books, three doubts: is monarchy necessary for the world's well-being, is the Roman people the right instrument, does the monarch's authority derive direct from God, or through some minister. Three doubts, but no doubt in the answers, and once more the separation of the spheres of influence: with two suns, one for the spiritual, one for the temporal scene. And this is proved by abstract argument, with the authority of Aristotle as a prime factor. For if many things are ordered to one goal, there must be one to regulate or rule. And is not this a simple correspondence to the plan of the universe? And justice is most powerful under a monarchy, for here the judge is placed above cupidity. 'But the monarch has nothing which he can desire, for his jurisdiction is bounded by the ocean only.' And concord and unity for Dante hang together, and must be whole. Book II proves that the Empire is the appanage of Rome (and though Henry of Luxemburg may seem to us off-centre he is, for Dante, Roman by election). In the third book the livest issues come, and the novelty of the *Convivio* is maintained: not one beatitude for man, but two, earthly, and heavenly, happiness. Two beatitudes, and two guides, distinct in their attributes. Dante knows the opposition that will come from the Pope and from his party: the zeal for the keys, and for the profits that come from sacerdotal usurpation. All the decretalists will be fierce antagonists of the imperial idea. But he stands resolute on this, plainly non-Thomist, ground.

Dante's procedure in the *Monarchia* is by syllogisms depend-

ing on first principles, and no practical considerations enter
into it. And he wrote when the Empire had been slowly and
painfully extruded from Italian soil. When Henry VII looked
hopefully in upon the Italian scene the factions in Lombardy
sprang into life, and Florence looked to Robert of Naples to
organize resistance. Why this discrepancy between arguments
so well-begun, and the realities of Italy? It is that concord
may be best, and may be unity, and this may be obvious
(though not necessarily); but it does not follow that you are
on the path to either by asserting this. Nor do monarchs lose
cupidity by having more: rather, *l'appétit vient en mangeant.*
What Dante prescribes is not a recipe for improvement, but
a formula for replacement. And between what should be,
and what is, there is no link but the futile enterprise of Henry
VII. To this we must add a word on the *Epistles*, for they offer
battle where the *Monarchia* offers theory. Though it is usual
now to deny that Brunetto Latini (*c.* 1220–*c.* 1295–1300, author
of the *Tesoretto* and the encyclopedic *Livres dou Tresor*) was
Dante's teacher, yet Dante's letters belong to the school of
rhetoric of which Brunetto was a master. He keeps faithfully
to the rules of the *ars dictandi* which dominated the writing of
medieval Latin, making embroidery more important than
plain statement. And here Dante, using language of biblical
exaltation for the rickety enterprise of Henry of Luxemburg,
shows up sharply the unreality of his political views. While he
confidently expects the judgement of God to fall on the
Florentines for their wicked opposition, it is Henry who
pays with his life for his rash intrusion into the troubled field
of Italian politics.

Dante's thirteen epistles have all been a matter of controversy: four are in the name of others, all have a public character, and all belong to the years of his exile. It is those round
Henry's enterprise which offer greatest interest: to the rulers
and peoples of Italy (autumn 1310), to the Florentines (31
March 1311), and to Henry himself (17 April 1311). The first
is the manifesto of the new order: all Italy will have peace,
justice, liberty, prosperity; the language of biblical fervour
and prophecy swells in this prospect of general submission.

But with the honey comes also the hint of gall: beware of not recognizing the divine ordinance, or the Emperor will shake you in your obstinacy! And when the Florentines rough-handled Henry's messengers Dante was goaded to write against them, offering a fate as harsh as Hannibal to Saguntum. The counterpart went to Henry: why was he dallying in north Italy, when his enemies were in its centre? He must turn against this snake that would bite her mother, this incestuous Mirra, this frenzied Queen Amata: and all these are Florence, seen through a new lens. And Henry made his expedition, and his little army lay outside the gates of Florence, too weak to attempt assault or encirclement, until at last Henry retired, harried and exhausted, on the road to Pisa. Similar in its appeal is the letter sent to the six Italian cardinals who went to Carpentras in 1314 after the death of Clement V. Here Dante draws the picture of the desolate nature of Rome, abandoned by the popes. Let the cardinals blush at what they have done, let them be unanimous for the Spouse of Christ, and for the seat of the Spouse, which is Rome, not Avignon. The papacy, like the empire, is a divinely ordained institution for the benefit of all mankind. Place it back in Rome, the world will return to a better, to half at least of the right shape. The best of being governed by ideals is that one is never without the simple formula which changes everything. But the six Italian cardinals took no notice, or were too few to make their voices heard. The papacy stayed where it was till 1375; and even then, return to Rome did not mean all that Dante thought it would. Perhaps of the next year (1315) is the very dantesque letter to his *Florentine friend*. A glimpse of hope for his return, but with conditions attached to it: the guise of a pardoned and self-confessing malefactor. All Dante's scorn bursts forth: in spite of his longing he will go back only if there is a path consistent with honour and dignity. Otherwise, never; nor will he lack for bread! There remains the letter which has given most controversy, that to Can Grande della Scala, with its famous statement of the title of the *Commedia*, and the addition for its author, *Florentinus natione sed non moribus*. If it were genuine, and were com-

plete, with Dante's exposition of his *Paradiso* (in a letter?),
it would be a document that might have saved a mountain
of exegesis. As it is, most doubt still clings about it.

In the fifteenth century Leonardo Bruni had seen other
letters, even in Dante's hand, but this small group is all that
now remains. And with this last, concern has shifted to the
major work. From the breaking off of the *Convivio* and the
De Vulgari Eloquentia all Dante's energies are absorbed upon
his poem; and it is plain that it dwarfs what he had done
before. Dwarfs, but not cancels, unless it be in the case of the
De Vulgari Eloquentia, since Dante's attitude to language
has changed radically. The ideas of the *Convivio* and the
Monarchia may be attenuated, more by implication than by
overt statement, but they are still as much the prerequisites
of Dante's poem as the Roman Empire was, in Dante's
view, the prerequisite for the birth of Christ and the whole
process of Redemption. And though it would be possible
to struggle over dating, with the *Monarchia* as the most
movable of Dante's works, and the question-mark first
entered by Boccaccio (on Dante beginning his poem before
his exile) as an appetiser to our reading of *Inferno*, yet there
is very little purpose or profit in such wrestling. The traces
of the *Convivio* and the *Monarchia* are visible even in what
might seem the alien world of the later *Paradiso*. But it is
true also that this vision is an escape from the trackless world,
or from the world off its appointed track, into the other world
where all is divinely ordered. When Dante is launched upwards on a voyage into boundless space whose goal is contemplation of the light that lights the universe there is no
reason to look back. Here the earth is cancelled as of no
account, and we may take Dante's prayer to Beatrice at the
moment when she hands him over to St Bernard as typical of
the direction. 'So I prayed, and she, as far off as she seemed,
smiled and looked down at me; then she turned back to the
eternal fount.' Here Dante seems to make return to the safe
fold, in the final affirmation of the contemplative ideal as
having precedence, even as dismissing all that is else. Yet
the final vision does not obliterate, it concentrates what

Dante has seen and declared before; and despite the contradictions which might seem to arise between the diverging
paths, Dante does not renounce his remedies for the world,
even when he has renounced the world itself.

We have leapt forward to the journey's end, but that is not
surprising, for the three parts of Dante's world are self-
revealing. In less than the count of twenty Lucifer rebelled,
and fell, crashing to the centre of the earth where he is chained
in endless impotence, and where his three faces make a trinity
of evil. For Lucifer an instant, for Adam only seven hours of
Earthly Paradise, then by the illusory gift of Free Will he also
fell, to lie in wretchedness through the 5232 years till Christ
appeared triumphantly in Limbo. Lucifer and the pit remained: a funnel subdivided by Dante's imagination of the
realm of evil and its punishment; and this counterbalanced
by another cone, caused also by the fall of Lucifer, so that he
provides the tomb, and the escape. For in the antipodes, in
a world which Dante imagined as a waste of waters, rises
a mountain of unexampled height, on whose truncated top is
the Garden that should have been the home of Adam and of
all mankind. Round the steep sides of this mount are circles
corresponding to the ones of hell. But there punishment is
without end, and the inhabitants look back on earth as on
the only world they know, nor have they lost the features
which were characteristic then, and will remain forever. In
purgatory sin is a disappearing element, and hope prevails over
pain. This is a transitional world, and before the canticle ends
we have emerged into the ever-vernal atmosphere of Eden.
Here Virgil vanishes, and Beatrice, the symbol of Theology,
confronts Dante before he sees the vicissitudes of man and of
the Church presented as a mistery play. Then he is ready to
soar with her to that first principle on which the world depends. From one heaven to another, faster than thought itself,
and with a growing emphasis on *light* and *bliss*, or on the smile
(*riso*) of Beatrice or others. And the orchestra of light is
varied with the grand figure of the imperial eagle, or the ladder
formed of souls, each mobile and each bright. And at the end
there is the concentred motion of the Rose of the Blessed,

with here the seats already filled, 'so that few now are wanting', and the world for Dante, as for many another prophet, in full sight of its ending. Here too the shortness of human vision, acknowledged increasingly through the last canticle, reaches its maximum. For what is most to be communicated is least capable of communication, and even Dante's sureness falters before what he hopes he saw.

Such is the theme, so sure the structure, and we may count its architecture, which is Dante's own, as a supreme achievement. Here all the chaos of medieval imaginings is brought to order, and Dante moves, with Virgil as his guide, without a trace of hesitation. It is reassuring if one's leader knows the way, especially if we are going from boundless gloom to endless bliss. And in this we may note a divergence from Jacopone, and St Francis. With them we have seen exultation in rejection and opprobrium, carried to logical excess with Jacopone in the privy writing lauds. But in the varied punishments of hell we shall find the flatterers immersed in human excrement. This represents a shift in Dante's standpoint. For St Francis the world, as God's creation, was good, and all one needed self-abasement. St Francis was not concerned with the organization of the world, and still less Jacopone. Indeed, for Jacopone the worse it was the better, with the greater compensation. But it is the sinners here who are bemerded, and by implication Dante prefers a different sort of world. It is one which should work rightly, having such a sponsor, and here the governing ideas of the *Monarchia* still apply: the world with the right remedies, under the right authorities, would itself be right. These were: Pope, Emperor, Aristotle, and at first sight it might seem that the latter should be Dante's guide. But in effect he keeps his place as 'master of all those who know': since that in theory what we need is the check that keeps mankind within the bounds of reason, not pure reason in itself. And here Virgil steps forward as the singer of the Monarchy which Dante sees as providential. Even St Peter, in the celebrated outbursts of *Paradiso* XXVII against his false successor Boniface VIII, lends his high sanction to the Roman claim: 'But that high providence which with Scipio kept for Rome the glory of the world will soon give rescue, this is my belief'. And in Canto xxx the seat is ready for Henry VII, who 'will come to put straight Italy before it is disposed' to follow him. Is not the implication that the twofold remedy still holds? that the pope must leave intrusion into the temporal realm? Nor of course is this yet the Renascence, in spite of the enthusiasm for the ancient world. Dante has an all-embracing formula in which the world will find its order, and he looks back, to Virgil or to Aristotle, not as entities to be discovered, but as fixed stars with an obligatory role in a heaven of his own making. He is not ready to explore antiquity, instead he has miscast it within the orbit of his time. And this implies as great a distortion as those pictorial representations of characters from Livy as medieval personages.

So it is not the practical importance of Dante's recipe that matters, for that never worked before him, and a universal pope is hardly more likely now than a universal emperor. What matters is the strength of Dante's presentation. On that ideal date of April 1300, half-way through the natural span of Dante's life, he finds himself in the trackless wood of sin. The straight path is lost, for him, as for mankind; and instead of the active life which should be, Virgil takes him down 'out of the quiet, into the trembling air'. The three aspects of this world are summed up in the three beasts of Canto I: incontinence, violence, and fraud. This is a fatal progression, with the first step leading onwards to the other ones. Punishment is governed by analogy (as with the lustful, tossed by passion's gusts, and now tossed on the squall of hell) or by the *contrappasso* (where those who rend are rent themselves or those who sank in sensual pleasures are sunk in stinking rain and mud). The anatomy of this world is in Canto xi, and that clear statement is accompanied by a banishment of the medieval grotesques which grew around the theme; as by Dante's care to give physical plausibility to his journey, especially to be observed at the tricky point where he crosses with Lucifer the very centre of the earth into a different hemisphere. All this gives graphic reality to Hell as a place, while its human filling gives it the relief which it assumes in comparison with the later canticles. Traversed by this pair of poets, Virgil and Dante, its episodes provide the background of the world of Dante's time; and almost all the figures which popular imagination associates with Dante are here in hell: as Paolo and Francesca, Farinata degli Uberti, Brunetto Latini, Pier della Vigna, Ulysses, Mahomet, or the Conte Ugolino. Seen also in their full earthiness, they have the fullest impact. There is a full range to Dante's attitude, as pity dies with acquiescence in God's justice; but the human note is rarely lacking. It may be in Virgil's subconscious recommendation of Limbo as the West End of Hell, with further down an unacceptable address: *basso inferno*. Or in the nostalgic glance: 'Up in fair Italy there lies a lake, beneath the alps which shut off Germany ...'; or maybe in the admiration wrung from Dante by some hero whose proud name dominated the period of his youth, as when Farinata, towering suddenly before us from his tomb, seems 'to hold all hell in high despite'. Or it may be in the affectionate cry of Guido Cavalcanti's father, 'Where is my son? and why not with you?' as it will be constantly in the tender, if ever-changing, relationship of Dante–Virgil.

So it is a human pilgrimage through an inhuman world. We may find the brutal note which exasperates the penalties of Malebolge, in the concentric pits which garner fraudulent sin, strong meat for squeamish appetites. But even here there is heroic stature: as with Ulysses, assimilated in his greed to know to Florence in her greed for wealth, and yet, from the first solemn latinism, treated with a high respect, and left to utter proverbial lines which have been taken for the voice of Dante. Or in the next canto Guido da Montefeltro, whose name epitomizes the recent history of Romagna, and brings again a sharp reflection upon Boniface VIII, 'the great priest – curse him!' So this 'prince of the new Pharisees', with all the proud claims of his bull *Unam sanctam*, stands for Dante as the arch-enemy of the programme which pervades his poem; and the shafts recur against the clerics who have followed the lead of the decretalists towards the things of earth. At the centre of this canticle, and realm, is Geryon, the threefold monster who is the 'filthy image of fraud'; and from Malebolge another pit, ringed round with the earth-giants, takes us down to where the cold wind fanned by the wings of Lucifer freezes the waters to ice, in which the souls of traitors are set, like meat in aspic. Here *whoever has betrayed forever is consumed*, and light and life are coming to their vanishing-point. But to the tragedy of Ugolino, gnawing the bloody scalp of Archbishop Ruggieri, Dante with a deft touch juxtaposes a little comedy. He meets Branco d'Oria, who 'never died at all, and eats and drinks and sleeps and puts on clothes'; and so he may, and yet anticipatorily be in hell. And so we come to the emperor of this dolorous realm, in which he does not rule. Lucifer's three faces have no corresponding mind, his only action is to raise the freezing wind which cancels life, and to maul in his mouths the traitors to Dante's institutions: Brutus and Cassius, who killed the founder of the Empire, Judas Iscariot, who betrayed the founder of the Church. Then down (and up) his fleecy flanks they go, to make their epic climb to Purgatory, the other side of the world.

Here instead of the bleakness of the bottom pit, we have the rising sun making the east to smile, and comforting to love. Nature wears a serene countenance, and Dante strikes the tenderest note with the 'sweet colour of the eastern sapphire'. It is a necessary counterpart that the nostalgic glance to parts of Italy is lacking here. For here all are looking forward, and the backward glance is blame, not regret. It is a pointer to that abandonment which is forced on Dante by the logic of his theme. Nor can any soul hold all Purgatory in high despite, or make therefore the strong, or harsh, impression made by the great figures which crowd the canvas of *Inferno*. The new note is struck in the notable encounter with Manfred, son and successor to Frederick II. Manfred – whose sins were horrible – might have been a candidate for treatment like that of Farinata. But in between has come repentance, whether historic, or presumed, and all is mild and placid. His wounds identify, but do not hurt; and though accustomed to be recognized Manfred is not moved to haughty scorn by Dante's ignorance of his looks, nor to indignation by the treatment given to his corpse. What matters of the world is the prayer that it can give to shorten expiation, *for here we profit much from prayer of those below*. In correspondence with this atmosphere we have at the centre of the canticle the theory of love on which it rests. Love, without which neither Creator nor created can remain, is of two sorts, natural and of the mind. The first is always right, the second may go wrong through a wrong object, by too little or too much of vigour in the loving. This is the basis for the disposition of the seven deadly sins around the slopes of Purgatory. Washed on the shore from the murk of hell, girt with the reed which marks humility, Dante passes up through the antepurgatory (with the souls of the excommunicate and negligent) to the gate of Purgatory proper, and has imprinted on his brow seven Ps which will be purged away circle by circle. Here pride and envy are at the root, and we proceed upwards to incontinence, with which we entered hell. Cardinal to this scheme is Dante's affirmation of free will, without which blame or punishment would have no reason. But with its play the unerringness of natural instinct disappears from view, and Dante's dream of the *femmina balba* serves to stress the falseness of the world's desires, leaving their rightness out of sight. From then on the lesson of detachment, which is to culminate in *Paradiso* with the panegyric of St Francis and St Dominic, becomes a leitmotiv for Dante's poetry; and Beatrice with her accusations on their meeting in the Earthly Paradise stresses this lesson: 'He turned his steps into a way which is not true, following false images of good, which never keep their promise whole.'

This world must then recede from view, as being a wrong start. And perhaps what is most present from it is the memory of its poetry, from the first reminiscence ·with Casella of Dante's youthful canzone, *Amor che nella mente mi ragiona*, via Sordello and Statius (each bringing their contribution to the praise of Virgil), to Guido Guinizelli and Arnaut Daniel, with Dante's own definition of the 'sweet new style'.

By the side of this, or welling from it, as with Sordello giving rise to the famous invective against Italy, we have lament for the distracted present. And still there is a symmetry of rebuke: to the clerics, who should let Caesar seat himself upon the saddle, to Albert or Rudolph of Habsburg, who might have healed the wounds of Italy, but left this for another. And still the apotheosis given to Virgil, especially in the encounter with Statius, shows that Dante keeps his own course, refusing to admit the world before Christ as wholly off its track. Were not natural powers left to man, had he not climbed toward moral precepts and universal rule? Was not Rome the sacred instrument? The light shone behind Virgil's back, but it was he who held the lamp. Virgil, who was in the *Convivio* 'our greatest poet', will keep this stature still in *Paradiso*, and Dante meeting Cacciaguida, his own ancestor, will strike the keynote of affection in Virgilian terms: 'So loving did Anchises' shade appear, if our greatest muse deserves our trust, when in Elysium he saw his son.' And Virgil can give to Statius news of the characters from the latter's poems now in Limbo, while Dante believes in the firm reality of the world of Virgil. It is only Dante himself, when he comes to the Earthly Paradise, and Virgil turns to go, who is back in a world of innocency where the providential remedies have no function; and here Virgil's words are specific, and notable: 'therefore over yourself I crown and mitre you.' But Dante has still to face the accusations of Beatrice (whether moral, political, or theological); and then he closes the *Purgatorio* with that elaborate representation of the vicissitudes of the chariot which stands for the Church, established by Christ, persecuted by Nero, assaulted by heresy, pampered by Constantine in that misguided Donation which marked the first moment of aberration and degeneracy, and finally outraged by Philip the Fair of France. Here in this allegorical miracle-play Dante has made use of all the elements which St John had laid in store; and according to our inclinations we shall find these enrichments and complications more or less poetic than the simple line which Mr Eliot once put forward as the essence of Dante's poetry, *e'n la sua volontade è nostra pace.*

So we pass to the incorporeal world, and to the zones of ineffable light; nor will Dante's emphasis on the fallaciousness of earthly goods and on the need of detachment from them to concentrate on the infinity which is waiting for us, fail at this point. This theme will culminate, after Dante's examination on Faith, Hope, and Charity, after he has been handed on to the mystic St Bernard, in the ultimate vision of God Himself, the point of dazzling light from which all else proceeds, and on which all else depends. But if this is the warp, announced by the first soaring of Dante and Beatrice, and by the twin panegyrics of St Francis and St Dominic, who choose the bare ground for their couch both nascent and dying, there still remains the weft of the earth as it is, and as it should be. And Dante may look down from seven heavens' height on the little patch of earth over which we squabble, but he still needs Beatrice to reassure him that he will see before he dies the punishment for what is wrong. These hints and prophecies, subscribed to by no less a personage than St Peter, betray at times the exasperation of long exile. Dante may stand foursquare against the blows of fate; but he wishes to assure himself that the wind will not always blow, and that the world's order waits on Providence. Has he abandoned in the *Paradiso* the programme of the *Monarchia*? In Canto VI he exalts the imperial eagle as a *sacred sign*, and looks back upon the peace of Augustus as a prophecy; in Cantos XVIII to XX Dante, as signwriter, blazons this same eagle, for the same reason, in the sky; and in Canto XXVII St Peter underlines these hopes with words that only the Dante of the *Monarchia* could have written for him. Dante would hardly play so high a trump if he had now abandoned his *idée fixe*. And at the centre of this canticle there is the longest space allotted to any figurant, given to Cacciaguida, to remind us that the earth, or Florence, is not really out of sight. True, in this encounter with the ideal ancestor, there is stressed the necessity of renunciation, and Cacciaguida himself has come from martyrdom in the fallacious world into *this peace*. But the picture of Florence as it was, and should be still, is relevant to Dante's political hopes. Here with the bitterness of exile there is the same reassurance that Dante will live to see the punishment of those to whom he owes his woes. Wrapped up with this there is a hint of greatness coming to Can Grande della Scala, 'things incredible' and so not stated. Did Dante, after the hopes in Henry had been dashed, transfer them lower, to one less than an emperor? The path of prophecy is hard, and those scattered through the *Paradiso* are unlike the dantesque sort (made after the event) which the ideal date of 1300 had rendered possible. Dante's plan awaits fulfilment, and as his life runs out he snatches what consolation can be found in hints of what he knows must come.

If we have left out the structure it is because this has less significance than before. Here the writ of paradise is everywhere, and in the passage from one heaven to another, up to the Primum Mobile, there is no landscape to make a difference. As we go so more light floods the scene, until in the empyrean the final vision is vouchsafed, and the pilgrim Dante, sponsored by St Bernard, the mystic devotee of the Virgin Mary, sees what can be seen of the eternal light which is the heart of all creation; and the poem ends with the noble prayer, addressed by St Bernard to the Virgin, which has to many seemed the summit of poetic discourse. The first note of *Paradiso* opening was a paean sounding full and strong after the half-lights of purgatory. And now, after the effables and the ineffables, after his high imagination has lost its power, Dante ends his great poem with an echoing line, the last word *stars* (connoting hope) aligned with the former canticles, but the whole line answering *Paradiso* 1, so that we come to rest with *Love that moves the sun and all the stars*.

CHAPTER 3

The Prose Tradition to Boccaccio

THE Duecento has little of original prose, and Dante's two works, the *Vita Nuova* and the *Convivio*, stand out as early landmarks. And Dante himself, who mentions Lancelot, Arthur, Tristram in his *Comedy*, coined a term – the *prose di romanzi* – for all the translations from the epic material of France. Translations will remain an important staple, sometimes providing, as with Fra Bartolomeo da San Concordio (*c.* 1262–1347, author of a compilation, *Ammaestramenti degli Antichi*), some of the purest Tuscan prose of a golden period for the language. But for us there is more attraction in a book which opens a legendary window upon the East: the Travels of Marco Polo (1254–1324?), more often called *Il Milione*. At seventeen this Venetian boy had set out with his father and his elder brother. Via the court of Kubla Khan they came to China, where Marco prospered. In 1295 he was back in Venice, and three years later taken prisoner in a naval battle with the Genoese. In prison he found leisure to narrate his voyages, taken down by Rustichello da Pisa, in French apparently, though an Italian version goes back to the first years of the fourteenth century. Long suspected of being a tissue of improbables, Marco Polo has gained in reputation with developing knowledge. Via the caravan routes he comes to the eastern sources of the spice trade, sees with his own eyes the fabulous realm of Cathay. Beyond the deserts he looks with a fresh eye on an unrecorded world, and leaves a book which has no parallel in its time, or in Italian literature.

Exceptional too, if in another way, is Dino Compagni (*c.* 1255–1324). Before him we have the *Historia Fiorentina* of Ricordano Malespini, and the same air of controversy has enveloped both these authors. Malespini writes of the origins of Florence in a naïve style, and has been thought of as cribbing from Villani. First printed in 1568, and Compagni not till 1728, either might have been the subject of forgery. Of the two it is Compagni who matters most. A *popolano* of Florence at that moment when the struggle is developing between the nobles and the rising power of the merchant class, Dino Compagni was spectator of the background of faction to Dante's poem. Here, instead of the flat accumulation of the medieval chronicle, is a narrative bursting with energy, and with a strong delineation of the major characters, as with Giano della Bella, or with Corso Donati, the haughty leader of the Blacks. Here all the characters are given life and motion, and the times of Dante set in strong relief. So strong, indeed, that the very usefulness of the book has seemed the reason to deny its authenticity. But Compagni keeps his place among the legitimate company of Italian authors more securely than Malespini. Of greater bulk, of equal importance, though with less imprint of personality, is the *Cronica* of Giovanni Villani (1276?–1348), later continued by his brother Matteo (d. 1363) and his son Filippo. Like Dante, Villani goes back to the beginnings, with Nimrod and the Tower of Babel; and in the alphabetical arrangement of chronology he accumulates all sorts of information, strung in short unrelated chapters. Equable in his judgements, Villani is a foundation-stone for our knowledge; but the duller surface, and the greater bulk, will send the reader back to Compagni, or else on to Machiavelli. Meanwhile with these writers, and with such works as Bono Giamboni's version of Brunetto Latini's *Tresor* and Ristoro d'Arezzo's *Libro della Composizione del Mondo* (c. 1282) – the first vernacular attempt at a scientific explanation of the world – the stream of prose works is developing into a tradition.

There are two paths to its great early monument, the *Decameron*: through the rest of Boccaccio's writing, and through the undergrowth of the short story. The first has been often rehearsed, the second is often left unrelated, following a scornful judgement of De Sanctis which made the search for sources a petty task, idle work for old women. And there are obstacles also: first in the fluidity of the oral tradition, where stories may float from India to North Wales; then in the equal fluidity of medieval Latin, so that collections which offer prototypes may come from all over Europe – just as they may come from outside, by a process of transvasation of a Sanscrit original via intermediary languages to Vulgar Latin. So the *Pantchatantra* and the *Libro dei Sette Savi* work their passage west, the former in a Spanish, the latter in an Italian version. In this fantastic traffic the strangest representative is that life of Buddha, written in Sanscrit in the sixth century, which by successive transformations ends as the biography of a Christian saint, appearing in Tuscan guise as the *Vita di Barlaam e Josafat*. And while the East supplies its quota (and offers the useful device of a frame), the West contributes to the birth of a new genre, from the *examples* (*exempla*) used in the pulpit. With Jacques de Vitry these short stories are culled from sermons given, and soon will be culled in the same abbreviated form to be preached. The emphasis falls on a single point, nor is there any regard for verisimilitude. This is indeed conspicuous by its absence, as in the case of the usurer, buried with his money bags. His relatives hasten to exhumation, only to find his gold red-hot with devils pouring it down his throat. ... Sometimes the moral is hard to extort; sometimes we may feel at the source the drift from the pulpit to the tavern.

But the start, at least, is pious; nor does this conflict with the elements of misogynism and asceticism coming from the East. Sometimes this surface will remain, as in the case of Fra Jacopo Passavanti (1302–57), Prior of Santa Maria Novella in 1348, who wrote *Lo Specchio della Vera Penitenza* about the same time as the *Decameron*. He takes from Bede the story of the Englishman who died in 806, then came to life again. Instead of listening to congratulation he fled, built himself a cell beside a river, heated a great cauldron, and alternated between standing in the water of the river up to his chin till his clothes were soaked, freezing in the wind upon the bank, then boiling in the cauldron. This process he continued till his death. It is a painfully obvious little story, and we hardly need the explanation, that he preferred to do justice himself rather than suffer what he had glimpsed. Passavanti quotes the names of his well-known sources, the *Vitae Patrum*, the *Homilies* of St Gregory, Caesarius of Heisterbach, the Bishop Jacques de Vitry; nor naturally does he betray the intentions with which they wrote. This is particularly true of one he takes over from Helinandus, and which we know because in the *Decameron* we find it in reverse in the story of Nastagio degli Onesti: here the lady is pursued in the next world for unkindness to her lover, not for its opposite. The same sea-change has taken place to the apologia of Boccaccio for his own indulgence towards love in the Introduction to Day IV. For this is an eastern story that came in with *Barlaam e Josafat*, of the youth brought up within a vault till ten years, taken to view the objects of the upper air, and wanting only one thing which he saw, though his mentors called this demonic. And the one thing was, of course, a girl. Told with misogynistic intent, it shows how deadly is the lure, and spread like wildfire through the collections of stories. *En route*, some preacher found the word *devils* too strong, and put *geese* instead, with which childish emendation it came to Boccaccio. But as with Nastagio, he reshaped its moral: no longer, beware the charmer! but instead, who can resist what Nature means for all?

That process is not peculiar to Boccaccio, and we could find it in Sacchetti; and with it also another development, by which the short, generic, canvas receives particulars, and expands. In this momentum a story which in its first version was a clear invention, with no habitat, acquires the aspect of observed reality. A glaring case will make this plain. Antiquity had offered little towards the short story, but one item was to hand: the Matron of Ephesus as told by Petronius in his *Satyricon*. This can be found rejunevated in a rhymed version of the *Libro dei Sette Savi*, as also among the *Cento Novelle Antiche*. And here it begins with some assurance, 'The Emperor Frederick hanged one day a great nobleman for some misdeed'. This general process of acquiring a surface that looks like reality is one that we must bear in mind when thinking of 'realism' in the *Decameron*. Meanwhile, we have come to the collection which is in some ways the foundation-stone of the Italian *novella*, the *Novellino*, or *Hundred Old Tales*. Its authorship is uncertain, though it must be Florentine, its date between the end of the Duecento and the first decades of the fourteenth century. Its aim is to be a model for conversation. Here the *exemplum*, still recognizable, steps to a lay usage; and since this had laid hands on all the scraps available the *Novellino* follows suit. All its stories are of the nature of a paragraph, and its uncertain grasp of what is comic (or can make a story) makes its brevity at times akin to poverty. A novelty is the introduction of Arthurian and Provençal elements which give a flavour of romance. Here the moralization has slipped out of the bottom, and there is one case where this tendency is strikingly attested: the story of the father who had his precious ring copied, then left one each to his three sons. In the *Gesta Romanorum* the real one (standing for the true faith, against the Saracen and Jewish) could be tested by its power to work a miracle. In the *Novellino* the story is told by a Jew to escape embarrassment, and leaves to the next world the decision which of the rings is real. 'And so it is with the three faiths. The Father above knows which is best, and the sons, that is ourselves, each thinks he has the good one.' Now this might be a scepticism potent as that of Montaigne, who saw religion as an accident of birth. And it is this version which finds consecration (if that is the *mot juste*) as the third story of the *Decameron*: 'Each one thinks his own inheritance the true Law and his commandments to be followed; but as to which one has it, as with the rings, the question still remains.' Now this is a story, and being detached from its original moral, it may have none at all. But along with the indulgence in natural sensuality it has been taken sometimes (and this is why I cited Montaigne) as the coming of the Renascence, setting men free from the restraints of religion and morality. But the very fact that we have found this in so patently medieval a collection as the *Novellino* is indicative of the objections to this view. Asceticism and religiosity are one side of the Middle Ages, but we can find another in such strongly marked works as the *fabliaux*, or the

Carmina Burana. And that enthusiasm for embracing all the works of the flesh, in what way it is different from what we can find in so medieval a work as the *Roman de la Rose*? There is no need to wait for the Renascence for the resurrection of the flesh.

We shall come back to some of these early stories as models for Boccaccio, and may leave them reluctantly, as a beguiling sea on which one longs to drift. But before we look to the *Filocolo* there is a pleasing author to whom we can put a name, and who is linked with the *novella*. This is Francesco da Barberino (1264–1348), who might – as his dates attest – have been among the poets of the *dolce stil* were his love poetry extant. As it is, he put the principles of love according to their view into his *Documenti d'Amore*, where allegorical figures give their teaching (that is the sense of *documenti*) on other matters than on only love. The manner is more pleasing than the matter. But it is the treatise *Del Reggimento e Costumi di Donna* (not earlier than 1318) which deserves our gratitude. In an age of misogynism it sees women in an attractive light, and illustrates in prose and verse precepts concerning their behaviour and position in society. In this way it paints a welcome picture of the social scene. And here also, roughly contemporary with the *Novellino*, we have short stories introduced, still thought of as *exempla*, but no longer in a sermon, and in less naïve language than in that collection. Once it has penetrated here the *novella* is ready to turn up in unexpected places, as in the *Volgarizzamento del Libro ... degli Scacchi* of Fra Jacopo da Cessole; and of course the scraps on which it fed, Valerius Maximus, Aesop, or Phaedrus, appear also in translation. So we have a manifold flavour to this new genre. The east was not bound to the single point of the *exemplum*, and tended to throw light on behaviour in a supple narrative sequence; and it provided the idea of a frame which was often, as with the *Libro dei Sette Savi*, as fragile as the stories. And everywhere we find the rudimentary story which only awaits the embroidery of particulars to give it life and movement. In this same *Libro dei Sette Savi* we can find the promising tale of the Jealous Man shut out of his house. It is one of the original inhabitants of this frame, coming from India, to be embellished in the *Decameron* (VII, 4), after appearing in the *Disciplina Clericalis* of Petrus Alphonsus, which is one of the most fascinating source-books of all. Written by a Spanish Jew (born 1065, converted 1106) with the object of improving people, its title sounds as musty as its purpose, or as the *Scenes of Clerical Life* of the late George Eliot. But it is fuller of meat than the proverbial egg, and the stories of Maimundus the servant, the weeping little bitch, or the half-friend, deserve to immortalize their author. And here also is the story of the well, with all the kernel of the invention of *Decameron* VII, 4, but with an aura of inverisimilitude in the setting which will be cleared away by the time Boccaccio comes to narrate the story about characters he seems to know.

Before we look to the *Decameron* to observe the progress he has made we have to look to that other progress, from the youthful *Filocolo*; and we have to look a little at the changing picture of Giovanni Boccaccio (1313–75). For a long time his epitaph, self-written, passed as evidence for his birth at Certaldo. But nineteenth-century scholarship discovered a whole web of autobiographical passages in his writings, and there was substituted the romantic version of birth in Paris, where his merchant father met a noble lady. And this was paralleled later. Sent as a boy to Naples to learn the ways of commerce, after one or two prosaic love-affairs, Boccaccio met and seduced Maria d'Aquino, natural daughter to King Robert of Naples, and immortalized her in various works, under the name of Fiammetta. And of course the critics had an easy task in pointing out the earthiness of Fiammetta after the ethereal or elusive Beatrice and Laura. Once more, the new age seemed inaugurated, medieval idealism dissipated by the spirit of enjoyment. But the inconsistencies of this web of pseudo-autobiography are now apparent. Boccaccio was romancing in this double ennoblement of his life, and following a literary bent of his own time. The earthy Fiammetta has now become more elusive, less real, than either Laura or Beatrice, a mere invention and a dream. That is not without its own irony, and may compensate for some of the difficulties of his chronology. In a statement which is above suspicion, in the late work *De Genealogia Deorum*, Boccaccio spoke of the six years wasted as pupil of a merchant, and of as much again under the same paternal compulsion in the study of Canon Law. Twelve years, but which? It all depends when Boccaccio went to Naples. In the clash of opinions about precise dates we may take comfort that it is other things than dates that are important. Even without Maria d'Aquino the atmosphere of Naples is decisive for the flavour of Boccaccio's youthful works. Turning his back upon the merchant world to which his father destines him, Boccaccio looks to all the pleasures of the courtly world of Naples, and to the chivalrous tradition. It is this that is reflected in the romances, in prose or *ottava rima*, which begin with the Filocolo, and continue with the *Filostrato* and the *Teseida*. The *Ninfale Fiesolano* marks the cleavage from the Neapolitan to the Tuscan scene, and to a rustic level which presages the bourgeois side of the *Decameron*. And at Naples too came the first distant view of Petrarch, glimpsed when he came to be examined by King Robert as a candidate for coronation with the laurel wreath upon the Capitol. Boccaccio watched as an onlooker, and was fired with enthusiasm. Henceforth he began to collect the scraps from Petrarch's table, to put together a *De Vita et Moribus Domini Francisci Petrarchi*, and to be stirred to a new fervour of production.

For the rest, the particulars of Boccaccio's life are not of much importance. He met Petrarch personally in 1350 when the latter passed through Florence to the Jubilee. He held minor offices in Florence, and went on minor missions to Romagna and Milan. Without the affluence of Petrarch he remains for the most part between Florence and Certaldo with the dis-ease of a poor scholar. With his enthusiasms too: and it is Boccaccio more than Petrarch who is responsible for those first strivings to bring Greek within the field of knowledge, and he bore with the impossible Leonzio Pilato in a patient effort to secure a grounding in Greek, and a literal translation of Homer. Less strong a character than Petrarch, he looks up to him with reverence; but he looks also another way, back to Dante. And this twin loyalty remains to the end: in his last years he is the first public exponent of the *Divine Comedy* in Florence, and his unfinished *Comento su Dante* is accompanied by a *Trattatello* in praise of Dante – a short life which has received more attention in recent times than formerly, when Boccaccio was thought a gossiping guide to Dante.

In spite of that reverence, Boccaccio frequently inverts the scraps he repeats from Dante; and has been thought of as a new departure, as if a difference in temperament must involve the opening of an era. But if Boccaccio perverts what he finds in Dante it is because he represents another side of the Middle Ages, not because he stands for the new world of the Renascence. As the light of recent criticism has played upon his work, and the old prejudices dissolved, it is a medieval Boccaccio that has emerged, in substance and in form. From Dante he derives the matter and the form of the *Amorosa Visione* (but with an undantesque twist), or the ambition to break new ground in the *Teseida*; from Petrarch will come the impulse to erudition, by which the last period of Boccaccio's life is given over to the compilation of encyclopedic works, of which we may take the *Genealogy of the Gods* as strongest representative. On both sides it is the spirit animating the original mind, Dante or Petrarch, which escapes Boccaccio; and in reality, the tendency to accumulated erudition is his from the beginning, in the *Filocolo*, which by this overlay has usually been taken to have been made illegible.

We have come back to this development of Boccaccio's minor works; and this first one should be a variant of the touching idyll, *Aucassin et Nicolete*, for it derives from a French congener, *Floire et Blanchefleur*. Only here the theme has been well-nigh drowned in a long accumulation, not so much of episodes as of irrelevant material. Most notable in this is the section in Book V, where the ardent Florio, in his pursuit of the abducted Biancofiore, is becalmed in Naples, and listens in the garden to those Questions about Love which bring the first crop of *novelle*: including two which will be repeated without a great deal of change in the *De-cameron*. Or if in one of them there is a change, in the story of Messer Ansaldo and the enchanted garden we may well prefer the verve with which the ingredients of the poisoned cauldron are produced. For though it is often taken that the *Decameron* comes down to earth, you can hardly convert to realism a story, the kernel of which is the creation of an enchanted summer garden in mid-winter to win a reluctant lady's love, by the mere process of omitting the mechanism of the magic used. The surface of the *Decameron* at this point can only be illusionary. Outside the *Questioni d'Amore* the *Filocolo* proceeds by amplification of a simple tale: brought up together, Florio and Biancofiore (what wonder when they have been educated on that book of Ovid in which 'il sommo poeta mostra ... i santi fuochi di Venere'?) fall in love, and Florio's royal parents go to all lengths to ward off the *mésalliance*. But who can fight against so general a thing as love? The ancient gods (whom Virgil had renounced in the *Divine Comedy*) fight openly for Florio, Biancofiore concurs upon the irresistible force of Love; and when Florio is finally united with her the sensual nature of Boccaccio runs riot in a full glow of warmth.

In the *Filocolo* all Boccaccio is in germ; nevertheless the reader may turn with relief to the *Filostrato* if only because the new verse-medium has shaken out the superfluous fat. Again Boccaccio is derivative, this time from the *Roman de Troie* of Benoît de Sainte-Maure: a guarantee there will be no classical quality to the treatment. Here Troilus, Cressida, and Pandar are launched on their European career, though Pandar, especially, has far to develop. It is he who presses on Cressida that advice of Jehan de Meung which used to do duty for the spirit of the Renascence:

> Querre doit d'amors le déduit,
> Tant cum Jonesce la déduit;
> Car quant Viellesce fame assaut,
> D'amors pert la joie et l'assaut.
> Le fruit d'amors, se fame est sage,
> Coille en la flor de son aage.

It does not lessen the piquancy that Pandar urges Cressida to yield to Troilus in words which Virgil used to spur Dante up the slopes of Purgatory. ... After this victory, the main subject of the *Filostrato* is the absence of Cressida, summoned by her father to the Grecian camp. And already there are touches which show Boccaccio happier in comic invention than in the effort towards solemnity of poetic devices. Yet it was a remark of Dante in the *De Vulgari Eloquentia* – that no one had sounded the trump of war in vernacular poetry – which prompted Boccaccio to the *Teseida*. And indeed it has twelve books, and as many lines as the *Aeneid*. But that is not enough to give it epic qualities: this element may be reduced to the enumeration of combatants, while the real subject is the competition of the captive knights, Palemone and Arcita, for the love of Emilia. Perhaps because the triangle is more normal, or Boccaccio more experienced, the handling seems firmer than that of the *Filostrato*. Here are the same commonplaces (as on Fortune), that medieval note of the springtime of the year, and stock epithets for Emilia; and in the victory of the appellant to Venus over the one to Mars we have a confirmation of Boccaccio's authorship.

The *Ameto* and the *Amorosa Visione* are by the way of being the dullest of Boccaccio's minor works, although the first has been given adventitious importance as a factor in the birth of pastoral. Seven nymphs, who should represent seven virtues, and whose recital of their often scandalous amours derusticates the swain Ameto. What is chiefly notable is not the allegory, which never holds together, but the emergence of the sensual Boccaccio without timidity. The *Amorosa Visione* also, the most pseudo-dantesque of his works, should contain an allegory, and might seem to be the *Ameto* in a different guise. But it is Boccaccio's erudition that is more evident here than his sensuality. Led by a Donna Gentile (a Boccaccian counterpart to Virgil-guide) he traverses the realm of spirits, harvesting a store of ancient stories (Pyramus and Thisbe, Orpheus and Eurydice, the loves of the gods ...): even Dante himself appears to him in the Elysian Fields. Characteristically, he falls for one of the fair ladies, and while the Donna Gentile leaves them discreetly to their own devices Boccaccio forgets the stairs that he should climb to virtue, wakes from his vision, and takes leave of us. As for the allegory, it is to be deduced that he thought no more of it.

The *Fiammetta* has been the most-rated, and the most controversial, of the minor works. When Fiammetta was thought of as being real, and as having jilted her lover, this book was thought of as being his revenge: annoying her by inverting the roles, and analysing the torment of Fiammetta, abandoned by Panfilo. As a revenge, it hardly seemed effective; and if Fiammetta had no existence, it must find other explanation. Here Boccaccio begins by renouncing the fanciful and the heroic elements of his earlier books ('here you will find no Greek fables adorned with many lies, nor Trojan battles foul with blood'), and it has seemed in consequence to be the first psychological novel, founded on experience. But without Fiammetta it becomes more plausible as a prose imitation of the *Heroides* of Ovid, and this story of a heroine abandoned owes not a little of its air of reality to the practice of that master. The place is Naples, the actors have a local habitation and a name, but the atmosphere and the details are for the most part what we should expect from the copybook of Love. Seen from this angle, this is a long epistle, not a short novel. Naturally, such an interpretation does not displace the *Fiammetta* from its eminence: it accounts for the sureness of its handling, on the base of literature rather than of life.

With the *Ninfale Fiesolano* Boccaccio is seen to change direction. Here is a rustic idyll localized in Tuscany, even though the shade of Ovid lingers round it. The classical baggage, the attempted elevation of tone of the *Teseida*, has gone; instead, Boccaccio has caught the air of popular poetry, never losing sight of the plump reality of Mensola. This is a climbing down, leaving his literary ambitions for something more artless, and more satisfying. Africo loves Mensola, and she is of Diana's nymphs (or if we like, a nun). She shuns him, but his stratagem is simple, and successful. When she is found with child there is left the indignation of Diana, and the metamorphosis into the streams that run through the Tuscan countryside. So slight the elements, so rustic all the tone, that the *Ninfale* will always please more than most of its company. More certainly than the *Corbaccio* (with which, setting aside the unimportant *Rime* and the *Caccia di Diana*, we are left). The *Corbaccio* runs away, not into pseudo-classical rhetoric or erudite examples, but into the vulgar Florentine. Once more, there is an autobiographical pose, the slightly elderly Boccaccio, back in Florence, jeered at by a widow to whom he made advances, and retaliating with a savage libel on women altogether. Was he blinded by a particular pique, or has he gathered here all the latent misogynism of the Middle Ages? At one point he uses the medieval word of *remedies*, and he may well be here sloughing off what had tempted most. Petrarch also will cogitate on *quid sit femina*, and Dante's vision of the *femmina balba* ended in a stench. The unction with which Boccaccio writes in the *Corbaccio* suggests that he thought of himself as fulfilling a traditional function. But the author of the *Decameron* had probably not the right, and the author of the *Corbaccio* carries the remedy to obscenity. Whatever we think of its origins we shall have no regret in leaving it for the *Decameron*.

By Boccaccio's indications the *Corbaccio* belongs to 1354; and for the *Decameron* we have a starting limit from the Black Death of 1348, so that the early 1350s are its traditional date. This plague which forms the frame has often seemed symbolic: out of the stricken world of Florence to the calm luxury of the villa on the Fiesolan hillside. Out of the ascetic world, with its emphasis on death and on eternity, into the gay light of the Renascence, with its note of enjoyment while you may. I have already quoted the *Roman de la Rose*, and might add the goliards, with the Archpoet at their head, as a reminder that wine and women is an old story, not reserved for the rebirth of learning. Indeed, if the coarseness of the *Decameron* is the sign of a new age, why were the medieval *fabliaux* coarser than the *Decameron*? And the frame is a device which we must not mistake for reality; nor can we accept the assumption of De Sanctis that the unification given by the frame extends to the stories themselves. They are obviously unequal in development and value. Some are of a kind which does not admit of any ripening: witness the arid day given over to witty sayings, where nine stories are run through in little more than the space taken by the longest one of the tenth day. Nor must we place too much reliance on the concept of the *Decameron* as an illustration of all the parts of Italy through which the exile Dante begged his bread. And here the experience we have made with the Matron of Ephesus is relevant: born in the pages of Petronius, yet attributed with all assurance to the time of Frederick II. But can we take it as casting light upon the latter? In the eighteenth century a historian of the *Decameron* took all its tales as having a historic basis. But the process is an opposite one: the weaving of a web of imaginary, but lifelike, particulars so that the surface can deceive us by its apparent reality.

It is time to see this in concrete instances. In Petrus Alphonsus there was a tale, of Indian origin, indicative of women's wiles. Taught by a wiseacre a young man built a house with high stone walls, one door, one window, and this at such a height that no one could get in or out. In the morning he went out and locked the door behind him, and locked it too on his return. When he was asleep the keys were safe under his head. Meanwhile the wife, so packeted, gazed from the window, and fell in love with a proper youth. She started to encourage her husband to drink, then stole the keys, and then stole out. But he knew that women's actions are never without guile, pretended one evening to be drunk, and when she slipped out, fastened the door, and waited at the window. The inevitable scene ensued, until she threatened to drown herself in the well, so that he'd have to answer for her death. And splash! she dropped a big stone in, and hid behind the parapet: he came out to see, she darted in, locking the door. He began to rail, she to reproach him for stealing out a-whoring every night, and in the morning her relatives came and laid about him, believing her. Now in this pretty tale the point is clear, but the circumstances sound unreal. Where did you leave the milk in such a sort of house? who did the shopping, or the housework? Turn to the *Decameron* (VII, 4), and all has sprung into a homely life which Boccaccio seems to know. There was a rich man in Arezzo, Tofano by name. He marries handsome Monna Ghita, and is jealous without cause. This she decides to give him. Amongst his bad qualities is drinking, which she encourages with a purpose; and when she has put him drunk to bed she slips out to see her lover, or, sure of the situation, brings him home. This goes on until he notices that she does not participate in the bottle. His suspicions aroused, he comes home roaring drunk, apparently, and the situation develops as before. As before, except that Boccaccio has listened to all the conversation. He's mistaken, she has been with a female neighbour who could not sleep. ... And then, when she threatens suicide in the well, 'May God forgive you, put my distaff away for me.' Then while he tries to fish her out, from the window, 'You should water it when you drink it, not afterwards at night.' He would wait patiently at the door, but she abuses him, he answers, the neighbours pop their heads out, and she informs them all how he distresses her, spending his substance *tout aux tavernes et aux filles*. With all the noise her family appears, to beat him up and take her home. He sees what jealousy has brought him to, and to get her back promises he won't be jealous any more, 'and furthermore gave her permission to do just as she pleased, but so prudently, that he should not know of it.' So to the Boccaccian moral of the tale: good luck to Monna Ghita.

I have reduced this till the two may seem the same, but it is clear that they are the same, and opposites. The unconvincing bare page of Petrus Alphonsus has become six pages which move with unflagging verve through detail which seems too rich to be invented, and the scene is in Arezzo not so far away. But who can say, knowing the first, that the second contains any realism? What has happened is that the bonds which held back the oriental apologue, or the *exemplum*, have been cut, and at this moment the story blossoms in its own right (facing, in so far as its 'moral' is concerned, in a precisely contrary direction). Sometimes, as here, the result is brilliant: because the ingredients of the intrigue, apart from a few externals which have been discarded, are human, and lend themselves to development. But sometimes also, and this tends to be the case in the closing days of the *Decameron*, the ground is less suitable, the scaffolding more elaborate, and defeats its purpose. Nowhere is this clearer than in another story from the same source, that of *Tito e Gisippo* (x, 8). In Petrus Alphonsus this contest of generosity is between two men who did not know each other except by hearsay, one from Baldach, the other an Egyptian. The first came on business to Egypt, stayed a week, a welcome guest. Then he fell ill, of love, of course, for the girl being brought up to be a bride to his host. As it was life or death, the latter waived his claim, and the guest with his new wife went back to Baldach. Later, the Egyptian lost his property, and set out for Baldach, but was ashamed to approach his friend. Taking refuge in a temple, he was the witness of a homicide, and arrested as the culprit. Thinking to end his wretchedness, he made no demur, but was rescued from the gallows by his friend who recognized him, and so offered to take his place. Whereat the real murderer was shamed to confession, and all eventually set free.

Not the best of Petrus's stories, it has an air of unlikeliness about it, and before Boccaccio it had been improved on to the extent of positing a strong bond of friendship between the pair. But it is Boccaccio who gives the most circumstantial scaffolding. Under Augustus a young Roman, because he was so clever, is sent to Athens to study philosophy, and recommended by his father to Chremes, who boarded him and brought him up with his own son. Their friendship grew so strong 'that it was never separated except by death' (albeit the story will soon demand their separation). Chremes dies, Gisippo's friends urge him to marry, choose Sophronia as his bride. Tito sees her, falls in love himself, and after debating for two pages on what to do decides to die. Gisippo gets his secret from him, nobly sacrifices himself (loving more temperately). But then the search for expansion and verisimilitude leads to the most impossible of situations. The match has been arranged by relatives, and it would cause a scandal to upset it: and they might marry her to someone else. So on with the ceremony, and when she's home she shall be yours! Tito's room is contiguous, and he slips in by night, and out of scruple asks if she will be his wife, and weds her with a ring, while she consents, taking him for Gisippo. So this goes on, with Gisippo her daytime husband, Tito so by night. I leave the rest because the point, I think, is clear: that this improbable story has been made more so by the elaboration meant to give it life. And there are others in the closing days in which the process has defeated itself. Indeed, if Boccaccio had in mind an overall plan resembling the *Divine Comedy*, starting with vice (condemned, or condoned?) to end with the praise of virtue, he may not have been more capable of keeping to the target in the *Decameron* than in the *Amorosa Visione* or the *Ameto*: only more interesting.

The *Decameron*, then, is neither the new world of the Renascence, nor a work of realism. It is a free work of the imagination, in which old tales are given as much life as Boccaccio can afford. It follows that it should be all the better mirror of Boccaccio. And here the germs which we have spied from the *Filocolo* on have come to flower. There are two high ministers to the world, Nature and Fortune, and who can resist the natural power of Love? Troilus gave thanks to Pandar and to God, for his conquest of Griseida; and nothing is more common as an ending here than a repetition of the thanks which Rinaldo d'Asti (II, 2) gives to God and to St Julian for their aid. And this was: stripped naked by robbers, and left chattering with cold outside the city walls, he was let into a house, found there a lady whose lover had not come, a bath, a meal, a bed and bedfellow, and in the morning had her late husband's clothes. While on issuing he found the robbers taken, his property returned. It is here that we must glance at Boccaccio's attitude to religion, so cynically revealed in this paternoster to St Julian. The easy comment is that he attacks, as Dante did, the abuses of the clergy, respecting dogma. That is convenient, but hardly adequate: for though Boccaccio does once or twice work up some indignation on this theme, yet he seldom fails to applaud where clerics indulge in the natural pursuits of the flesh (let I, 4 or III, 1 be witnesses). Nor does he stop short of doctrine: does he not invert the story out of Helinandus, so that Nastagio degli Onesti (v, 8) sees the pains of the next world punish continence in this? And we may compare the story of Passavanti told above with that of Ferondo (III, 8), returning as he thinks from the next world, where he has learnt that the sin of jealousy is punished; or, if this is merely playing, with the revelations of Tingoccio (VII, 10) on penalties in the next world. All these support that surprising sequence of the first three stories of the *Decameron*, with that transformation, by *purity of faith*, of Ser Cepperello into San Ciappelletto. There we might read into the story all the lessons of Anatole France's *Île des Pingouins* on the nature of saintliness, seen at first hand. And this is followed by the story of the Jew who would not be converted without a pilgrimage to Rome; whereat his Paris colleague fell into despair, only to find on his return that having found Rome a 'smithy of devilish works' he was ready to be baptized, because to grow and shine in spite of this there must be a divine basis to the Christian faith. It is a brutal story, but it may not be ill-meant. Yet how does it fit, if so, with the following one, of the three rings, where we have seen the conclusion, that the question is still open, which of the faiths is the true one? And what should we say, to look no further, of the cynical conclusion to the whole *Decameron*, where Boccaccio tells us, if we have laughed too much, we can soon be cured by resort to the lamentations of Jeremiah, the Passion of the Saviour, and the regrets of Mary Magdalene? Nor is this flippancy at all at odds with the texture of the book.

The *Decameron* remains a medieval monument, crowded with rich stories, of which we may make the old comment, *se non è vero è ben trovato*. In this addition of a lifelike habitat it is natural that much of the surface of Boccaccio's Italy transpires: elsewise, the invention would not have so much life. But there is little of that indelible stamping of some locality which we can find in Dante's snap-shots. Where Andreuccio meets adventure in the streets of Naples we may be sure Boccaccio

knows his way about, or a dark wood may be on the merchants' route from Naples to Florence. But when a story comes
out of Petrus Alphonsus the fact that Boccaccio has confidently transferred its venue to Arezzo must not make us
think we end with any genuine knowledge of Arezzo. What
is truer is that characters, as Fra Cipolla, live with an intensity
which the lay figures of the *novella* had not known before,
and will hardly know again. Nor, as has been often said, are
all the stories vulgar, and among the thirty salvaged for
presentation to the young there will be found the firmness
and tragic dignity of Ghismonda, the tragedy of Guglielmo
Guardastagno's heart, and the touching tale of Madonna
Beritola. Here, before in the last days Boccaccio over-
developed the formula of the *novella* (following success too far
along the road), it burns with its brightest flame, lighting the
two sides, the Neapolitan-chivalrous and the Florentine-
bourgeois, of Boccaccio's make-up. It is a plaguy, roguish,
greasy world, and Boccaccio sees its undersides most sharply.
But he did not write the *Decameron* with any firm programme
of ideas in his mind, and we must take it for what it is. Which
includes, of course, that periodic style, so cumbersome at
times, and yet so often interwoven with some short plebeian
pith. It was De Sanctis who said, He writes like Cicero, and
thinks like Plautus. And now this needs emendment, for this
style – whose imitation was to burden Italian prose for several
centuries – was born of medieval rhetoric, and looked to
Livy for its Latin air. But the mixture was individual to
Boccaccio, and is one of the richest parts of the flavour of the
book.

CHAPTER 4

Petrarch and the New World of Learning

IT was only slowly that the Petrarch of the *Rime* took priority. Even the *Trionfi* at first outshone the *Rime*, though we should regard them as an appendage. Indeed, they echo, but do not renew, and in the series, from the Triumph of Love through those of Chastity (and Laura), Death, Fame, Time, and Eternity, we may see no more than a rationalized version of the *Rime*, in dantesque *terza rima* and with a coating of erudition. But here, where all the flecks that made the pattern of the surface have been removed the interest has dwindled. Nevertheless, worked on from perhaps as early as 1340–2, and not divulged till after Petrarch's death, they show a larger number of manuscripts in the next century than do the *Rime*. This is partly because they could seem a side, subordinate but palpable, of the learned Petrarch who loomed most large for his contemporaries, as for the first generation of the Quattrocento.

Even with Dante it has been impossible to disguise the fact that Italian Literature includes books still in Latin; and if these were marginal with Dante, yet here we have come to a point where the highroad of Italian culture switches into Latin. Nor, since the Rebirth of Learning is crucial for Europe as for Italy, can we dismiss it from our thoughts as outside our writ. If we did, we might find it hard to understand the literature of the fifteenth-century ending, as of the High Renascence. And we may come to this episode now with the knowledge that there is no clear, clean break, and that the sets of opposites, dear to the nineteenth century, apply no longer. Have we not seen that the Middle Ages were not wholly dominated by asceticism? Do we not know that Dante gave the strongest allegiance to Aristotle, the warmest enthusiasm to Virgil? Do we not also know that Petrarch, short of being another character, cannot mean to usher in a pagan world? The problem of the Renascence will be simpler if we remember that there is a continuity between the world of the Middle Ages and the new world of Humanism. But this must not be stretched so far as to imply that those three terms are indistinguishable, or that we can never say, Here we have left what was for what is going to be. And however much we find Petrarch medieval in many of his final attitudes, none shows more clearly as the hinge on which the future turns. And it is this Latin Petrarch who overshadows for a long time the poet of Laura.

His creative Latin may be limited substantially to the *Africa*, the epic poem in praise of Scipio on which his fame was to rest, and which won those offers of the laurel wreath in 1340 of which he took the Roman one, with its preliminary of examination by King Robert of Naples in the spring of 1341, when Boccaccio in the audience may have derived his first enthusiasm for his 'master and preceptor'. But the *Africa*, like the *Trionfi*, remained in Petrarch's hands until his death, and knew little of their diffusion afterwards. Even nineteenth-century scholarship dismissed it as a mere versification of Livy, and it has been left for our own time to see its subjective connexions with the attitudes of Petrarch, and to rate its achievement without prejudice against neo-classicism. Here also is that emphasis on death, more Christian than Roman; and in this narrative which centres on the victory of Scipio over Hannibal, Rome over Carthage, we still find insistent that note which is best known from the closing line of *Italia mia*,

I'vo gridando: Pace, pace, pace.

The *Africa* is eloquent of Petrarch's allegiance to Christianity, but it has not the impact of his prose-writings, nor their importance.

It was through his Letters principally that Petrarch was known to his contemporaries, and before he collected these into the *Familiares*, the *Seniles*, the *Sine Nomine*, there were enthusiasts like Boccaccio who treasured individual epistles in their first form, and added round them copies of what others they could find. Outside the Letters there is a long series of other works in Latin, sometimes the fruit of devotion (*De Vita Solitaria, De Ocio Religiosorum*); sometimes engaging in polemic, as in the best-known of these invectives, the *De Sui Ipsius et Multorum Ignorantia* (1367), written against the blind adherents of Aristotle and the formal logic of the Schools. Then there are the long collections, lives of famous men (*De Viris Illustribus*), remedies against the haps of fortune (*De Remediis Utriusque Fortunae*), with what should have ranked with these had it been finished, the book of memorable things (*Rerum Memorandarum Libri*). The *De Viris* and the *De Remediis* look in opposite directions, the first indicative of a shift in interests, the second a medieval concept, even if illuminated by a new width of learning. Then outside the series of works which Petrarch meant to give the world (even if he kept them to revise), there is the *Secretum Meum* (1342–3, revised 1353–8), whose very title expresses its personal nature, and the intention not to publish the secret conflict of his cares. Here, in years of spiritual crisis, Petrarch anatomizes – in the presence of St Augustine and Truth – his attitude to love and glory, the twin appetites to which he holds most dearly, and the problem of his own will. This last is an element which had no emphasis in Dante's poem, but which is of cardinal importance for Petrarch. The *Secretum* is not the whole of Petrarch, but it has always, and rightly, been taken as holding one of the main keys to the conflict revealed in the *Rime*.

Nor must we forget with this the Letter to Posterity. For in both we may sense the vanity which people have blamed in Petrarch. This is other than the haughtiness of Dante: Petrarch, so much more successful in his life, can presume not only his own worth, but also the concern of future generations for his personality. We left him as a young man at Avignon, and with his foot just on the ecclesiastical ladder he is able to live free from want with a succession of benefices. These, together with the patronage of the great (from the Colonna via the Visconti to the Carrara, Lords of Padua), open for him the life of the scholar and the traveller, the first independent observer of the European, as of the ancient, scene. And at times the Petrarch who takes for granted the laurel wreath, the homage of posterity, who collects his letters as of importance for the world at large, has been an object of dislike, as one who presumes too readily on our acquaintance. Nor was the nineteenth century slow in drawing the contrast between the steadfastness of Dante, defeated in his life, but unyielding in his mind, and the wavering nature of Petrarch: not only as recorded in the *Rime*, but in his hesitations, for instance, between Cola di Rienzo heir to the Roman Republic, Pope, and Emperor as the rightful lord of Rome. But there is a continuity in Petrarch's thought, and a rigidity in formulas may, as with Dante, only lead to a decreasing contact with realities, and opportunities.

We have seen implicit in this the sense of contrast, and must draw a dividing-line between Dante and Petrarch. Not that Petrarch has a new enthusiasm for the classical world unknown to Dante, or that he has abjured the world of medieval Christendom. The lines are subtler, but not less strong. Let us remember the distorting hand which Dante lays on Virgil to turn him into the sponsor of the Holy Roman Empire, and his guide; on Aristotle, to make him a 'catholic opinion'; on Cato, to make him worthy to signify God on earth. These are signs that Dante looks to antiquity not for its identity, but as a part of the medieval system. Dante in fact looks to absolute authorities, and to an order for the whole world. Let the whole be right, the individual will be right as well. He is not concerned with the candle to be lit by individual effort, but with the order of the world, the anatomy of its arrangement. And of course we know that Dante put his system forward at the moment when his absolute authorities were absent, or were wrong. In these conditions it is not Dante who discovers Virgil, it is Virgil who discovers a new field of action, where we may fail to recognize the poet of the *Aeneid*. His enthusiasm for the classical world is that of one looking away from it, not to it, and his mind is fastened in a rigid scheme seen as the one solution for the world's problems.

Now Petrarch also makes medieval assumptions about

antiquity. Could Providence have been silent then? Are not the moral truths of ancient writers proof of the contrary? Does not Cicero speak in part as if he were a Christian? All truth is true from the Truth; and one part – the moral world – was mapped in antiquity, and needs no changing after Revelation. But this is less dantesque than it may appear: for Petrarch sees no world order to appeal to, and envisages the moral world, not as something to be imposed by legislation for the whole, but to be achieved by the effort of the individual. Dante's authorities disappear without an echo: Aristotle can be wrong, or Cicero's eloquence more helpful in the pursuit of virtue. And while Dante wrote the *Monarchia* (what history must be in order to be right), Petrarch writes the lives of famous men, because in them lies the example of what we may achieve, or must avoid. The sense of the medieval mind is the anatomy of the world's ordering by theological argument; and only when it is abandoned is the scholar free to look back to the classical world to see what it really was. With Dante the individual fits into a niche, with Petrarch we become concerned with the effort of the individual to improvement. *Ignorance is a great poverty of the mind, than which there is no greater except vice.* Man is not just a pawn whom Pope or Emperor arranges rightly or wrongly on the chessboard: he is an individual with the possibility of development on the basis of man's experience and man's history. It is this building on experience, not theory, which is the mark of Petrarch; and in going back he has found food in the literature of Rome, while longing for a similar draught from that of Greece. Virgil, Horace, Livy, Cicero have been his constant friends: 'These books have impressed themselves so familiarly upon me that they are fixed not only in my memory, but in my bones, and have become one with my mind, so much that even if I never read them more in all my life they would still cling, having taken root in the innermost portion of my mind.' And this fervour leads to something new: in Verona (it seems) Petrarch discovers the letters of Cicero to Atticus, to Quintus and to Brutus (1344), piercing behind the literary works to the soul of Cicero, revealed at the crucial point of

Roman history. Nor can the process stop with this search for
the true face of the past as personality, or with the unearthing
of forgotten texts: it is prolonged into that second stage
which has seemed to some the true centre of Humanism. This
is the effort of philology, to use the Italian term, or of textual
criticism, which is ours. For the texts which came to light
had been immersed for centuries in an encrusting medium.
The task opening for scholarship was their restitution to a
pristine clarity.

Boccaccio stands with Petrarch in the discovery of texts,
and ahead of him in appreciation of the importance due to
Greek. For Petrarch, Latin literature eclipsed its predecessor,
and Cicero outshone Demosthenes. Boccaccio showed in the
De Genologia Deorum a truer apprehension of the merits of
Greek authors. And with him there comes back a knowledge
of Tacitus and Martial, with texts of Cicero, Seneca, Ovid,
and Apuleius; while from 1360 his house is the channel by
which the fervour of Petrarch is transmitted from north to
south, and the meeting-place of that circle (including Coluccio
Salutati and Luigi Marsigli) from which Florentine humanism
is to spring. In spite of his industry there is, as on that other
axis Boccaccio–Dante, some shrinkage on the way. In the
Filocolo Boccaccio revealed his bent for erudition, and for all
the eloquent defence of poetry in the *De Genologia* it is to
compilation that he turns in his later years. That marks him
off from Petrarch. Nor does Coluccio Salutati (1331–1406)
measure up to either, though he receives a strong imprint
from Petrarch, and is the first Florentine Chancellor to be a
scholar-humanist. Open to medieval influences Coluccio
reverts to the idea of a static universal empire willed by God,
and from Petrarch he inherited chiefly a vein of Christian
stoicism. It is another Chancellor of the Florentine Republic
who took the lead, in the person of Leonardo Bruni (1374?–
1444), when Florence met the threat of the Visconti, lords of
Milan, aspirants to an Italian monarchy. At one moment
Florence stood alone, with defeat imminent, and was retrieved
by the sudden death of Giangaleazzo Visconti (1402). As
the representative of liberty Florence looked to her traditions,

and her scholars solved the problem of her origins in a symbolic manner. For Dante the medieval legends hooked Florence on to Caesar: but now were found the republican origins of Florence, predestined champion of liberty in Italy. In the second part of Bruni's *Dialogi ad Petrum Histrum* there circulates a conscious Florentine and civic sentiment, which swells visibly in the *Laudatio* of Florence of 1403, and is later to find its full expression in the great *History of the Florentine People* (1415–1440s). The civic humanism of Bruni looks forward to that of Savonarola and of Machiavelli, while the Florentine attitude to history begins here with the omission of providence in history, and the search for human causes and effects. Nor is this due to a pagan attitude, for Bruni – accepting the identity of the moral aim in the ancient and the Christian world – clings firmly to religion as the most necessary of elements. Nor is the fifteenth century set, as used to be averred, towards incredulity, and the library of Lorenzo will still begin with the Fathers of the Church, as did Duke Frederick of Montefeltro in his studies. Nor is the present dismissed, and alongside Bruni, whose work is a paean for the new achievements of Florence, we can find a Benedetto Accolti who will write *On the pre-eminence of the men of his own time*. Nor can this pride be made compatible with a contempt for the tongue of Dante, Petrarch, and Boccaccio. Bruni wrote their praises in the second Dialogue *ad Petrum Histrum*, and in Italian wrote the Life of Dante. There is nothing here of that old equation between humanism and tyranny, Latin and a contempt for the free past of the commune. Indeed, the Latin tongue itself acquires the suppleness of a modern idiom instead of the stiffness of ancient speech. And in Bruni's orbit we have the vernacular history of Gregorio Dati, written 1407–8, under the impact of the struggle against Giangaleazzo, and pulsing with a Florentine pride. 'E puossi dire che tutta la libertà d'Italia stesse solo nelle mani de'Fiorentini, che ogni altra potenza li abbandonò.'

To reinforce this emphasis we have (*c.* 1430) the treatise of a disciple of Bruni, Matteo Palmieri (1406–?), *Della Vita*

Civile. The language is proof that Florentine humanism does not eschew the vernacular, the title redolent of post-Petrarchan impulses. Here after the groping for theological systems it is the active life of the citizen which is explored and extolled by the new generation. The ideal is a social one, reversing the values of the active and contemplative life, bringing a distrust of monasticism. And Palmieri writes off also the 'sciocche maraviglie' of medieval art, painting before Giotto, sculpture and architecture before Ghiberti or Brunelleschi. This idea of renewal echoes through the Quattrocento, long before it finds codification in Vasari. And cognate with this there is the attitude which vivifies the century: that of the dignity and possibilities of man. Even philology is strictly related to this theme, as we can see in the noble definition by Leonardo Bruni of the *studia humanitatis*, so called because they perfect mankind. From Salutati on, through writers like Poggio or Platina the theme of the active life recurs, and in Giannozzo Manetti (1396–1459) it soars into a paean. The very title, *On the dignity and excellence of man*, speaks for the content, where the achievements of the Quattrocento are met with full enthusiasm; and where the aim and point of man is written in terms which can sum up the century: *to do and to know*.

Agere et intelligere: the pattern for the formula is Leon Battista Alberti (1404–72). He too speaks this language, and is its obvious fulfilment. In the *Della Famiglia* he quotes, from Aristotle via Cicero, the idea of man 'come uno mortale Iddio felice, intendendo e faccendo con ragione et virtú': where the additions are as important as the citation. With Alberti we have at once writer, theorist of the arts, and their practitioner; his activity flares in half a dozen different fields. In the contemporary anonymous *Life: Whatever was done by the mind of man with elegance, that he thought almost divine*. In his own work on architecture, the *De Re Aedificatoria: The eyes especially are by their nature eager for beauty*. And elsewhere in the same book: *How many cities we saw as boys built all of wood which now are turned to marble!* If we wished to sum the Quattrocento in one breath we need look no farther: here in the spirit of humanism is both the impulse and the action, and we must not divorce the two. For the blaze of achievement which begins with Masaccio and Brunelleschi is born in this atmosphere. The façade of Santa Maria Novella, or the Temple of Rimini, is there to show that humanism is not exhausted in an unpractical world; and Alberti can legislate for painting, sculpture, and, supremely, for architecture. His great *De Re Aedificatoria* appears after his death, edited by no less a figure than Politian, setting the course of European architecture towards the humanistic trilogy, necessity, convenience, delight, until the eighteenth century. Meanwhile he promotes the poetic contest of 1441 (the Certame Coronario) and the interests of the vernacular. His eclogues start the vogue that is to lead via the *Arcadia* to the *Aminta*; nor is he shy of using the vernacular elsewhere, as notably in the *Della Famiglia*, which reflects the eager spirit of the age, with the conviction that man can do what he wills, as also the surface of Florentine society.

Elsewhere the heritage of Petrarch develops in different ways. Firstly, with the humanist educators, and such household names as Vittorino da Feltre (*c.* 1373–1446) or Guarino Veronese (1374–1460), with whom the new world of classical studies has a profoundly practical character, and is not divorced from piety. The theme of humanistic education nourishes a flourishing literature, from names we know, as Leonardo Bruni, Poggio, or from others, as Maffeo Vegio, P. P. Vergerio, or Enea Silvio Piccolomini. And then there comes the growth of criticism, the spirit of inquiry, implicit from Petrarch's first turning back to find the true surface of the past, not taking it for granted as an admitted element in a theological scheme. Lorenzo Valla (1407–57) is the great example: his *Elegantiae* sets out to recapture the Latin tongue in its purity, and provides a tool for the next two centuries, and the new weapons serve in his examination of the Donation of Constantine. Here the forgery of papal claims by the Decretalists is brilliantly exposed in the *De Falso Credita et Ementita Constantini Donatione*. Even more, he carries his criticism into delicate fields, and the *Annotations on the New*

Testament bring the new method of philological investigation to the Vulgate, opening the way for Erasmus and textual criticism. All this allows us a deduction about his most controversial work, the *De Voluptate ac de Vero Bono*. With Aquinas Aristotle had been absorbed into the Christian sphere; with Petrarch, Cicero, and by anticipation Plato; now in the enjoyment of man's heritage Epicurus also claims his place. The extreme views are put forward, appropriately, by Panormita, but the moderate assertion of beatitude as *voluptas*, and pleasure as a part of life, is not meant as anti-Christian. It runs parallel with Alberti's views on the enjoyment of the whole man, and is the logical consequence of the new directive towards the active life.

In the *Momus* of Alberti, amongst its Lucianesque humour, there was the idea of the need for a ruler to observe the past, think of the future, and look round upon the present; and we have seen with Bruni history as observation, replacing the dogmatism of Dante in the *Monarchia* and the amorphous chronicle. We shall find this new historical awareness echoing through the writings of one of the ablest popes of the fifteenth century, Enea Silvio Piccolomini (1405–64), elected in 1458 as Pius II. Unceasing in his literary activity, leaving from his carefree youth one of the successful stories of the Quattrocento (the *Historia de Duobus Amantibus*), and a bawdy play (*Chrysis*), as views on the supremacy of the Council over the Pope – all part of that famous abjuration as new pope (*Hold to Pius, spit out Aeneas*), his mature work throws strong light on the Germany he knew so well and so long as Imperial secretary, and his *Commentaries* to his own life contain the best descriptive writing of his time. And his astringent comments look clearly to the *verità effettuale*: as in *Europa*, 'All things were done according to the victor's will: nor did laws defend whom arms had not protected'; or in the *Commentaries*, on the defeated Sigismondo Malatesta, 'No pacts avail the vanquished, and treaties are dissolved in the process of defeat.' Such utterances, which could be multiplied, would till a little while ago have been called (had Pius II received due notice as a writer) pre-Machiavellian. Now they serve to show that there must be some other field for Machiavelli than the mere acceptance of reality, where perforce he comes too late to be a pioneer.

The first generation of the Quattrocento in Florence plays its share in the life of the state. With the coming of the Medicean principality a new attitude ensues, and a new category, the *letterato di corte*. The chief representative is Marsilio Ficino (1433–99), protégé of Cosimo de'Medici, and centre of the Platonic Academy, translator into Latin of all Plato's writings, author of the *Theologia Platonica*, with its attempt to fuse the Christian and Platonic traditions; but author also of a subtle shift in emphasis, by which the contemplative goal reasserts its primacy. And it may not be coincidence that this comes when there is no longer place, under the Medici, for Coluccio Salutati, Leonardo Bruni, or Donato Acciaiuoli, all free actors on the political scene. With Ficino beauty becomes something spiritual, and though he may not repeat the condemnation of the natural world as under the taint of sin, yet it is clear that with him the full inspiration of the Quattrocento world has lost its basis. This is even clearer with that phenomenon of learning, Giovanni Pico della Mirandola (1463–94), who stood ready to dispute *on all that can be known* (*De omni scibili*). Now by the title of his treatise, *De Hominis Dignitate*, Pico has been taken as following, even as consummating, the earlier tendency. But the dignity of man has here a different significance. Man has become the intermediate between the angel and the beast, capable of which he chooses. But who for Pico, being initiate, will look downwards? 'Who is there who will not desire, spurning all human interests, despising the goods of fortune, neglecting those of the body, to banquet with the gods while still on earth, and dewy with the nectar of eternity to receive, a mortal animal, the gift of immortality?' That is not a continuation from Manetti or Alberti, still less the climax of this theme of the dignity of man: it is its renunciation, more medieval than renascence in its temper. And this is echoed through his work, as in a letter to Aldus of 1491: 'Apply yourself to philosophy, but with this law, that you remember there is no philosophy which can call us away from the truth of mysteries. Philosophy seeks truth, theology finds it, and religion possesses it.' With Petrarch we abandoned speculation, to concentrate on the moral world; with Pico we have gone back to scrutinize behind the veil. There are mysteries to elucidate, and in the Septuagint the initiated reader can discover the Trinity, the incarnation of the Word, the divinity of the Messiah, and so forth. With Pico we come to hermeticism and cabalistic learning, and shall not do well to take it as the summit of fifteenth-century thought. It is, of course, substantially the rejection of what has gone before.

With the other major scholar of Medicean Florence we are on more non-committal ground. This is Angelo Ambrogini (1454–94), called Politian from his birthplace, Montepulciano. For with Politian scholarship has become an end in itself. In his *Letters* we shall find, not the play of ideas, but controverted points, mainly linguistic and textual; and this is the main concern of his *Miscellanies*. In Latin poetry he indulges his taste for delicate embroidery, and lays under contribution the poets of the Latin decadence whom we shall find amongst his inspiration in the *Stanze per la Giostra*. This is an eclecticism which makes him stand against the imitation of any single author, or any single style, ready to use the full range of the Latin tongue, even to its more curious recesses; and in this he is an abettor of Francesco Colonna and that quaint phenomenon, the *Hypnerotomachia Poliphili*. But on the other side he is one of the sharpest instruments in the battle to amend corrupted texts. The splendour of Renascence learning is maintained by both Ficino and Politian, but the world of Leonardo Bruni is with them in abeyance.

With Politian we have come to Latin verse instead of Latin prose, which is the main vehicle of the early Quattrocento, and its true voice. Even in this rapid survey we must still add Flavius Blondus, as Biondo Biondi (1392–1463) called himself, to the major figures of the first tradition. In his *Roma Instaurata* we have Christian Rome as the heir of Latin grandeur; and in his major work, the *Historiarum ab Inclinatione Romanorum Decades*, covering the period 412–1441, we have the first Decline and Fall of the Roman Empire. For Valla, in the pulsating prefaces to the whole and to the separate books of the *Elegantiae*, the Roman language was the foundation and the cement for the fabric of learning, more vital than the Empire itself. And here the heritage of Rome appears all the more august for its disappearance, and for the first time the Middle Ages appear as a concept, and as something past. Then in the venerable figure of Cristoforo Landino (1424–1504) we can still find echoing, with his *Disputationes Camaldulenses*, the theme of social virtue in the age of Ficino; and in his Commentary to Dante (embellished with the designs of Botticelli) we can find, in the full tide of Latin humanism, a strong enthusiasm for the major poet of Florence. And this continues that directive of Bruni, for whom there was no exclusive virtue in Latin, and Italian was awaiting its perfection. With Landino we stand upon the verge of the other theme of vernacular literature.

Before returning finally we must look briefly at the second half of the century in its Latin side, as verse now, more than prose. The change goes back, perhaps, to Antonio Panormita (1394–1471), the notorious author of the *Hermaphroditus*; and is associated with the south of Italy. The principal name is that of Pontanus (1426–1505), born in Umbria, but linked with Naples. His production in prose and verse is ample, but it is as the supple poet of sensuous impressions, in a Latin which has all the appearance of an individual creation, that he is most memorable. Nor does he stand alone: on the one side he inaugurates the didactic poem (not without echoes of Lucretius), bringing the *Zodiac of Life* of Palingenius, and especially the *Syphilis* of Girolamo Fracastoro (1480–1553). On the other, we have a lyric continuation, if in a chaster tone, with Marullus (1453–1500), a Greek born in Constantinople, but as a Latin poet of the Neapolitan school; and more conspicuously with the elegies and epigrams of Sannazaro (*c.* 1455–1530), and with his elaborate poem *De Partu Virginis*, which stands with the *Christias* of Marco Girolamo Vida (1485–1566), the last twin monuments of the effort to write the Latin Christian epic. Freer, and more successful, in his more personal poems, Sannazaro is capable of the sharpest shafts in his epigrams against the Borgias. With Vida we have moved a further stage, and his *Poetics* bring us to the six-teenth-century love for theory. Perhaps because with Vida this is in a clear and elementary form, close still to Horace, the *Poetics* will survive the seventeenth century, to find a vogue awaiting them in England in the age of Pope. And for a long time Vida takes second place (Horace, Vida, Boileau, Pope) among the four poets of the *Ars Poetica*.

To this we must add the tombstones to the line of living Latin works. For we must not forget that this abundant literature was not an artificial growth, and that it did not stifle the Italian tongue. Some sorts of book had always been in Latin, and the change in writing Latin does not alter those categories, though it expands production. And we have seen that Leonardo Bruni pays tribute to the *volgare*, and desires its advancement. With Cristoforo Landino the principle of symbiosis for the two languages is asserted, and in the second half of the Quattrocento we find that native genres either receive enrichment from classical sources, or begin to wither, and to be replaced. It is at this moment that we meet two curious hybrids, the illegitimate offspring, so to speak, of this marriage of Latin and Italian in one living culture. The first is the *Hypnerotomachia Poliphili* of Francesco Colonna (1432?–1527?), for which a much earlier date than its noble Aldine edition of 1499 is claimed, and indeed asserted in the book itself. *The Strife of Love in a Dream* has always attracted notice by the beauty of its physical form as a book, the excellence of its woodcuts; while from the obscurity of its text has come an attitude of reverence which it does not quite deserve. Following Politian's lead, the obscurest corners of the Latin language have been ransacked, and the products of this process intruded, undigested, into what is only nominally an Italian book. So irksome the form: what of the matter? At its root this is a romance, the love of Polifilo for Polia, but its story is not told till the second, shorter, book, while in the first, in a dream within a dream, Polifilo passes from the mighty works of antiquity to the ordered world of Queen

Eleuterylida and to the island of Cythera, letting loose at all points a riot of description. As a tour de force the book is notable enough: one cannot foresee what realm of art or nature will next add its store of rarer names; and Polifilo's love stands still – in spite of the burning furnace of his breast – while a bewildering variety of trees shaped by topiary-work to naval battles or to colonnades is visited, or the isle of Cythera measured out to the last yard. As a romance it is a failure, as a practical recipe for architecture, a failure also. But its concern with the visual at every turn (reminding us of Alberti's dictum about the eyes) may have for us, who live in another age, some merit in intention.

The *Hypnerotomachia* is the pedantic, or rather the pedant-esque, solution, and it never has the vigour which is the birthright of its vulgar twin, the macaronic poem. Teofilo Folengo (1496?–1544) burlesqued the epic in his *Baldus*, or *Macaronicae*, which first appeared in 1517. Here Latin and Italian again have fused, but this time by the intrusion of plebeian (even dialectal) elements into what still purports, by syntax and endings, to be Latin. Here, in a work which Rabelais looked to, are the prototypes for Grandgousier and Panurge (with the scene of the bell-wether thrown into the sea for all the sheep to follow ready made for imitation); and here already is a rich vein of comic invention, which we may instance in the case of the poor traveller in the (inevitable) epic storm. When all are throwing their heaviest possessions to the greedy sea, he, having no luggage, snatches his wife and hurls her to the waves, because he has no burden of a greater weight. And she bobs up and down, to drown amid the white horses of the sea,

> Sic vadant quantae sunt bruttae, suntque bizarae.

The flavour of the joke is acrid, and the monk Folengo relishes the misogynism of the Middle Ages. It is, of course, the vigour of this new material, the local life of episodes, not the plan, or the whole, which is deserving of our praise. But to a reader who comes with adequate preparation the *Macaronics* may offer (it was Billanovich who made the suggestion) the most amusing and ingenious reading of the early Cinquecento apart from the *Orlando Furioso*. But this must not make us lose sight of the fact that historically both the *Hypnerotomachia* and the *Macaronics* are sports which offer no legitimate descent, and therefore close, in differing ways, this chapter of the intrusion of Latin into the modern literature of Italy. And by 1517 the battle has been won, since the year before the *Orlando Furioso* had also made its first appearance, while for the next fifteen years Ariosto will lovingly correct it in the spirit of Bembo's rules for the vulgar tongue; so that it beomes the pattern of Tuscan usage in the hands of a non-Tuscan, one of the main instruments for the victory of Tuscan as the Italian language. Which henceforth we may use instead of the inadequate middle terms, vernacular or vulgar, which have done service hitherto. And now finally, after this interlude, we are free to return to Italian literature, safe in the assurance that it will no longer be supplanted by a Latin counterpart.

CHAPTER 5

From Petrarch and Boccaccio to Lorenzo and Politian

IT is no accident that at first the chronicle of the successors in the Trecento, or of the pioneers in the Quattrocento, will seem unimpressive. They are dwarfed by the two comparisons, with the giants behind them, and with the contemporary growth of Latin writing alongside them. It is not that this last stifles the vernacular: it is, instead, that it has left until recently Italian production unregarded. But it is the first comparison which has crushed interest in the later writers of the fourteenth century. After Dante the *Dittamondo* of Fazio degli Uberti (*c.* 1305–*c.* 1367), with its historical and biographical information, and its touches of poetry in a dry theme, has slight claims on the reader; and this is true of the long *Quadriregio* (the journey through four reigns, Love, Satan, Vice, and Virtue), born also under dantesque influences, the work of Federigo Frezzi (*c.* 1350–1416). Even in the early Quattrocento this imitation of Dante is continued in the *Città di vita* of Matteo Palmieri. Where we have no imitation, the qualitative comparison still acts as a shield against acquaintance. This is true of Domenico Cavalca (1270–1342), author of the *Vite dei Santi Padri*; and despite the fervour and the occasional burning eloquence it is true of the *Letters* of St Catherine of Siena (1347–80) or of Giovanni Colombini (1304–67), who is best remembered by the life that Feo Belcari will write of him in the next century. Nor do the continuers of Petrarch find their task an easy one. If for the Florentine Cino Rinuccini, long unnoticed, there is now a stirring of interest, others (as Buonaccorso da Montemagno or Rosello Roselli) remain forgotten; and the best-known, Giusto de'Conti (d. 1449), author of the *Bella Mano*, keeps his notoriety as one who brought coldness to Petrarchan imitation.

It is the inheritance from Boccaccio which deserves most notice, though no rivals to the *Decameron* are in sight. Indeed, with Giovanni Sercambi, of Lucca (1347–1424), we feel a painful gap. His *Novelle* remained unpublished till 1889, owing to scruples about their morality. The frame is a loose imitation of the *Decameron*, with a company of persons fleeing Lucca's unhealthy state in 1374, and telling tales during their tour of Italy. The style is unlettered, full of anacolutha and of Lucchese dialect; nor does the matter redeem the style. In fact Sercambi shows up more favourably in the *Monito* which he addressed to the Guinigi family whose rule he preserved in Lucca for a long period, and in the *Croniche* which he wrote, maybe also for their instruction. But flatter still in his attempt to recreate the setting of the *Decameron* is the unfortunate Florentine who has been handed down as Ser Giovanni Pecorone (still alive in 1406?), the unflattering title shared by him and by his book. The ideal date of the *Pecorone* is 1378, the year of the Ciompi, but we have two interlocutors only, Suor Saturnina and Frate Aurecto, who has come from Florence to Romagna to be her chaplain out of love for her reputation. In the convent-parlour they meet for 25 days, each tell a tale, then sing a *ballata*. But they do not notice that half-way through the author starts to copy long chapters straight out of Villani, continuing with effusive thanks as formerly. ... In the genuine stories we have a succession of events, but Ser Giovanni cannot create a character to rule them, and hold our interest. It is a point in his favour that the story of Giannetto (IV, 1) offers all the ingredients for Shakespeare's *Merchant of Venice* – the pound of flesh, the judgement, and the ring. And here is one of those circumstantial stories, set with a wealth of detail in Venice, but coming from Herodotus where it was told about the treasure of a Pharaoh. Apart from these intricate and ingenious stories the most appealing is 1, 2, where Bucciuolo learns the art of love at Bologna, at the expense of his tutor.

But rather than these Franco Sacchetti (*c.* 1330–1400) is the first continuer of Boccaccio with a personal flavour. His family was ancient, and he filled many public offices in and outside Florence, keeping an unblemished character. His verse at times anticipates the light-hearted note of Politian, and he always writes with liveliness. But neither his verse nor his *Sermons* have quite the interest of his *Trecentonovelle* (now mutilated, and reduced to just over 200). The Proem, surprisingly, proposes imitation of Boccaccio: for here there is no frame, and the story itself has reverted to the single incident, but treated now as something to be dramatized, and centring chiefly on the bourgeois world of Florence. Outliving Petrarch and Boccaccio by a quarter-century Sacchetti shows none of their influence on that side from which the Renascence is to come, and in a letter confesses to scant Latin. This may have helped in keeping him from the latinizing style of the *Decameron*, and the essence of his manner is a presentation of things as happening, not as having happened, with the most vital movement given by a staccato criss-cross of brief-sentenced dialogue. This sense of movement can be seen at its most brilliant pitch in CLI, where Fazio da Pisa, claiming to be able to foretell the future, is pressed ruthlessly back to the confession that he cannot tell the past, even that most close and familiar. How often up the stairs? How many steps in them? – and Fazio gives up his claim to know at all. In these fast-moving episodes the comedy may be low, the *beffa* (or practical joke) be cruel for our taste; but we can remain sure of the commonsensical honesty of the narrator, expressed especially in comments added after the narration ends. Here it is so much easier to grasp his view than in the ambiguous attitude of Boccaccio. And in most ways he remains an opposite, attractive at any given point, but with perhaps too many of these breathless short stories jostling each other, since they lack the richness of character which Boccaccio rose to.

Even Petrarch translated the improbable story of Griselda into Latin. It was a sanction to other sporadic *novelle* in the fifteenth century from scholars who might have eschewed the genre. Foremost among these was Enea Silvio Piccolomini with the *Story of Two Lovers*, and even Leonardo Bruni wrote in Italian the *Novella di Seleuco*, a story with a classical source, intended as a counterblast to the cruelty of the Prince of Salerno in the famous story of Tancred and Ghismonda; while a tale of love between rival houses (*Istorietta amorosa fra Leonora de' Bardi e Ippolito Buondelmonte*) has even been attributed to Alberti. More interesting is the rise of the *Facetiae*, associated primarily with the sharp wit of Poggio Bracciolini (1380–1459), the most successful also of discoverers of ancient manuscripts. A papal secretary (later chancellor of Florence), he was the centre of the school for scandal of his fellow-secretaries. Poggio's malicious *Facetiarum liber* enjoyed enormous popularity, and was imitated in the vernacular by the Ferrarese Lodovico Carbone, and others. With the latter's praise for the vernacular we may associate his jest on using Latin for public acts: for when the Marchese Niccolò d'Este sent a letter to a *podestà* asking for an *accipitrem bene ligatum in sacculo* he received the archpriest suitably trussed up. ... The *Facezia* did not need the warning, and many Italian collections succeed Poggio, the best known being the *Facezie del Piovano Arlotto* (Arlotto Mainardi, 1396–1484), not collected by himself, nor all authenticated.

Meanwhile the *novella* also continues on its course. Exceptional importance attaches to what its editor Wesselofsky called the *Paradiso degli Alberti*, by Giovanni Gherardi da Prato (*c.* 1366–*c.* 1446). Here is a company which leaves Florence in 1389 for a pleasant sojourn in the villa of Messer Antonio degli Alberti, and Luigi Marsigli and Coluccio Salutati are among the number, the villa being the paradise which supplied the title for this acephalous work. Wesselofsky took it as evidence for a humanist society in the fourteenth century in Florence, which seems now to be mistaken. Written *circa* 1426 it mirrors the ideas of the circle of Leonardo Bruni, and does not anticipate them. What is important is not so much the predominance of learned conversation over mere story-telling, but the continued esteem for Dante, and the parallel respect for the Italian tongue: both patent proofs that Florentine humanism did not act as a stifling blanket. By the side of the *Paradiso degli Alberti* the stories of Gentile Sermini, of Siena, seem uncouth. Put together some time after 1424, they were sent as a 'basket of salad' to a friend at the spa of Petriuolo, all supposedly plants plucked from his own garden. We know the licence reigning at spas, and Sermini's stories suit with that. Rather than his matter, it is his rich Tuscan, with a strong Sienese flavour, and no Latinisms, which recommends him. With Sermini there is another spa-collection: that of Giovanni Sabadino degli Arienti (*c.* 1450–1510), secretary to Andrea Bentivoglio in Bologna, who takes us out into the Apennines, where a noble company take the cure, and sixty-one stories, in 1475. Here is a laudatory picture of Bologna and the Bentivoglios; but the construction is loose, and if he is no Sermini or Sercambi, yet Sabadino has rather an elementary sense of humour. The better stories hardly exceed a score, and are sometimes repeated from a written source. An example of the small change is the story of the abbot robbed of his mantle and preaching to the thieves. But what moved them in his eloquence was the far-off term of the Day of Judgement, so that they took as well his mule, horses, clothes, and saddle-bags. At stories such as this the company bursts with laughter, drying streaming eyes with fingers or handkerchief. But *Le Porrettane* (from the name of the Spa) will never find again so consenting an audience.

To close this series we have one of sterner substance, who aspired to the lash of Juvenal. Tomaso Guardati, better known as Masuccio Salernitano (*c.* 1415–*c.* 1480), wrote only fifty stories in his *Novellino*, and he has often been accounted the most important prose-writer of his century. One copy only of the first edition of 1476 survives, because of the sharpness of his attack upon the hypocrisy of friars. The book is divided into five parts, each with an introduction, and each story with a dedication to a noble person from the Aragonese court of Naples (a circle soon to perish in the Conspiracy of Barons of 1485); and each close has a moral note by the author. The scope is not different from the *Decameron*, but the spirit, and the style, are wholly so. Ignorance of Latin saves Masuccio from pedantry, giving a humble and by no means unpleasing touch to his prose; and he has none of the enigmatic tolerance of Boccaccio, always ready to crack the lash of scorn. Thus his indignation against 'feigned religious' carries him to pray God for the quick destruction of Purgatory so that unworthy ministers, 'unable to live on alms, may go back to the spade from which the most part drew their origin'; or knowing what Machiavelli will say about Italian mercenaries we may feel the force of his contention 'that it is easier to find among a hundred soldiers half of them good than one in a whole chapter of priests without the foulest stain.' His attack on women has behind it the medieval traditions of misogynism and his conviction is that his invective did no more than draw 'a bucketful of water from the ocean'. His protestations on the truth of all his stories we need not take quite seriously, though he has localized his narratives most strongly. But his first derives from a fabliau, his second from Caesarius of Heisterbach by way of Boccaccio: on the whole, however, written sources are lacking. It is the harsher emotions which he best portrays, the tragic vengeance of Nicolao da Guitone against the Moor and his own wretched wife (her head crushed by the heavy lid of the chest in which she is searching); or else that masterpiece of the macabre, the flight of the star-crossed lovers Martina and Loisi, who lose their way, and seeing a light take refuge in a leper-house, where Loisi is killed at once, and Martina escapes her fate by killing herself. The theme of love and death reaches here an intensity which it is hard to parallel elsewhere in the *novella*.

It may be a relief to turn to the field of the lyric, which is more varied than we might have thought. First, the odd figure of the Florentine barber, Domenico di Giovanni, called Burchiello (1404–48), whose bizarre and grotesque fantasy points on to Berni via such imitators as Antonio Cammelli, called Il Pistoia (1436–1502). Some of the reactions of the latter against what seemed amiss in the closing stages of the Quattrocento give him an honourable niche: more honourable than what belongs to the contemporary petrarchists. For with Tebaldeo (Antonio Tebaldi of Ferrara, 1463–1537) and Serafino d'Aquila (Serafino Ciminelli, from Aquila in the Abruzzi, 1466–1500), the petrarchan lyric turns to the mere elaboration of *pointes*. Nor does Benedetto Gareth (called Il Cariteo, born at Barcelona *c.* 1450, but living at Naples, d. 1514) in his *Endimione* bring this tradition back to vitality. More pleasing is the vein of popular poetry exploited by the Venetian Leonardo Giustinian (*c.* 1388–1446); and more impressive the single *Canzone alla Morte* of Pandolfo Collenuccio of Pesaro (1444–1504), unpublished till the time of Leopardi, on whom it left an impression perpetuated in some details of the *Canti*. Then rising above the run of petrarchism are the three *Amorum Libri* of Matteo Maria Boiardo (1441–94). They commemorate his love, between 1469 and 1471, for Antonia Caprara in a *canzoniere* with a Petrarchan structure, and final mood of repentance, but with a different spirit. This is clear in the opening sonnet, *Amor, che me scaldava al suo bel sole*, where 'puerile errore' echoes Petrarch, but the last tercet proclaims that those who live the flower of their life without the warmth of love may seem to live, but live without a heart. Such a creed (reaffirmed in the *Orlando Innamorato*) takes all the *angst* from Love, leaving jealousy in the second book to be the disturbing note. And with this theme of the naturalness of love (*Chi tole il canto e penne al vago augello*), goes that of its ecstasy (*Datime a piena mano e rose e zigli*). In the third book time presses on, but brings not the petrarchan note of Death (and of repentance), but that of disappointment ('Il Sol pur va veloce, se ben guardo, E il tempo che se aspetta mai non viene'), with the alternative of resignation.

Freshness and sincerity, in spite of the echoes, has been the dominant impression of Boiardo's readers. And he takes sparingly too of the pirouetting which we call petrarchism; bringing also that slight hybridization with the local speech of Ferrara which gives colour without adding obscurity. There are, too, more frequent contacts with classical poetry than one might imagine from the slightly rustic surface of his verse. To this we can add the homogeneity of mood which comes from the period of composition (between 1469 and the first dated manuscript of 1477), and the association of the whole with the youth of Boiardo (from twenty-eight into the early thirties). *Ocio amoroso e cura giovenile*: an expatiation where an innocent appetite finds firm and full expression. Boiardo, perhaps, is not caviare for the general because his note is neither quite strong, nor quite obvious, enough; but by discerning readers he has often been rated the finest Italian lyric poet, even in the age of Politian and Lorenzo. It is a compliment which should not be overlooked.

Before coming to these there is one who otherwise may find no place in the narrative: Jacopo Sannazaro (*c.* 1455–1530), author as we have seen of some of the most elegant of Latin poetry, but also of a slender body of *Rime*, and of a work which knew in its time an enormous vogue, the *Arcadia*. Both composed in the fifteenth century (the *Arcadia* mainly by 1489), and published in the Cinquecento, they are swallows flying in the direction of the spring: in contrast to Masuccio, that is, here we have a Neapolitan using already a pure Tuscan idiom, long before this is codified by Bembo for the literary usage of all. It is the language of Petrarch that makes the deepest imprint on the *Rime*, their themes only sporadically Petrarchan, so that they are a vehicle for the wistful personality of Sannazaro more than a body of love-lyrics. Here it is the complaints that are most memorable (*O vita, vita non, ma vivo affanno*), and once only does Sannazaro on a general theme rise to a fuller note which caught the ear of later poets (*Icaro cadde qui; queste onde il sanno*, translated by Desportes amongst others). But it is to the *Arcadia* that Sannazaro's reputation is tied, and whose fading has wrought his eclipse. With all pastoral there should be the label *Non tibi spiro*, with the old picture of the rosebush and the pig. For the pastoral is aristocratic, and not popular. Moreover, we have here an added difficulty: when Sannazaro as a Latin poet imitates Horace or Catullus he yet must do something different; but when he turns to imitate the pastoral in Italian? Then it may seem sufficient novelty to make a mosaic from Virgil and Theocritus, changing only the disposition and the language. Impregnated with the same gentle melancholy this was enough to bring vast fortunes in the Cinquecento, and is the reason for later neglect. The form comes from Boccaccio (his *Ameto*), the matter from all pastoral literature, seen more as apparatus than as sentiment. This is the divide from Tasso, who dismisses the apparatus of shepherdom to leave the atmosphere of Arcadia. The boccaccian style adds to the complication, and to the deterrents now. Yet this is the beginning from which will flow an ocean of literature: not only Tasso and Guarini, but Ronsard and Belleau on to the *Astrée* of Honoré d'Urfé and the novels of Madeleine de Scudéry, from the *Diana Enamorada* of Jorge de Montemayor to Spenser's *Shepherd's Calendar* and that other *Arcadia* of Sydney. But it is significant that none of these subsists on direct imitation of Sannazaro, whose languorous melancholy offers less reward than the quintessence of feeling which the pastoral will attain to in the hands of Tasso. The *Arcadia* must have a larger place in literary history than in the hearts of its readers.

No one who has looked on the harsh features of Lorenzo the Magnificent (1448–92), whether in the portrait by Vasari or the Ashmolean bust, can fail to think of him as the central point of interest amongst the authors of the Quattrocento. That is not to imply that his production will be also, like his person, the most valuable. Nor has time resolved the enigma of his personality, stated by Machiavelli in the *Florentine Histories*, 'there being in him two different persons, almost with impossible conjunction joined'. The virtual ruler of Florence, in a short life exercised by public misfortunes, and by such private griefs as the death of Giuliano de'Medici in the Pazzi conspiracy of 1478, Lorenzo looks fleetingly to poetry, and never with the application which might have deepened statement to full poetic life. It is the contrasts which hold attention mainly: Lorenzo, saviour while he lived of Florence and Italy together; Lorenzo, tyrant and corruptor; author of spiritual lauds, as of carnival songs whose immoral content goes to the same tune; best known for the chorus to *Bacchus and Ariadne*,

> Quant'è bella giovinezza,
> Che si fugge tuttavia!
> Chi vuol esser lieto, sia:
> Di doman non c'è certezza.

Opposite which, obligatory, quotation we may set another to point the contrast:

Sola sta ferma e sempre dura Morte.

It is inevitable that we should begin with the least hopeful side of Lorenzo's poetry. He made for Frederick of Aragon a collection from which we know that his gaze had penetrated past Petrarch to Dante, even to the early poets. He sees the superiority of Guinizelli to Guittone, recognizes Cino da Pistoia as the first to put off the old awkwardness. This, with his praise for the Italian tongue, is of some critical importance, more perhaps than the *canzoniere* and the commentary which Lorenzo writes under these influences. Here he adds also an infusion from the neo-platonic ideas of Ficino, with the appetite for beauty a matter of the mind, the eyes and ears. 'The delights of the other senses, unworthy and unfitting for a gentle mind, are repudiated.' This, after Valla and Alberti, is a demonstration of how little Ficino travels in the same direction as the world of humanism. The Commentary is unfinished, the *Rime* without direction (and without foundation, since he chose a lady to justify a petrarchan *canzoniere*), and just a little touch of nature – the picture of the ants and bees – prophetic for a side of his poetry which is often put forward as the best. Certainly it appears again in the *Selve* (the title from Statius, the metre, *ottava rima*, part of a new tradition which will lead on to the *ottava d'oro* of Ariosto), which offer more than the *Rime*. The naturalism of Lorenzo has perhaps been overrated: it is of the sort that can be easily recognized for what it is even by those who are slow to the appreciation of poetic quality, but its danger is that it replaces sentiment rather than creating it. More interesting in the *Selve d'Amore* are the personifications, Hope or Jealousy, foreshadowing those central motifs of the *Orlando Furioso* which we may think of in many ways as its dynamo.

Lorenzo's most-remembered poetry is elsewhere. If we consider classicism as an insidious menace to free expression we shall find our attention taken by such poems as the *Caccia col Falcone*, with the naturalistic baying of hounds and the

Origen, Jerome, Albertus Magnus ...) in twenty-two months. Such were the achievements of Vespasiano just on the threshold of the printed page, with which he or his clients had no truck. Seeing the prominent men of his time, and counting them as worthy to stand with the heroes and sages of antiquity, he thought of recording something of their lives. Hence his *Vite di Uomini illustri*, though from his humility comes an air of one assembling materials for others to write the life itself; and here there is a Petrarchan moral sense of biography as example, and his gallery is full of men of virtue, in the ordinary acceptance of the term. And when we see upon his list Nicholas V, Frederick Duke of Urbino, Cosimo Pater Patriae, Giannozzo Manetti, Leonardo Bruni Aretino (for him the main renovator of the Latin language after its long rusting), Vittorino da Feltre, and so forth, we may feel it is a testimony to the quality and the direction of learning in the Quattrocento. Perhaps Vespasiano, as a writer, is not quite equal to his clients, and is best read in samples, rather than as a continuous narrative. Naïve, and a little unconvincing, on the whole, we never feel him though as feigned or false, and the candour of his character outweighs his shortcomings as an author. The more so as in his *Vite* there is contained a picture which we cannot find repeated elsewhere for the noble figures which crowd the century of humanism.

The other marginal figure is Girolamo Savonarola (Ferrara 1452–Florence 1498), with whom we may record a minor revolution in a point of view. Savonarola was for long the voice of the Middle Ages crying in a pagan wilderness, the other extreme to Machiavelli, whose cynical face (in a famous image of Carducci) leered at the ascetic monk from a corner of the piazza. As prejudice has dwindled, Savonarola and Machiavelli have drawn nearer together: both heirs of the civic humanism of Bruni and the early Quattrocento, both pillars of the new Florentine Republic, and the first the begetter of solutions for its working which will be adopted by the second. Nor, since the course of the fifteenth century was not set towards incredulity, is there any need for surprise that the religious fervour of a Savonarola should dominate

Florence, even though it met a tragic fate at the unclean hands of Alexander VI. Though we are concerned primarily with Savonarola as writer, no one can help thinking that it is ultimately the dramatic intensity of his life, together with its brutal ending, which mainly counts. The keynote of one side we may find in the youthful treatise which he wrote before he left Ferrara, with the significant title *Disprezzo del Mondo*. His first fervour for essential Christianity was not dimmed by the acquisition of theological learning, and his period of preaching in Florence saw the composition of inflammatory writings, simple and straightforward in form, meant to encourage germination of the seed sown in teaching. It is perhaps by accident that he reached the full height of notoriety in the period after 1492, through his prophecies that the sword of the Lord would come speedily to punish current wickedness (GLADIUS DOMINI SUPER TERRAM CITO ET VELOCITER). These seemed dramatically fulfilled by the arrival of Charles VIII (even if we may doubt now whether the latter was the Soldier of the Lord); and when Piero de'Medici fled from Florence in 1494 the influence of Savonarola swelled to be the dominant voice of the revived Republic. To this period belongs his *Trattato sul Reggimento di Firenze*, which embodies his hatred of Medicean tyranny. Here is set up the ideal of a civil government, not of the plebs, but with councils and institutions, and in this Venice may be a model, though not an obligatory one. In this treatise are to be sought the ideas which link him to Machiavelli, in spite of all the differences we may see between the two. The greatest of these is perhaps the fanatic conviction that he was the instrument of God and this pride may partly have been cause of his downfall; that and the opposition of the Borgia pope, Alexander VI, whom he most naturally denounced and who replied by excommunication; as also of the forces in Florence which he had displaced from positions of authority. He was in difficulties with Alexander from 1496, and in the intervals of silence imposed he wrote his major devotional treatise, *Il Trionfo della Croce*. But it is the last period with his arrest in San Marco in 1498, after the fiasco of his followers' appeal to ordeal by fire, on which our interest is focussed. In his bare cell in the tower of the Palazzo Vecchio he wrote his last work, the few pages of the *Regole di Ben Vivere*, a brief *profession de foi*, and in the May of that year there followed the scene, poignant as the martyrdom of Joan of Arc, of his degradation preparatory to being hanged and burnt. The Archbishop of Florence, in his commotion, mistook the formula, 'I separate you from the Church of God militant and triumphant', and Savonarola intervened, 'From the Church militant, not from the Church triumphant, for that does not pertain to you.' And few will think now that Savonarola is more separated than his arch-separator, Alexander. For in the end those who speak with the weight of institutions win only temporary victories, and the voice of the individual speaks louder finally, if only it speaks right. Would not the Church now, had it the choice, cast out Alexander from its bosom, or its record, to embrace Savonarola?

CHAPTER 6

Machiavelli, Guicciardini, and their Heirs

THE name of Savonarola may now lead us on to Machiavelli, who inherits his conception of the Florentine Republic which he served. Than this there is no more beckoning name in all Italian literature, none which has won more admiration or more obloquy. Even now a recent book could trade under the happy title *Machiavelli Antichrist*; but from the first there have not been lacking those who, like Bernardo Giunta in his dedication of the first edition of the *Discorsi* (1531), spoke of the excellent and more than human wit of Machiavelli, his labours aimed at nothing else than the profit of mankind: to whom, said Giunta in this glowing testimonial, we owe immortal obligation. And now, perhaps, the scale has tipped definitively. The distrust, which still animated Villari in a work which remained canonical for sixty years, is dissipated, and Ridolfi in his authoritative life of Machiavelli speaks of the injustice done him in the past as though the present was a different matter.

Niccolò Machiavelli (1469–1527) was of an honourable, but poor, family, and till recently we knew nothing of him till at the age of twenty-nine he entered the Florentine Chancery. Now we have the *Ricordi* of his father, Bernardo. These belong to a category with rich contributions in the Quattrocento: especially the *Diario Fiorentino* of Luca Landucci and the *Ricordanze* of Bartolomeo Masi; and with these in mind we may feel disappointment at the meagre scraps that can be gleaned from the jottings of Bernardo. Here we find Niccolò learning Latin from the age of seven, and on to authors by the age of twelve; but we also find Bernardo projecting an index to the whole of Livy. Here also are other books: Cicero, *De Officiis*, Flavius Blondus (including the *Decades* which will be a source for the *Istorie Fiorentine*), Pliny, Justin (also a prime source for Machiavelli). And with the culture of Bernardo there is the testimony to his honourable quality. However brief the snippets about Niccolò, in view of all the prejudices this is a golden acquisition. One other detail has recently come to light: the circumstances of his election to a public post in 1498. It is the moment following the fall of Savonarola, and Machiavelli comes in, plainly enough, on an anti-Savonarolan ticket. That does not commit his final attitude, and nothing has disappeared more irrevocably than the old strident contrast between the believer and the cynic. Indeed, for the readers of Villari nothing will be more symptomatic of the change in the climate of opinion than the emergence of Machiavelli as '*il grande appassionato*'. Whatever the circumstances of his appointment, Machiavelli serves from 1498 to 1512 the Florentine Republic, and will inherit from Savonarola's treatise on its government as much perhaps as he rejects. And it is the passionate nature of his concern with political problems which leads to the statements which have shocked his readers.

This public service produced the series of *Legations* which are of the first importance in the maturation of his thought. They began with the redoubtable Caterina Sforza of Forlí, in whom Machiavelli more than meets his match; and they continue through journeys to the court of France, to Caesar Borgia (in contact with whom he was supposed to have caught fire with admiration for ruthlessness, though he retained his Florentine suspicions), to the court of Rome when Caesar Borgia was slipping politically into his tomb; and later to the Emperor, then joining in the grab for Italian money. In all this some salient points impressed themselves on Machiavelli: the blackmail of those small states which supplied Florence with mercenary troops; the clear advantage, which he saw with Caesar Borgia, of having forces of one's own for making firm, and fast, decisions. Both of these lessons he will hammer into his works; and for the second he gave strenuous service in the establishment of a Florentine militia during the long struggle for the recapture of Pisa, after it had been left by Charles VIII in 1494 with contradictory promises to the Pisans and to Florence. That is a symbol of what Machiavelli expressed graphically, in a phrase of the *Legations*, with the French King as 'maestro della bottega', now that the old balance of power in Italy had gone, its needle broken with Lorenzo's death. If that had remained so, Florence might still have survived, as being traditionally liege to the French alliance. But when the fatal victory of Ravenna (1512) presaged the collapse of all the French holdings in Italy, Florence lay exposed to the appetite for change of the Spaniards and Julius II. The Medici were restored after the sack of Prato, where Machiavelli's militia had a smaller part in ignominious defeat than used to be stated. With the fall of the Republic Machiavelli loses office, suffers imprisonment, even the *strappado*, as suspected party to an anti-medicean plot, and is afterwards confined out of Florence. This is the period he describes in one of the most eloquent of all Italian letters, that to Francesco Vettori of 10 December 1513, with its contrast between the trivial and tumultuous occupations of the day, and the putting on by night of 'panni reali e curiali' to commune with the historians of antiquity. And in this communion Machiavelli found a fame transcending what would have been his had he continued undisturbed as functionary. There is a symmetry to his life, cut into almost even halves by 1498: twenty-nine years of preparation, then twenty-nine till his death; and this cut also into half, the 'lunga esperienza' till 1512, and than a similar period for his major works, with seven years for the *Prince*, the *Discorsi*, the *Mandragola*, the *Arte della Guerra*, and all the rest for the *Istorie Fiorentine*. It will be seen how much the latter gain as the final, most considered, word of Machiavelli.

Machiavelli's political thought had begun to erupt in 1498, with an analysis of the Pisan war (*Discorso della Guerra di Pisa*), in which it is obvious why the Signoria will rely on him for its missions, and value his reports. It continues with the *Del modo di trattare i popoli della Valdichiana ribellati*, which has been held to contain *in nuce* the essence of his attitude: history as experience, and Roman history as the supreme experience, with the lesson from it that half-measures damn while whole measures save; with the famous alternative, to cherish or to extinguish. And in the celebrated *Descrizione del modo tenuto dal duca Valentino nello ammazzare Vitellozzo etc.* men have seen the plain proof of Machiavelli applauding the wickedness of Caesar Borgia: though neither side of that may be quite right. Then in the vigorous *Parole da dirle sopra la provvisione del danaio* he fires the first shot in that campaign for a Florentine armed force, in a world where faith depends on force, and others' swords depend on others' will. Then lest we think he admired decision to the point of ruthlessness, or the Borgias to the exclusion of morality, there is the *Decennale Primo* (covering 1494–1504), with not poetry perhaps, but pithy comment on those troubled years: and with the sharpest condemnation for the Borgias, *père et fils*. In its close, with its lament over the storm still raging, Machiavelli's mind is all on fire (he whom Villari made out so cold!), but would find reassurance if the Florentines reopened their old temple to Mars. In this ardour the early attitude of Machiavelli shows clear: in spite of the whirlwind he makes bold to see the port, if only one has the courage to make straight for it. For some, all Machiavelli is contained in such an attitude, taking it as prevalent in the *Prince*, and the *Prince* as definitive. But this is a youthful ardour, and Machiavelli will not remain convinced that hundred per cent solutions are practicable in a conflicting world, either for the weak, who cannot put their hands to them, or even for the strong, who will end up in his judgement as the *insolent*, condemned and not desired.

For want of a surer place we may look here at one of the most revealing of Machiavelli's unregarded writings, the *Allocution to a magistrate assuming office*: two pages, and the theme of Justice in the time when men were good, and the gods dwelt on earth. Then vices grew, the gods returned to heaven, Justice the last of these. With its going came the fall of kingdoms and republics, and ever after Justice has come only sporadically to some city, making it great and powerful. So with Greece and Rome, so now with Florence. Justice brings union, union power and maintenance. 'She defends the poor and impotent, represses the rich and powerful, humbles the proud and bold, checks the rapacious and the grasping, punishes the insolent, scatters the violent. She generates equality in states, which is desirable for their maintenance.' And finally Machiavelli quotes the 'golden lines' of Dante on Trajan's justice (*Purg.* x, 73–93), reaffirming its close,

Giustizia vuole, e Pietà mi ritiene,

as showing how much God loves 'e la giustizia e la pietà'. He ends with an exhortation towards Justice in Florence, to make 'this city and this state glorious and perpetual'. This *Allocution*, rich with authentic touches, extends a hand towards the *Esortazione alla Penitenza*, though that seems the fruit of a later mood.

It is plain (though it is not usually made so) that if these pieces, with the *Legations*, were what remained of Machiavelli they would make an exciting legacy; in which there would still arise a conflict between those who read only the startling passages, and those who look patiently to the whole, and to the abiding elements. But in 1512 Machiavelli was turned from actions to words, and his major works come like a pent-up torrent. In this one problem of dating remains obscure: the *Prince* belongs firmly to 1513, with the addition of its Dedication to Lorenzo de'Medici (replacing one to his uncle Giuliano) in 1515 or 1516, before he became Duke of Urbino. The *Discorsi* seemed to have been begun before the *Prince*, and now may tentatively be taken as started only two years afterwards, under the impulse of the meetings in the Rucellai Gardens, and covering a period which we may loosely take as 1515 or 1516 to 1519. Here there is still no general agreement, but the problem is of acute importance only for those who see an acute contrast between the standpoint of the two books (as with Taine, who saw the *Prince* as the manual of monarchy, the *Discorsi* as that of the republic). Naturally, in such a case, it is helpful to envisage the one as replacing the other, not both jostling for the light in the same lapse of time. But for those who see some unity to Machiavelli's thought the problem will not give too much embarrassment.

However we resolve these doubts, it is the *Prince* which meets us first; and which has always fascinated men by what seemed the naked statement of harsh truths in a harsh world. That the world of 1513 was harsh, after twenty years of tempest, there is little doubt: and it would be well if readers of the *Prince* began with the last chapter as a reminder of what Italy had suffered, and of the redeemer Machiavelli hopes for. 'In this there is great justice', and he reinforces that appeal with a tag from Livy, on war as just when necessary, and arms pious when there is no hope but arms. Have we not just seen Justice and Piety meeting in the 'golden' lines of Dante? And here Machiavelli offers the task to the Medici, half done for them already by the incredible good fortune which had swept them from exile to rule in Florence, and, even more than that, to the papacy in Rome (with the election of Leo X, March 1513). All Florence was convinced that no heights were beyond their reach, and kingdoms in the south or in the north for both Giuliano and Lorenzo were universally predicted. And what other dynasty in Italy could at this moment aspire to anything? Venice, Naples, and Milan were all abased: only Florence and the Church, backed by the power of Spain, and with the rising star of the Medici, had power to act. Is it not obvious why Machiavelli offers the redemption of Italy from 'these cruelties and insolence of the barbarians' to the Medici?

That they did not listen is their affair, rather than his. But what did he propose? The outcome was to be the general good, with the new prince establishing new laws, building a basis on *armi proprie*, and ending *reverendo e mirabile*. Under the spur of these ideas the chapter catches fire with a biblical eloquence, and ends with the prophecy of the ennoblement of Florence and with the lines from Petrarch on Italian valour being not extinct. It is not accidental that this fervour finds correspondence in Ch. VI, where Machiavelli sets up the noble patterns, Moses, Cyrus, Romulus, and Theseus, sees their opportunity in the morass in which their peoples floundered, and concludes with the same terms as in Ch. XXVI: *donde la loro patria ne fu nobilitata e diventò felicissima*. The aim of

Machiavelli's *Prince* is constant: it is not directed to the un-
fettered greatness of a despotic ruler, but to security and
glory. Hence the reminders, running through the book, of
the need for a ruler to keep the benevolence of his subjects,
on whom he must base his state. The foundations of rule are
good laws and good arms: it is by their establishment that
Italy, plundered, traversed, *vituperata*, can hope to escape
towards *la securtà e il bene essere suo*. In this dilemma, the new
prince must imitate as little as he can the harshness of Severus,
only what necessity dictates, and as much as possible those
parts in Marcus Aurelius which 'are fitting and glorious for
the preservation of a state already established and secure'.
Here is the context for cruelty rightly or wrongly used. For
in a world of turmoil security is not to be had as a paper
arrangement. Well used (if it is lawful to speak well of ill)
are those harsh actions which are converted to the usefulness
of one's subjects, and which die away as the state settles down.
For those who use cruelty as a normal instrument of policy,
'it is impossible that they should maintain themselves'. Here
Romulus and Caesar Borgia meet in the same bracket: their
intentions judged by the result – in the case of Romagna, the
mending of that distracted province. And now that the Borgia
threat to Florence has been removed by time, Machiavelli
can look to the parallel: Cesare Borgia with the favour of
Pope and King of France, but looking to his own foundations.
It is the obvious pattern for the younger Medici, who can,
if they will only see the opening, accelerate the establishment
of a stable state as barrier against the ultramontane flood.

Granted the distinction between the external threat, against
which the prince must do what he can, as he can, and the
internal situation, where he can only build on the good will
of his subjects, the chapter on faith in princes reads in a
different light; and in the chapter on the Papal State, where
Machiavelli seemed most ironical, it is more than clear that
he skates over the surface, to emphasize the revived prestige
of the papacy as a temporal power, and the hopes to be placed
on Leo X: hopes which can seem hollow now, for Leo, like
his younger relatives, was unequal to the moment, but which

were vital to the case as then presented. But the *Prince*, not printed till 1532, when its context was long past, was read for centuries as though it had no filaments in its contemporary situation, or in the body of Machiavelli's thought. This worked a double change, for it meant that the sharpest statements were read in the wrong connotation (as if directed at oppression within the state); as also that the staple of the *Prince*, its proffers of honour and stability to a prince capable of creating *ordini*, and of rebutting the foreigner, was left neglected and unseen.

There is another document to which a new dating gives special weight. This is the *Canto degli Spiriti Beati*, written in a moment of hope in 1513 when Machiavelli had been released in the amnesty on Leo's election. It breathes compassion for the state of Italy, looks to Petrarch's keynote of peace, appeals for an end to internecine strife, in order to unite against the Turk, hoping in Leo's power to correct, and ending eloquently,

> Dipartasi il timore,
> Nimicizie, e rancori,
> Avarizia, superbia, e crudeltade;
> Risorga in voi l'amore
> De'giusti e veri onori,
> E torni il mondo a quella prima etade;
> Così vi fien le strade
> Del cielo aperte alla beata gente,
> Né saran di virtú le fiamme spente:

which is clearly Machiavelli's rewriting of the lines from Petrarch with which he closed the *Prince*. Here, as in the *Allocution*, justice and piety go hand in hand; while *just and true honours* are an earnest for the sort of honour offered in his treatise to the new Prince.

In the circle of the Rucellai Gardens Machiavelli continued his exploration of the ancient historians, and out of his meditations come the *Discorsi sopra la Prima Deca di Tito Livio*. The *Prince* had not been based on a conversion to the cause of monarchy (let alone of tyranny), but on an opportunity, unique in that it concerned the Medici, and gone when they had failed to take it. Specifically in the *Discorso delle cose fiorentine dopo la morte di Lorenzo* Machiavelli presses the advice of creating a true republic in Florence on Leo X; and in the *Vita di Castruccio*, which by mere prejudice was taken for too long as a rehash of the *Prince*, he condemns the violent, and therefore unsuccessful, ruler, offering the plain lesson that another path was needed. In short, there is for Machiavelli no going back to the moment of the *Prince*, but since that work was not born out of any theoretic attachment to the cause of monarchy there is no opposition to account for between the *Prince* and the *Discorsi*. In the former one can find beneath the surface his concern with laws and arms as the substance of the state: in the *Discorsi* and the *Arte della Guerra* respectively this becomes the open substance of his work. The world is a flux in which human institutions go up, or down; hence his search for maintenance, stability, security, hence the need for a guard on liberty; and hence, in the backward glance to learn the lessons of history, his gaze rests on the Roman Republic as the prime exemplar. Here is a book expressing all he knows, dedicated not to some prince more meriting of blame than praise, but to his Florentine friends Zanobi Buondelmonti and Cosimo Rucellai; and he writes, spurred on by that 'natural desire' to do what will bring 'general benefit to all'. Hence this commentary to Livy, written with the desire to draw fruit from the knowledge of history, and to look back to the political wisdom of antiquity. Human affairs are in perpetual motion, up or down, and it depends where one is whether praise for the past as superior to the present is right objectively. But now there is no possibility of mistake, for the ancient past was marvellous and the present shameful, here 'where there is no observance of Religion, none of laws, or of militia, but it is stained with every sort of ugliness'. Here is a Machiavelli with substantially the interests we have found within the *Prince*; and unequivocally he speaks with the voice of a moralist, as well as of an idealist. Machiavelli is one who sees, or thinks he sees, what is wrong, and also what is right in order to amend it.

As with the *Prince* there is for the *Discorsi* a key-chapter to read first: it is Book I, Ch. x which has the inspired warmth of the end of the *Prince* or of the *Discorso delle Cose Fiorentine*. Here there is praise for those who found, and infamy for those who destroy; and none will be so foolish as to mistake the categories, though in their own conduct they may choose the worser path. But read history, and no private individual will fail to prefer Scipio to Caesar, no prince desire to be Phalaris rather than Timoleon. And Machiavelli adds, from Tacitus, a strident contrast between the good and the bad emperors of Rome, to burst out with the conviction that beyond all doubt any born a man will be dismayed and turned from imitation of the bad, and will *catch fire with an immense desire to follow the good*, times of Rome. Here we may learn what debt we owe to Caesar (or to any other whom men wish to make the despot on the old pattern of the *Prince* misread), and Machiavelli ends by asking, what greater glory could be hoped for than to inherit political corruption, not to complete it as Caesar did, but to reorder one's city, as did Romulus. And he returns, so wont is Machiavelli to strike with the same word the same essential key, to the proffer of glory and security, contrasted with eternal infamy.

Such is the idealism underlying the *Discorsi*, so strong the pulsating conviction of Machiavelli looking for the *ordini*, the constitutional devices, which shall stabilize the flux. And here, perhaps, the latent contradictions lie. Machiavelli gives importance to the *ordinatore*, the legislator who can see the public good, and can best provide for it. A state legislated for by one man is fortunate; a state in the power of one man is unfortunate, because power corrupts, him or his partisans. To go back to the beginnings, to the principles (to use the term which will attract the notice of Montesquieu) on which the state rests, is a wholesome operation; and a state that is not planned on the right lines from its start has difficulty in finding them afterwards. But with this Machiavelli has taken from Polybius the account of the cycle of human government, the slipping from monarchy to tyranny, with aristocracy as a reaction against the latter, from aristocracy to oligarchy, with democracy as its reaction, and popular licence as the last phase before we start again. And with this goes a casual origin to the human polity: from scattered anarchy via the gratitude of offspring slowly towards civil institutions. In the history of the world, unless we take Rousseau's view, or start from the Earthly Paradise, there is nothing sacrosanct about beginnings, and the improvements, as with Machiavelli's account of Rome, may come with time, rather than be there for reversion. Civilization, that is, is a development, something to be achieved, always before us, never going back to a pattern once existing. It is here that Guicciardini, in his *Considerazioni sui Discorsi*, will criticize Machiavelli for his infatuation with the Romans (as if conditions were the same!); and here also that Machiavelli comes nearest to Dante, who also saw a pattern in the past to be returned to.

The whole of Book I revolves around the search for *ordini*, with the praise of those which preserved the Roman Republic. And here Machiavelli watches the long struggle between the plebs and the patricians, seeing Rome free so long as it preserved a balance in those forces, and enslaved when mastery, with Marius, Sylla, Caesar, passed to the latter. In all this, the guard to liberty is best placed with those who have not, rather than with those who have; and the constant care of Machiavelli is to see that power and influence do not lead to insolence. To cap this, Book I ends with a crescendo of fervour for the popular state against the monarchy. Here Machiavelli rejects all the adages on the fickleness of the people, passes beyond the statement in the *Prince* on a ruler having no other base to build on than his subjects, to maintain that a people bound by law is superior to a prince, and that a prince unbound by law is far worse than a people. 'The governments of peoples are better than those of princes.' Here the republicanism of Machiavelli is amply borne out, but the *Discorsi* as a whole are more the theory of the rule of law and *ordini* than a theory of the republic as distinct from a kingdom. The later books, with their emphasis first on the external side of Roman history, then on the influence of individuals, are not as epoch-making as the first, but they do not change the essentials of Machiavelli's attitude.

The *Arte della Guerra* is a twin to the *Discorsi*, the only one of Machiavelli's works to be printed as soon as written (by the Giunta of Florence in 1521). For the first time it lays down the principles on which our National Service is still based, and it looks to peace as the object of war, not to war as the object of peace. In the Proem Machiavelli separates himself from the general view that civil and military life are opposites. The body politic is formed for the general good of men, but all the *ordini* set up for them to live in fear of the laws and God are useless without their defence. And if the ancients strove to keep men faithful, peaceful, full of the fear of God, they did so doubly with their militia. Where is more faith needed than in those who may have to die for you? Machiavelli draws the contrast between the *true and perfect* military discipline of antiquity and the vicious habits of modern soldiery. A citizen army, ready to go back to civil occupations, Rome decaying when it let its generals be masters of their armies, no professionals, for they will want their profession to be flourishing ...: all this first book is full of characteristic ideas, in the most typically Machiavellian language. The details of military organization (relying on the Roman use) are less helpful now, but at the end Machiavelli returns to his same contrast. Here once more Italy, without *ordini*, is the *vituperio* of the world; and in a celebrated passage he paints the portrait of the fifteenth-century princes, with their display, caught by the crisis of 1494, with its stern realities. But optimistically, in a land which has resuscitated 'Poetry, Painting, and Sculpture', Machiavelli ends, as in the *Prince*, with hope that this other resurrection may prove possible.

The *Istorie Fiorentine* is the only work to be commissioned, but that does not change its animating spirit. Begun in the fall of 1521, it was ready for presentation to Clement VII in 1525. For the first, preliminary, book which sweeps through the anterior history of Italy to bring us to the fifteenth century, and in the ones which deal with the internal history of Florence up to the date 1434, Machiavelli relies heavily for his facts upon the earlier writers, as Flavius Blondus in the *Decades*, Giovanni Cavalcanti, or Villani. But it is he who sees the outlines in their assemblage of the details; and we may judge from a remark at the end of Book I, when he is about to turn to the real theme of Florence, how much it is the author of the *Discorsi* and the *Art of War* who writes the *Histories*: 'Of these idle princes, then, and of these cowardly arms, my history will be full.' It is an indication of the contrast Machiavelli sees between the history of Rome (the basis of example in the *Discorsi*) and that of Florence (here a pattern for a warning). In the speeches here we may often find the purest Machiavellian statements, and in that of a citizen in 1372 there is the epitome of all that he believes. Here is the love borne to one's native city, the sense of corruption (including the lament of 'religion and the fear of God lost'), the sense that laws, statutes, civil *ordini* have followed ambition, not been in accord with the *vivere libero*; and as a close the hope of better *ordini* bringing better fortune, putting a check to ambition and faction, recreating 'il vero vivere libero e civile'. Since this history of Florence is a chronicle of what should not have been, this characteristic vocabulary, built up by Machiavelli in the *Discorsi* especially, tends to be crowded into key passages at the opening of the separate books. The beginning of Books IV and V underline the consistency of his aims. Up and down, order to disorder and downfall; order wrested from this, and valour resting on order, both together bringing glory and fortune (Book V); and in Book IV, in the variation of cities, which is so often between licence and servitude, instead of being (as many think) between liberty and servitude, the hope of some *wise, good, and powerful* citizen to ordain laws so that his city may be free, stable, and secure. And we may take as final his comment on Veri de'Medici who, had he been more *ambitious* than *good*, could without hindrance have made himself prince in 1393. These are not the words of one who hankers after a prince. Here for the first time in Italian the reasons of history reinforce the recital of its details; and though Machiavelli may have often gone too hastily in his acceptance of these last, the interest which accrues from this sense of purpose is enormous. The *Istorie Fiorentine* open the way for Guicciardini, and for the rest of written history.

No two names in Italian literature are more linked than Machiavelli and Guicciardini, yet they both exactly touch, and remain discrepant. Francesco Guicciardini (1482–1540) comes from the ruling class of Florence, and is not destined for the subaltern positions which are in Machiavelli's reach. As a sign of this, he was designated in 1512, in spite of his youth, ambassador to Spain to plead Florence's case; and maintained, unlike Machiavelli, after the Medici return, he came back to Florence author of a *Relazione di Spagna* which is one of the rich store of unpublished writings now coming from the Guicciardini archives. Soon he began a dignified career as papal administrator: as Governor of Modena and President of Romagna he showed civil and military qualities. He strove to bring the virtues of Florence to strife-torn Romagna: justice, taxation, communications, buildings. Austere in person, no fortune accrued from his offices. He showed his courage in 1517 when Modena was threatened, and in 1521 when Reggio was attacked; and he saved Parma after the death of Leo X. Amongst the tergiversations of papal policy in the fatal years after the battle of Pavia (1525), he played a leading part in the organization of the League of Cognac, only to find that others' weakness – leading to the Sack of Rome in 1527 – brought odium, as if he were responsible. When the Florentines took their opportunity, making Niccolò Capponi *gonfaloniere* of the Republic and rising against the Medici, he threw up his Presidency in Romagna and hastened to be counsellor: only to find himself unwelcome on all sides. In the crisis of 1530 he won concessions for Florence from that interview between Clement VII and Charles V at Bologna: but Florence refused the terms, and condemned him *in absentia* for his pains. Even when Florentine liberty had died Guicciardini returned with hopes of moderating absolutism in the direction of an aristocratic republic. But Alessandro would not listen, and Guicciardini went back to papal service, at Bologna. But in 1534 the Farnese pope, Paul III, succeeded Clement, and a Medici nominee was not desired. He returned to Florence, even averted the direct intervention of Charles V by pleading Alessandro's cause at Naples. But before long the youthful Lorenzino stabbed Alessandro, for Cosimo de'Medici to take his place. Guicciardini hoped at last to be the mature voice of counsel (was not Cosimo's mother a Salviati, of the family into which he had married?). He urged a senate, and the drastic limiting of absolute power. But Cosimo had no wish for fetters: Duke he was, soon to be Grand Duke, and Guicciardini retired to his villa to write his magnum opus, the first great *Storia d'Italia*.

Guicciardini saw his policies baffled in a continual malignity of fortune. *Post res perditas* was a marginal scrawl of Machiavelli which allows us to glimpse the bitterness he felt, but with Guicciardini the iron has entered into his soul. It is for this that, since De Sanctis at least, he has had a more depressing reception than even Machiavelli. None more than Machiavelli looks to the general good; but in the *Ricordi* Guicciardini offered as compensation to the trials of the public weal one's private interest, the *particulare suo*. And for De Sanctis, anxious to stimulate the moral sense, he seemed to codify Italian corruption. A Machiavelli without ideals, became the usual label for him; and it is only slowly that revision has been made. Slowly, of necessity, for though the *Ricordi* (which have seemed most scandalous) are as brief as the *Prince*, the bulk of Guicciardini is *ondoyant et divers* as Montaigne, himself, daunting the inquirer, leaving him clinging to the scepticism of some lapidary utterance, and to the reiterated judgements of De Sanctis's successors. And we must start with the contrasts with Machiavelli. In the *Cose Fiorentine* (which has recently come to light to join the *Storia Fiorentina* published a century ago), Guicciardini put his general attitude: 'The world's affairs depend upon so many accidents, and thus are so uncertain that the judgements made of them are often most fallacious, and one sees by experience that almost always the opposite happens of what men, even wise men, have thought.' Let us look back to the eagerness of Machiavelli to wrest a precept from a mere outline of facts: 'From which one may draw a general rule, which rarely or never fails. ...' These are opposites; and so is Guicciardini on the people: 'He who said *people* said indeed mad animal, full of a thousand errors, a thousand confusions, without taste, without delight, without stability.' And nothing offends the Machiavellian more than that last word, for in the last chapters of *Discorsi* I stability was the attribute of popular, in contrast with monarchical, government.

The way is open to the characteristic attitudes of Guicciardini, as lighted by the *Ricordi*. Here is that strident contrast between his aspirations, to be rid of the ambition, the avarice, and the softness of the priests, and his *particulare mio*, the private interest that casts him in the role of papal servant. Here is a scepticism which points us on to Bayle, with all those who scrutinize the supernatural uttering follies, men in the dark about the world, tasking their minds without discovering truth. Or even it may point us further, in the direction of Pirandello, with a veil between people and ruler, and men with no real knowledge even of present things. And is not this the burden of the last weary question, after all the theoretic demonstrations of monarchy as best, yet worst because it slips so soon to tyranny: which should a new city desire, the government of one, or many, or of few? And this weariness has been seen also as a coldness of vision. For Philippe de Commines *Dieu donna saige conseil au roy*, even in the smallest details (though was he wiser for the counsel?), but with Guicciardini men's motives have a lower keyboard. In the *Ricordi* his father quotes St Augustine, on ill-gained riches not reaching the third heir, and he doubts first the truth of this: 'ma quando fussi vero, potersi considerare altra ragione'. To this we may add that general weariness of spirit which finds expression in one of the most revealing of all the *Ricordi*:

When I consider to how many accidents and dangers of infirmity, of chance, violence, and a thousand other sorts, the life of man is subject, how many things must go together in a year for the harvest to be good, then there is nothing at which I wonder more than to see an old man, a fertile year.

Bayle and Pirandello come to mind in reading the *Ricordi*; and Leopardi also, as with that observation that

A more than mediocre mind is given to men for their unhappiness and torment; because it does not serve for more than to keep them in more toil and anxiety than those who are more positive.

For we shall find with Leopardi that sentience is an undesirable inheritance. But is not here a way of escape opening from the negative judgements on Guicciardini? It is because he feels the tragedy that he is baffled by it. Nor must we exaggerate the gap between his political doctrine and that of Machiavelli: that is a result of the accident of birth, by virtue of which Guicciardini looks to a republic which gives weight to responsible citizens, where votes are weighed, not counted. For the rest, he will come close to Machiavelli's aspirations, and when he writes *Discourses* (as on the government of Florence) he will inevitably use the Machiavellian words, with the need for a guard on liberty, the *vivere libero*, their common aim, achieved by *buoni ordini*. And though he may rule out the Romans, yet he looks to the Venetians – not out of sight for either Savonarola or Machiavelli – with their doge bound by *ordini*. Whereby he also proposes the *governo misto*, compound of the various forms, which is the contribution of the *Discorsi*. And underneath the apparent scepticism of the *Ricordi* lies the unceasing effort of all his life. The austerity of his conduct must modify the facile judgements on the *particolare mio*, and his care for the humble people qualify his declarations on weight to an aristocratic circle.

Meanwhile what we have seen of his belief in the scant value of experience conditions his writing of history: that and the new screen on which the eye must focus. Machiavelli has the limited viewpoint of Florence, but with Guicciardini the stage has widened: the Empire has followed France and Spain into the picture, and now dominates Italy. If policy for Italy is made outside Italy, the *Storia d'Italia* must tremble on the verge of becoming a History of Europe. It is a fault which will run through Venetian history-writing that, because of her involvement, we get a scattered history of world affairs rather than a history of Venice. It is Guicciardini's merit that he halts upon the edge of this predicament. But where Machiavelli, seeing the connexion between phenomena, and quick to draw the line that links them, and the lesson they afford, can be brisk in narrative, Guicciardini comes inevitably to a different method. Since it is the detail, the divergences, which baffle experience, preventing general judgements, it is natural that this should grow into an intricate web. If we add to this the complication of Guicciardini's style in the *Storia*, eschewing the full-stop in favour of the semi-colon, so that sentences meander over pages, and the breadth of the canvas, we can see why Guicciardini remains less apprehensible than Machiavelli; and why Italian criticism has not yet grappled with the task of examining the accuracy of his record. His impartiality has been accepted (though the Venetian Leoni wrote against his animus in relation to Venice), but impartiality and veracity are not synonymous, and there is room now for a full study of Guicciardini, covering both the old and the copious new material recently become available.

Machiavelli and Guicciardini both reflect, in differing ways, the heroic age of the Florentine Republic, when the reserves of strength, undissipated in the brilliant days of Lorenzo's prime, grew up into the light. It is only natural that after them, in the changed climate of the sixteenth century, we should meet with men of lesser stature. First is one who stands close to Machiavelli, whom he knew, and whom he succeeded as Secretary in 1527. This is Donato Giannotti (1492–1573), who continues directly the work of Machiavelli for a civic militia, one that this time gave a good account of itself in the siege of Florence. And Giannotti both admired Dante, and was the recipient of Michelangelo's bust of Brutus: this last denoting a republican fervour, still Machiavellian in tone as in vocabulary, and displayed in Giannotti's two treatises on the Florentine and Venetian Republics. With Venice Giannotti looks to those *ordini* which hold sedition at a distance, and since before him Savonarola, Machiavelli, Guicciardini looked in the same direction it is natural that we should follow their gaze to find the expression of this oldest and most stable of European polities in its most influential form. This is with Gasparo Contarini (1483–1542), whose treatise *De Magistratibus et Republica Venetorum* was written about 1523, published the year after his death, translated into Italian in 1544, and in both forms had a European impact. Written before the *Discorsi* this looks the same way. Soon we shall find Tacitus replacing Livy, the monarch the republic, but here from the start is the principle that as man rules animals, so mind must rule man, therefore *summam imperii commendandam esse legibus non homini*. Here also, in that dilemma of the theoretic arguments for and against monarchy, comes the solution of a *mixtionem quandam*, corresponding to the *governo misto* of Machiavelli; and the Venetian constitution turns out to be, as the Roman for Polybius, a balance between contrasting sorts of government, with the Doge looking to unity, but prevented from abuse of power. It is for these reasons, as well as from the physical inviolability of Venice, that the latter is from 1530 on the last citadel of Italian liberty.

While Venice looks to her constitution the Florentines look back to their history: Jacopo Nardi (1476–1563), Benedetto Varchi (1503–1565), Bernardo Segni (1504–1558), Filippo de'Nerli (1485–1556), G. B. Adriani, Jacopo Pitti, throw valuable light on the periods of Florentine history with which they deal, especially when these are near to their vision, and their heart. And in one or two minor pieces, as in the *Vita di Antonio Giacomini* of Jacopo Nardi, or the *Recitazione del caso di P. P. Boscoli e di Agostino Capponi* of Luca della Robbia, or in the *Apologia* of Lorenzino de'Medici (the assassin of Alessandro), there breathes a warm and graphic eloquence which carries us into the spirit of the time. This seems now a more welcome achievement than the ambitious *Istoria d'Europa* of P. F. Giambullari (1495–1555), covering the years 887–947, the first wide vision of the past, giving to the remoter time an attractive legendary touch, but hardly valid now as testimony. Here Paolo Giovio (1483–1552), who loomed large in his time and then slumped heavily, stands in better case. His biographies of famous men have been recommended by the portraits he collected (including the Titian one of Aretino), but the long *Historiarum sui Temporis* (quickly translated as the *Istorie del suo Tempo*, 1556) was for long invalidated by his reputation for a malicious tongue and a facile pen. But the qualities which went into his search for tangible evidence of the characters of history, portraits, inscriptions, documents, went also into the history, and while we shall not find here the acuteness which is the companion of history for Machiavelli there is a wealth of detail which will not mislead.

Naples, with Camillo Porzio (*c.* 1526–1580) and Angelo di Costanzo (*c.* 1507–1591), also produces her historians; and in Venice they range from Pietro Bembo down to Paruta, nor are all her official historiographers yet published, as witness one of the most attractive, Nicolò Contarini (1553–1632), whose *Historie Venetiane* stop tantalizingly short of the struggle over the papal interdict of Venice. But there is something symptomatic in the appearance (actually in the early seventeenth century) as the last historic monument of the Cinquecento of the great translation of Tacitus by Bernardo Davanzati (1529–1606). His motto was *Strictius Arctius*, his intent to match in the allegedly looser fibre of Italian the nerve and sinew of Tacitean brevity. But more than a *tour de force*, it is a portent. The age of absolutism had dawned with Charles V, and it is the right-minded thinkers who concoct the *Ragion di Stato* (the phrase belongs to Giovanni Botero, 1533–1617, his book of this name to 1589), with all the doctrine of kings answerable to God alone. In the old criticism this was the very breath of Machiavelli's nostrils, the title and the content of the *Prince*. Instead, there is a compact republicanism in the first half of the sixteenth century, and it is only with the age of Charles V, and of the Council of Trent, that the blameless writers of the orthodox persuasion will produce the monstrous doctrines that lead on to revolution.

> Le droit des rois consiste à ne rien épargner,
> La timide équité détruit l'art de régner,
> Quand on craint d'être injuste, on a toujours à craindre,
> Et qui veut tout pouvoir, doit oser tout enfraindre,
> Fuir comme un déshonneur la vertu qui le perd;
> Et voler sans scrupule au crime qui le sert.

That is Corneille in the climate of the seventeenth century, writing what would long have done duty as machiavellian concepts; and Bossuet, with his *Politique tirée de l'Écriture Sainte* (where he discovered that kings may do what they will without their peoples having the right to murmur), is round the corner. In this new world Davanzati brings out the text of Tacitus translated, and the commentaries on Tacitus pullulate. We have left the age of Machiavelli for the age of machiavellianism.

CHAPTER 7

Epic Poetry from Pulci to Tasso

HISTORY for us now is not a part of literature, and though none can exclude Machiavelli or Guicciardini from the record of Italian literature, there will be some who come back with relief to poetry. As in Latin times, Italy imported its epic themes: not Troy, but the *matière de Charlemagne* and the Arthurian legends. Paolo and Francesca read of Lancelot, and Dante also sang of the horn of Roland in the dolorous rout of Roncisvalles. And this enthusiasm, commemorated for an early date by a door-carving at Modena, is variously attested in Ferrara. Borso d'Este writes in 1470 for as large a load as possible of French romances from his ambassador in Paris, lends them out, and has sisters and other relatives with Arthurian names. These two cycles could not live transplanted without suffering some sea-change. The *Chanson de Roland* mirrors the clash between Christian and Saracen in the eleventh century; its atmosphere is hieratic in its simplicity, with Charlemagne laying waste the land of Spain for the excellent reason that he is right and they are wrong. And when the Saracens submit he offers them the straight alternative of death or baptism, so that 100,000 become *true Christians*. In this world of black and white Charles and his paladins loom up before us with unrelieved majesty, and the traitor Guenes (Ganelon), another Judas, stands opposite them unredeemed, and dies torn asunder by four proud horses till all his nerves are stretched apart, his clear blood split on the green grass: *Hom ki traist altre nen est dreiz qu'il s'en vant*. Two centuries before the *Divine Comedy* the note is similar to that which damns the traitors to the deepest pit, where *whoever has betrayed forever is consumed*.

It was inevitable that this should lose its urgency, and its dignity, as it passed over the Alps and into the market-places as the stock-in-trade of itinerant singers (*cantastorie*), unconcerned with resistance to Moorish Spain. Moreover, where, as in Florence, feudalism had been defeated, the spirit of chivalry could not survive untravestied. In the *Fatti di Spagna*, a northern prose text of the fourteenth century, we find Charles threatening to hang Roland with coarse insults, while Roland almost draws his famous sword against the king. He leaves in dudgeon, finds an enchanted fountain, ends up in the Holy Land as Constable of Jerusalem. Here the treachery of Ganelon has become a well-worn device to stir distrust in Charlemagne and send his bravest paladins in search of unrehearsed (but predictable) adventures; confronted with their monarch, both sides are robbed of all dignity by the intemperance of their language in trivial terms. Nowhere is this process of disintegration better seen than in the *Morgante* of Luigi Pulci (1432–84). Belonging to the circle of Lorenzo Pulci is on the side which produced the *Nencia* or the *Beoni*; and he also wrote his *Nencia*, the *Beca da Dicomano*. The first part of his *Morgante* is a reworking of an earlier poem on Orlando, to which he soldered later from another model, the *Spagna in rima*, the close of the campaign in Spain with its obligatory tragedy. The action of the first part is monotonous and repetitive, based on the device we have just seen: Gano pours drops of poison in Charles's ear, and Rinaldo sets out on adventures. As their spring runs down we come to reconciliation, only for Gano to begin again *daccapo*. The reduction of the characters is carried near to caricature (what is left for a king so constantly deceived but to appear a daft old dotard?); and for all their knightly accoutrements they have the appetites of the plebeian. Metaphor and simile turn on appetite in the most literal manner: Two lovers to one lass? – 'two gluttons at one trencher'; making a wrong approach? – 'it needs a different cheese to such a macaroni'. Even the fighting is in such terms, with the killing, 'slicing melons, marrows, turnips, bread'. Rinaldo as a highwayman is not out of place in this loutish world: to which Pulci added of his own invention the episode of Morgante and Margutte, who personify all this low life.

Morgante, the good-humoured giant, lives for eating;
Margutte, the mere half-giant, lives by his wits, confesses
cheerfully to seventy-seven mortal sins; and is, of course,
as gluttonous as Morgante. At times this runs to blasphemy:
but does not Rinaldo also believe more in food than in
religion?

> Venne un romito e disse: Ave Maria.
> Disse Rinaldo: se del pan ci fia.

This low rampageous world, shot beneath the conventional
opening stanzas with irreverent sentiments, brought hostility,
and the accusation of heretical opinions from no less a person
than Ficino. It is a reaction that Pulci went on to make the
Morgante the *Morgante Maggiore*, adding after the transitional
cantos XXI–XXIII the last five (XXIV–XXVIII), with Gano and
his final treachery, in the effort to reach a tragic note. Here
the literary elaboration is more obvious; but the reader's
interest, as with the first part, has often gone to what is
marginal – to the episode of the devil Astarotte, from whom
Rinaldo parts *as from a brother*. This has seemed the frankest
rehabilitation of the devil before Carducci; and it is significant
that Roland himself speaks the most sceptic words. He grieves
at the end of Charlemagne's glorious reign, and recognizes
that all things which rise must also fall:

> Ma ciò che sale, alfin vien poi in bassezza:
> Tutte cose mortal vanno ad un segno;
> Mentre l'una sormonta e l'altra cade:
> Cosí fia forse di cristianitade.

As Astarotte peeps through the heroics of Roland, so the
Pulci of the first part endures in the close.

The most popular of all purveyors of this material was
Andrea da Barberino (1370–after 1431), author of *I Reali di
Francia*, still in cheap editions on the book-barrows of Italy,
and with this of other titles (*Guerin Meschino, Aspromonte*), all
just a little below the level of literature. It remains for Boiardo
to bring Ferrara into the picture, and to give a new direction
to this old material. Matteo Maria Boiardo, Count of Scan-

diano (1441–94), belongs to the court we have seen avidly
consuming French romances; and it is left for him to amalga-
mate the two sides (Charlemagne and the Breton cycle) into
a new composite world. From his environment comes too
some little infusion of nobility. We know from his love-poetry
something of Boiardo's interests; nor is that here belied.

> In fede mia,
> Tutto è perduto il tempo che ne avanza,
> Se in amor non si spende, o in cortesia,
> O nel mostrar in arme sua possanza.

Love, courtesy, and war: they should exhaust the pattern of
the *Orlando Innamorato*, were not Boiardo's hand forced in
several ways. Firstly, in the matter of courtesy, the imprint
of the *cantastorie* is still visible, and all the characters, from
Charlemagne down, speak and act like boors. With the stock
epithets, this draws attention to the elementary qualities of
Boiardo's art. But there is something even more noticeable:
with this new world of separate adventures in a perilous, often
enchanted, environment Boiardo is hurried off into a chaotic
poem, which can be summoned to no unity, and might have
been hard to end at Roncisvalles even if its author had lived
to finish it. In his opening stanza he equates the pleasing and
the strange, and this naïve appetite for the monstrous, the
horrible, and the cruel, runs through all the *Innamorato*.

> Che la piú strana cosa che abbia il mondo,
> E la piú dilettosa e piú verace
> Vi contarò, se Dio ce dona pace.

Such formulas repeat themselves, and we are always being
led to a crescendo of impossible enchantments and strange
metamorphoses. In these conditions the characters lack
stability, and the episodes a human sense. Let us look to that
episode of the enchanted garden which will bring the richest
poetry with Ariosto, Tasso, and the Bower of Bliss in Spenser's *Faerie Queene*. Here it is an abode of genuine grotesques,
and Orlando, who has a handbook to its magic wiles, smears

himself over with Siren's blood to be safe against the bull with the iron and the fiery horn. ...

It was a misfortune for Boiardo that his gentle dialectal flavour gave offence in the age of Bembo, so that his poem was rewritten by Berni and Domenichi, leaving the original to languish till the nineteenth century. Since then his native qualities have been recognized: the constant resilience of his zest, the touch of gentle malice (as in the famous portrait of Astolfo, always unhorsed, always attributing his fall to the tripping of his horse), the idyll of amorous episodes, often franker in outspokenness than we shall find with Ariosto. But if we think of this in epic terms, it is however parody, and both the Arthurian and the Carolingian elements are in dissolution. What is clear is that the epic has no historical basis left, cannot be explained in relation to a period (the Middle Ages) with which its has no connexion, or to an institution (feudal chivalry) which it does not know. It is with Boiardo the detritus of old themes, redeemed by many endearing qualities, but outside reality. It is no accident that the *Innamorato* breaks off abruptly with the famous stanza on the coming of Charles VIII. That is the touch of the outside world, and with it Boiardo's poem is doomed to supersession, not so much by *rifacimenti*, as by some poem which can bring order and the semblance of reality to this chaotic world.

This task belongs to Lodovico Ariosto, and makes of the *Orlando Furioso* a new creation, hinged only casually on to its predecessor. In between, to emphasize the need for a new start, we have in the last years of the fifteenth century *Il Mambriano* of Francesco (Cieco) da Ferrara. This is a knot of fantastic adventures, the looseness of whose texture is underlined by the intrusion of seven *novelle* which join, and interrupt, the narrative. Here too is a coarseness worthy of the fabliau (from which one of the stories comes). If we add to aimlessness and near-obscenity the further caricature of the staple theme of combat, we shall see how this is the smoky candle-end of the epic, not the rosy dawn from which the *Furioso* springs ready-armed. Here is the clash, all unbeknowing, of Roland and Rinaldo:

E i troncon de le lancie andar sí insu,
Scrive Turpin se l'è vero io nol so,
Che ben tre giorni sterno a tornar giú.

If we follow the plain lie of the land we shall find that the old attitude to Ariosto, sanctioned by the great name of De Sanctis, and reduced to its extreme by his successors, makes no sense. Theirs was an Ariosto who ignored the harsh realities of his contemporary Italy to plunge into a dream world with a magic air, where nothing mattered but the beauty of images or the fluidity of his stanzas. The truth, of course, is contrary, and it will be the work of Ariosto to rescue this material from the plight into which it had fallen: to remove the coarseness of the *Mambriano*, to attenuate the magic and the strangeness of the *Innamorato*, to bring the ideal of courteous behaviour within the reach of Christian and Saracen alike, to bring towards order a chaotic world, giving it a human content.

Seen in this light the *Furioso* can escape some of the old questions. Was it the satire of, or a nostalgia for, the Middle Ages? And when in a celebrated line Ariosto exclaimed

O gran bontà dei cavalieri antiqui,

was he pointing a contrast with the harsher habits of modern soldiery? All this is wide of the mark, and the same process is at work as was defined once by Sainte-Beuve for the development of Le Cid: all of whose noble qualities had been foisted on him by writers looking for a contemporary ideal. And Ariosto does not come to the epic via or in search of history: he comes to it as he finds it, and transforms it by the operation of his own standards and the ideas and ideals of his time; so that the gap which looms between his poem and those of his predecessors is the measure of his abilities, as of his character. Nor must we ignore the herculean effort by which he brought the epic uphill from the morass into which it had descended, making of it the first shining monument of the poetry of the Cinquecento: one that could capture the whole century in a long series of editions, and enthuse Europe for several centuries. La Fontaine (*Je chéris l'Arioste et j'estime le Tasse*), Voltaire (*Je vous avoue que cet Arioste est mon homme*), Gibbon (*the incomparable Arioso*), and Charles James Fox (*For God's sake, learn Italian as fast as you can in order to read Ariosto*) are sample customers.

It was essential to put the *Furioso* in perspective, for no poem has been more consistently misread. Lodovico Ariosto (1474–1533) was born at Reggio, eldest son of a rather unsavoury servant of the Estes, by whose comparatively early death he became head of the numerous family in 1500. A member of the household of the Cardinal Ippolito till he refused to accompany his patron on a visit to Hungary in 1517, Ariosto was shortly after accepted among the dependants of Duke Alfonso. The irregularity of ducal pay led him to seek a post, which turned out to be the governorship of the Garfagnana from 1522 to 1525. His *Letters* are mainly concerned with this period, and throw a kindly light on his character, showing that in the most awkward of situations it was not his impracticality which was unable to cope with real life. His reflections on this period, and on other aspects of his experience, will be found in the good-natured *Satires*, more autobiographical than satirical, and with the *Letters* the most valuable evidence for his character. His poem he may have begun as early as 1504–6, after the Latin of his youthful production. It came slowly to the first edition of 1516, and was constantly revised, according to principles which we have seen, until the definitive edition of 1532.

Boiardo broke off with a despairing note on Italy in fire and flames with the coming of the French – who knows with what purpose? It was the symbol of the unreal world crumbling on contact with the real; and it is a measure of the contrast that among the references to contemporary events studding the *Furioso* there is an answer to this bewilderment,

> E che brevi allegrezze e lunghi lutti,
> Poco guadagno et infinito danno
> Riporteran d'Italia; ché non lice
> Che'l Giglio in quel terreno abbia radice.

What is the difference that makes these intrusions of the real world possible without destruction of Ariosto's as of Boiardo poem? It is that the poem is no longer based on monsters and impossibles. Fit Boiardo's key to Ariosto's door, try him with the adjective *strange* which rises incessantly to Boiardo's lips: we shall find it almost entirely lacking, and when, rarely enough, it does occur it does not lead to horrible adventures. This change of atmosphere applies also to the enchantments which Boiardo so enthusiastically, and irresponsibly, employed. The monsters have departed, and the epithets which went with them. Such magic devices as Ariosto retains are no longer taken seriously for their own sake. They are transparent, and they do not dictate or distort the actions of the characters. This is not a launching into magic, but its spiritual disappearing-point, so that it remains as a diaphanous veil in parts, at once serving the purposes of the action, and to give a sparkle to the colours. It is a world in which physical inconveniences are removed, and where being lucky one may travel faster by hippogriffin than by aeroplane, but it is not a fanciful world either in geography or content, and the actions which it chronicles are human ones.

That is why the magic which Ariosto retains is always trembling on the brink of allegory or rationalization: it is because his sanity of outlook is impatient with a lack of meaning. Amongst the often-praised openings of Ariosto's cantos none is more illuminating in this connexion than Canto VIII:

> Oh quante sono incantatrici, oh quanti
> Incantator tra noi, che non si sanno!
> Che con lor arti uomini e donne amanti
> Di sé, cangiando i visi lor, fatto hanno,
> Non con spirti constretti tali incanti,
> Né con osservazioni di stelle fanno;
> Ma con simulazion, menzogne e frodi
> Legano i cor d'indissolubil nodi.

And to make this point explicit the next stanza desires the ring of Angelica, or rather, that of reason, to see truth under the show of falsehood. We have only to put this against the constant boasts of Boiardo of stranger enchantments to see that Ariosto comes with an opposite intention. He dissipates the magic elements so frequent in Boiardo, keeping a little only with an indulgent irony to fit the management of his episodes, being always on the point of giving it a human significance. We may test this with that enchanted castle of Atlante, near the beginning of the poem, perched mountain-high, and flashing with stainless steel. It seems outside experience, yet when it is dissolved, and the ladies and the knights find themselves ruefully out in the cold, his comment (IV, 39) brings at once a sense which we can relate to a moralist's conclusions. 'Doth any man doubt, that if there were taken out of men's minds, vain opinions, flattering hopes, false valuations, imaginations as one would, and the like; but it would leave the minds of a number of men, poor shrunken things; full of melancholy and indisposition, and unpleasing to themselves?' Bacon's reflection helps to show that Ariosto is not the poet of illusions, or of an unreal world, but rather of a gentle disillusionment: one who has the maturity of the *nosce teipsum* to offer us. And we have to take cognizance of the modest personality of Ariosto, for the old criticism of the Renascence saw fit to blame that age for its glorification of man and its insistence on the idea of Fame, yet these are singularly lacking in the poet of the High Renaissance.

Nowhere is the revolution more visible than in the characters. Instead of the swearing and brawling of Charlemagne, we have the dignity of his prayer in Canto XIV; Rinaldo is no highwayman, but brother to Bradamante, with no breath of vulgarity. Indeed, urbanity and courtesy is so pervasive that it becomes the uniform accompaniment of all. Ariosto keeps the promise of his opening lines, but they are different from Boiardo's,

> Le donne, i cavalier, l'arme, gli amori,
> Le cortesie, l'audaci imprese io canto.

And this is distinct from Virgil, offering already a streak of civilizing feminism which runs through the poem. Nor is the old idea of a sensuous Ariosto right. The spirit of Boccaccio in Boiardo, or of the *fabliau* in the *Mambriano*, is repelled by Ariosto with a chastity we must not underrate: and if we look to Angelica or Olimpia exposed naked on the rock, or the central episode of the love of Angelica and Medoro we shall find a reticence which does him honour. This episode, with the luck of the outsider Medoro (not in the race, yet carrying off the prize), struck the imagination of Europe; and may show us that the characters are not unrecognizable, even if they are not yet wholly in the round. They have come back to human shape, motives, and actions. It is here that the personifications turn out to be one of the mainsprings in this humanization of the material. Though Ariosto restores dignity to the struggle against the paynim hosts, it is too remote to resume the significance it had in the *Chanson de Roland*. But while in the *Innamorato* there were no motives to replace the old conception, here there is a struggle of good qualities against bad, and in this the personifications, Fraud, Silence, and Discord, play a central part. Nothing is more admirable than the inextricable knot of disputes by which Agramante's camp, flushed with victory at the gates of Paris, dwindles and evaporates. It is not religion dooming them to be slain or baptized: it is Discord which prevents the exploitation of their strength, and this is a symbol of the way in which human motives have intervened to supersede the search for the impossible.

In snatches Ariosto will arrive at allegory, but it is a glory of his poem that this is a tendency and not a system. He writes at a golden moment, before the quest for conformity to rules; and as the heir to the Quattrocento he gives to the *ottava rima* the pictorial qualities bequeathed by Politian from the *Stanze per la Giostra*. While Boiardo was carried away in a breathless succession of adventures, Ariosto has always leisure to look round upon the scene; and brings, as in the celebrated episode of Astolfo's journey to the moon (Canto xxxiv), a gentle satire of sublunary beings. There remain the attacks upon the *Furioso* as a decorative poem, and here perhaps we have to make our individual choice and stand. It is sometimes taken for granted that the realities of life are grim, and that it is better to be cradled in the ugly, as being real, than in the beautiful, which may be only an escape. But those who built the fairer buildings in the world may have been just as much in earnest as the most extensive erectors of slum-property, and the choice between two sorts of reality is not necessarily the worst. In short, there was an age which looked to the creation of the beautiful as its proper business: what other sense have we seen for Alberti and the Quattrocento? It was not ashamed to add a storey here, a vista there. That age was the Renascence, and its chief poet was Ariosto, nor is there any pressing need, in the name of ugliness or squalor, to be ashamed of either.

The *Angelica Innamorata* (1550) of Brusantini may serve as indication of the attempt to go forward, while looking backward in imitation. More noticed were the poems of Luigi Alamanni (1495–1556), whose opposition to the Medici led to refuge in France, where he drew on a French romance for his *Girone il Cortese*, where Girone loves the wife of his best friend, and ends with suicide in the name of loyalty. The names, and the situation, we shall find in Leopardi's *Telesilla*. But neither *Girone* nor the *Avarchide*, meant as an imitation of the *Iliad*, have much poetic life, and Alamanni did better with the didactic *La Coltivazione*, where the rural world seen through the eyes of Virgil fuses with his memories of Tuscany and France. Here he followed the example of Giovanni Rucellai (1475–1525), whose short poem *Le Api* is based on the fourth book of the *Georgics*. To this respectable pair there will be added later *La Caccia* of Erasmo di Valvasone (1523–93), and *La Nautica* of Bernardino Baldi of Urbino (1553–1617) – this last, with *Le Api*, the best of this series. Then in this interlude between Ariosto and Tasso we must insert a poem best known by its not being read: the *Italia Liberata dai Goti* of Gian Giorgio Trissino (1478–1550). He was a man of the highest culture, equally prepared to fill the gap formed by the absence of a regular tragedy, or by the non-existence of an Italian *Iliad*. Taking his matter from Procopius he wrote in blank verse on the model of Homer a long poem in twenty-seven books that cost him twenty years of work, which won a modicum of praise, but no readers. And to this company of forgotten aspirants belongs the father of Torquato, Bernardo Tasso (1493–1569). As courtier and secretary he had a chequered life, but managed to write in various genres. Better than his long *Amadigi*, from a Spanish source, and attuned to the climate of the Counter-Reformation, is the fragment broken from it, *Floridante*, posthumously published by his son. But the respect we can accord to Bernardo is as father rather than as poet. There is left the celebrated version by Annibale Caro of the *Aeneid*. Written between 1563–6, and published after his death in 1581, the *Eneide* maintained itself until the nineteenth century. Less severe than Virgil, it pleased where it weakened the original; but contemporary in appearance with the *Gerusalemme Liberata*, it shares some of the latter's qualities, and has some of its success.

Torquato Tasso (1544–95) is more casually linked with Ferrara than were Boiardo and Ariosto. He was born at Sorrento when his father was in the service of the Sanseverino family, and hardship dogged his footsteps after their disgrace. The sunshine was his youthful period at the ducal court of Ferrara, where he came in 1565, and which he was to know for the best part of twenty years. It was from 1572–4 that fortune, and Duke Alfonso, smiled most on the accomplished courtier, and to this time belong his two chief works: the *Aminta*, a court entertainment on a pleasure-island of the Estes in the summer of 1573, and the *Gerusalemme*. These spring from the same mind, in the same lapse of time, and are conceived before troubles crowd on Tasso, and affect his mind. The *Gerusalemme* was completed by 1575, though neither appeared in print till five or six years later. In the interval Tasso was seized with scruples, fearing the censure of the Inquisition, adding an allegory, and embarking on the process which will lead him to the stillborn *Gerusalemme Conquistata* (1587–92), in which he set out to eliminate the elements which make the attraction of the earlier poem. The first authorized edition of the *Liberata* (1581) brought hostility from the supporters of Ariosto, and from Leonardo Salviati, just forming in Florence the Accademia della Crusca to

maintain the purity of the Tuscan tongue. And then, from
1577, the seeds of disorder had appeared in Tasso's mind,
so that, from 1579 to 1586 he endures imprisonment in the
Hospital of St Anne. Around this melancholy period was
woven the legend of Tasso persecuted because of his genius,
and because he dared to love Alfonso's sister Leonora. Meanwhile the battle raged around his poem, and his apologies for
it alternate with his efforts at revision. His poetry continues
to be pirated by the printers, though he made an attempt to
gather in one corpus his copious lyric output; and his path
is studded with lesser prose works, usually in the favourite
dialogue form of the Cinquecento. There is left, with his
tragedy *Il Re Torrismondo*, the poem of his last years, the *Sette
Giornate del Mondo Creato*, only printed after his death (in
1607), and making little impact then. In the meantime Tasso's
wanderings, resumed when Alfonso set him free, had taken
him from Mantua to Naples (where his protector Manso, his
first biographer, links him with John Milton), and from
Naples finally to Rome. Here he found tranquillity in the
monastery of Sant'Onofrio, where later Leopardi wept over
the simple letters marking his tomb.

If the emphasis of a short history could be upon biography
nowhere before Leopardi would one pause more naturally
than with Tasso. There is this distinction to be made, that
for Leopardi the melancholy facts of his life are inextricably
woven into his poetry, while for Tasso the main sector of his
work stands in the sunshine. With the *Gerusalemme Liberata*,
in spite of all the controversies, he takes his place as 'le prince
de la Poésie italienne', and will keep it till Dante is reinstated.
It may be that the line of La Fontaine which was quoted earlier
may serve to point the contrast in temper between Ariosto and
Tasso (*Je chéris l'Arioste et j'estime le Tasse*), for there we have
suggested the playful and buoyant quality of Ariosto as
distinct from the solemnity and decorum aimed at by Tasso.
But Tasso is not all on one front, and the spirit of the *Aminta*
makes its contribution to the contemporary *Gerusalemme*.
Here the pointers marked out by his youthful *Rinaldo* aim at
both these works, though on the surface they might seem

contradictory. The *Rinaldo* was completed by 1562, in obvious immaturity. To his readers Tasso offers the assurance that he will look to ancient models, but not, he adds, to the severer rules of Aristotle: he will, instead, strive to temper precepts with the desire for *delight*. No *profession de foi* could be truer, or more prophetic. At seventeen, his new unity turns out to be no more than that of a single main character, Rinaldo, and the tone is from the start ariostesque, with Rinaldo caught between *Desir di gloria, ed amoroso caldo*. Nor can Tasso help falling back towards the world of Boiardo, with strange enchantments to which neither sense nor importance can be attached. But in this inchoate world there are hints of the coming Tasso: as in the Palace of Courtesy and the episode of Floriana which rehearse the Gardens of Armida. And here to confirm Tasso's main interests is the prelude in the minor key to the *Aminta's* paean on the universality of Love.

> O gran contrasto in giovenil pensiero,
> Desir di laude, ed impeto d'amore

was Ariosto's reflection, and love and glory are to be the twin staples of the *Gerusalemme*; but in spite of the earnestness with which Tasso pursues the second it is the first which commands his natural allegiance, and to which his poem gravitates. Since Tasso means return to high seriousness he does what he can, with a Virgilian decorum, to ennoble the chivalrous material. And he added his views in the *Discorsi dell'Arte Poetica* (later elaborated as *Discorsi del Poema Epico*) to those sketched in with *Rinaldo*. Here matter and ornament stand separate, with the marvellous – thought of as a great part in Ariosto's success – as the best embroidery. Since dogma is thrust as resolutely aside as it will be by Boileau it follows that this will come from the outer fringes. Tasso must give this element (as with the magic wood) as much seriousness as the subject demands, but in the end it will detract, not add effect. The Archangel Michael calls off the devils, but Argante fights on as fiercely as before. The supernatural as Tasso uses it to support the theme of the First Crusade is something to which he has to give solemnity, but for which he has no real use. It makes us regret the abolition of magic under way with Ariosto. And there is another dubious element: the Crusaders are encamped outside Jerusalem, and all the apparatus of siege and war has to assume a dignity of treatment in its own right. Ariosto had shifted the emphasis away from carnage, and short of abandoning the combat epic, or treating it as parody, no more could be done in this direction. Now Tasso returns, more towards Virgil than towards Boiardo, with set pieces finely wrought from the antique, and that nobility of diction which pervades his poem. And in this direction too is the conversion of Ariosto's knights to be the grave companions of Goffredo, while Godfrey himself,

Augusto in volto, ed in sermon sonoro

(In shape an Angel, and a God in speech), may be taken as a pattern, looking plainly to *pius Aeneas*, not to Orlando.

It is because Tasso aims so obviously at the correct and solemn that one hesitates to see here, as is usually posited by Italian criticism now, the verge of the baroque in poetry. Those who had aimed at an imitation of the *Iliad* are not betrayed by Tasso: does not the anger of Rinaldo echo that of Achilles? It is a symbol of a neo-classicism which extends to all his poem. And if we look to one or two telltale points, as when Armida's anger fades when she gazes on Rinaldo, *E di nemica ella divenne amante*, or when Tancred finds that he has slain his Clorinda unawares, *Ahi vista! ahi conoscenza!*, we shall find nothing of the theatricality, the blaze of conceits which Marino will contribute to Italian poetry. But with these names, Armida and Clorinda, it is plain that we have come to a side of the action not advertised in the title; and it is well to remind the reader that Tasso still in the *Discorsi sul Poema Epico* reserves the right to temper the severity of the rules with softer things. *Le grand art, c'est l'art de plaire*, and no one more than Tasso bequeaths this lesson to the French seventeenth century. This licence he wrote in no uncertain terms in the *Discorsi*: 'thinking that all most beautiful things are fitting for the heroic poem: *ma bellissimo è l'amore*'. And once Tasso

141

has lighted a candle to this saint its brightness threatens to steal the picture. True, the Hermit catechizes Rinaldo, after the abandonment of Armida, in words which improve with Edward Fairfax's brilliant englishing,

> Not underneath sweet Shades and Fountains shrill,
> Among the Nymphs, the Fairies, Leaves and Flowrs;
> But on the steep, the rough and craggy Hill
> Of Vertue stands this Bliss, this good of ours:
> By toil and travel, not by sitting still
> In pleasures lap, we come to Honours Bours;
> > Why will you thus in sloths deep Valley lie?
> > The Royal Eagles on high Mountains flie.

But the end of the poem brings a significant epilogue. Armida, the woman scorned rather than the enchantress unmasked, had sought revenge among the hosts of Egypt, and when her champions fail her is overtaken by Rinaldo himself. It is a scene of reconciliation, with Rinaldo at her feet, and occupies more space than the Crusaders' homage to the Holy Sepulchre. The steep and craggy hill of virtue is less prominent than it ought to be, and Tasso expatiates where he is launched on to this softer side of Love, from the first episode of Sofronia on.

> But what avail'd her Resolution chaste,
> Whose sob'rest looks were Whetstones to Desire?
> Nor Love consents that Beauty's Field lie waste.

What is true of Sofronia holds for the poem. That is why Tasso's version of the gardens of Alcina and Ruggiero (itself so civilized after the enchanted garden in Boiardo) in Canto XIV, and Armida's world itself in Canto XVI, ring truest, and outlive in their appeal the less urgent themes of war and piety. And here supremely the sensuous element, so lacking in the elastic verse of Ariosto, comes into its own, and brings the *Gerusalemme* for all its epic qualities within the ambit of the *Aminta*. The picture of this Fortunate Isle we shall find in XVI, 11, and here is its law, proclaimed in XIV, 63:

> Folli, perché gettate il caro dono,
> Che breve è sí, di vostra età novella?

Nomi, e senza soggetto Idoli sono
Ciò, che pregio, e valore il mondo appella.
La fama che invaghisce a un dolce suono
Voi superbi mortali, e par sí bella,
È un Eco, un sogno, anzi del sogno un'ombra,
Ch'ad ogni vento si dilegua, e sgombra.

O Fools who Youth possess, yet scorn the same,
A precious, but a short abiding Treasure,
Vertue itself is but an idle Name,
Priz'd by the World 'bove Reason all and measure,
And Honour, Glory, Praise, Renown and Fame,
That Mens proud Hearts bewitch with tickling Pleasure,
   An Echo is, a Shade, a Dream, a Flower,
   With each wind blasted, spoil'd with every shower.

This is only nominally the world of Heroic Poetry: it is a cross-current which carries Tasso into his other world of the *Aminta*, in which he lives more fully than in this one. Just once in the *Gerusalemme* Tasso finds a line,

L'aspra tragedia dello stato umano,

full of commotion for the scenes of war; but on the whole the eyes of all these warriors close decorously, not tragically; and in an old phrase, Tasso found poetic life for his poem by going outside his subject to this more seductive world of Sofronia, Clorinda, Erminia, and Armida.

CHAPTER 8

The Italian Theatre from the Sacra Rappresentazione *to the* Pastor Fido

THE dramatic possibilities of the liturgy led in Europe to an independent drama, by the stages of representation in the chancel, within the nave, out in the *parvis*. Each stage saw a weakening of the sacred character, a fresh intrusion of the spirit appropriately named *farce*, as being the stuffing to the mistery play. Long thought of as a French phenomenon, this is yet something diffused all over the Italian peninsula, exemplified from its germination to full misteries on the central dramas of the Church, fusing into such cycles as those of Easter, Christmas, or Old Testament. Alongside this is the work of the *giullari*, or *joculatores*, who might by a stretch of the evidence or the imagination be taken as continuers of the ancient masks. Nor must we forget that in old Italian poetry the *Ritmo Cassinese* begins,

> Signori, se io favello, vogliate prestarmi orecchio,

or that the famous *Contrasto* of Ciullo d'Alcamo may be a dramatized scene of seduction needing only the simplest apparatus to be played by two actors. To these elements we must still add others. We have seen the Flagellants, and from their ejaculatory *lauda* there develops in Umbria not only the dramatic mono- or dia-logue which we have seen in Jacopone's *Donna del Paradiso*, but others whose first intent is to stimulate to penitence. The first subjects are the Passion, the grief of Mary, and so forth, and to these are added soon legends of saints. With the *giullari* the *malmaritata*, the girl anxious for a husband, had been dramatized, so now the repentant sinner, or the devotee of the Virgin. In Umbria the name *ripresentazione* first appears, though the main collection of *sacre rappresentazioni* is Florentine. Here the formative

stage was complete by 1440, after which there are only
rappresentazioni in eight-lined stanzas, with a total repertory of
nearly a hundred compositions. They continue on into the
sixteenth century, though by then they are an outdated form.
It was natural that they should be the vehicle of considerable
display, and Vasari writes that Brunelleschi, among others,
added to the perfection of their mechanism. With writers also,
the old anonymity gives place at the same time to names:
as Castellano Castellani, Feo Belcari, or Lorenzo himself.
In all this there is a constant tendency: for the material to
come from the religious side (with, for Florence, a predominance of the hagiographical subject), and the liveliness from
the Florentine scene. Thus we may prepare for the Massacre
of the Innocents with nurses' gossip on others' charges (R.
della Natività di Cristo); or on the way to Emmaus (R. *della
Risurrezione*) the innkeeper tempts the passers by,

> Venite qua, ché ci è lesso e arrosto;
> Promettovi di farvi trionfare ...

and when Christ and His companions have accepted he stirs
up his scullion in the roundest terms to bring kid, fat capon,
a basket of lettuce ... From which we follow to Christ
blessing the table.

The naïvety of such juxtapositions speaks for itself; but it
may be supposed that the genre should be tested where it
can boast a known, and not despicable, author. Feo Belcari
(1410–84) is a noble Florentine who held dignified offices,
and was not unacquainted with the Medici. All his small
corpus of work has a pious character, and himself a vein of
humility, as in one of his sonnets,

> Fo versi rozzi e non paio uom civile,

which was a salutary assessment of himself. In his *Rappresentazioni* of the Annunciation we can sense the inherent
defect of the religious theatre, with no development of
character, and all the figures fixed in attitudes we know. This
is shown painfully in the first one, where the angel calls on

the army of sybils and prophets, and thirty-two respond, each with an octave. Better the second, where the Incarnation is preceded by a debate in which Mercy and Peace plead for Adam's seed, while Justice and Truth are not satisfied with 5,000 years of penance. But the most dramatic scene is an insertion by Belcari into an older R. *del Dí del Giudizio*, some thirty-seven stanzas added at the point where St Michael has separated off the sheep and goats. We start with St Michael spying a hypocrite among the sheep, and then proceed with an assortment of sinners anxious to plead their case, or fathers pointing to their children their own merit in not having spared them chastisement. The clerics, the merchants, even the *femmine disoneste*, all make some shift to change their lot, though uselessly. Then finally, Christ with a voice of wrath utters the Last Judgement. Feo's contribution ends, and the dullness of the original resumes.

It might have been kinder to look at the life of the Beato Colombini which Feo wrote in 1449, in its naïve candour one of the charming books of the Quattrocento. By his wife's encouragement Colombini is converted, and carries his charity so far as to bring beggars home, washing their sores, giving them his bed. His wife complains, 'Io pregavo che piovesse, ma non che venisse il diluvio', and the narrative continues to heroic heights of what may seem folly or saintliness. But it is hard to think that the theatre is advancing with Feo Belcari towards any valuable conclusion. And if we turn to a more famous name, to Lorenzo de'Medici, whose wideflung *œuvre* includes the R. *di SS. Giovanni e Paolo*, we shall not find ourselves on firmer ground. Here is something in which the shapelessness of the beginning is matched by the flatness and inconclusive quality of the *ottava rima*. What hope is there from this amorphous work? It is hard not to see Lorenzo's *rappresentazione* as the death-knell of a form from which vitality has gone. And from the anonymous works we may add one corroborative particular. Nothing is commoner in the *rappresentazioni santoriali* than for young converts to be under strong pressure to abjure, and for miracles to preserve them from their tormentors. So in the R. *di Santa Margherita* stripping and whipping and torches applied to the bosom do no good; even, an earthquake frees her from this predicament. But she must be a martyr, as well as a saint, and in the end nothing is left but to take her on one side and chop her head off. But then, what point is left to the miracles? In short, it needs a firm conviction of the rightness of the old to claim that it was disaster for the classical theatre to offer a new start.

Even in Dante's time an attempt had been made to learn from Seneca the art of writing tragedy; but Albertino Mussato (1261–1329) is exceptional in his *Ecerinis*, with its fearful picture of the tyrant Ezzelino da Romano; nor had he much dramatic quality. It was left to Politian to break out from the *sacra rappresentazione* towards the classics, with the R. *della Favola d'Orfeo*, turned later to a tragedy in Acts. Here the form and stage technique is applied to alien material, with Mercury instead of an Angel, and the stage allowing for the underworld to which Orpheus makes descent. The primitive version belongs to 1480, and in spite of the briefness of the whole and the slightness of the *intreccio*, Politian brings to this his qualities as poet. But this is a deceptive flash, and the *sacra rappresentazione* was unable to beget other of these hybrids. It follows then the general law of the fifteenth century: that those genres which are not fertilized from the classical side tend to wither. In view of its poor and uneven quality at its best it is difficult to regret its going very much.

As with the epic, it is Ferrara which is prominent in the development of the theatre, and in its three kinds, comedy, tragedy, and tragicomedy. As early as 1486 Duke Ercole had caused Plautus's *Menaechmi* to be played, and from then on translations from both Plautus and Terence continued to be given: a process in which the young Ariosto had his part. And from translation Ariosto passed to imitation with *La Cassaria* (1508). Here there is no change, except by complication, to the structure of Latin comedy: with two miserly fathers, two young men in love, two slave-girls in the hands of a ruffian, and two sharp-witted servants to contrive the stratagems. But *I Suppositi* (of 1509) has shifted to Ferrara,

147

the central character a would-be student at the University, tempted by a pretty face, and changing clothes with his valet, he to serve the young lady's father, while his servant studies in his stead. Again Ariosto has quickened the pace of this initial comedy of errors by complicating the criss-cross of real and feigned characters, and out of a simple mechanism he has contrived a comedy which moves most briskly. The lay humour, of that sort which fits all times and places, is still untarnished, as with the lament of Damon when he finds his daughter's shame is known:

Whoever wants to confide a secret well, let him tell it to Pasifilo: only the people and those who have ears, and no others, will ever hear of it.

There is a reminder in the agnitions that these are still puppets to whom a role is assigned, but in surface this is the brightest of Ariosto's plays. Like the *Cassaria*, this was written first in prose, then later recast in verse, but with an opposite effect: the inexperienced *Cassaria* gains in verse, in spite of the rather unhappy *sdruccioli* endings, the *Suppositi* is best in prose. The other two of Ariosto's finished plays, *Il Negromante* and *La Lena*, are usually taken as continuing his advance, but in reality mark a regression. Their titles suggest the emergence of a single character to dominate the play, but though the Astrologo, or necromancer, gives rise to some pretty dialogue (as notably with Temolo's scepticism, or the Astrologo's own account of the gentle art of milking purses), this contemporary topic never becomes the centre of interest, and in the first version the Astrologo himself was forgotten in the ending. This is even truer with *La Lena*, often taken as the apogee, but instead showing a tiring of Ariosto's imagination. Here we have gone back to the 'esercito delle bugie' which were the spring of action for *La Cassaria*, and the girl for whose winning stratagems must be devised, and money be forthcoming, is safely back in the power of a *ruffiana*, who gives her name to the play without dominating it any more than does the Astrologo the *Negromante*. There are still deft touches from Ariosto's world, especially the commentary on legal costs, or on the ducal gamekeepers who are the main suppliers of the black market in pheasants and other game. But in some of these there is more weariness of spirit (the date of *La Lena* is 1529) than comic inspiration. It is the possibilities of the new medium rather than the actual attainments of Ariosto's own comedies which seem important.

The path which Ariosto opens is followed by many authors in the Cinquecento. Priority, and the particular of being a cardinal with close connexions with Leo X, gives prominence to Bernardo Dovizi, called Il Bibbiena (1470–1520), and to *La Calandria*, played first at Urbino in 1513. Like the *Suppositi* this is a comedy of errors, with the basic device of identical twins of different sexes and changed clothes to give it speed and point. This comic motiv is reinforced by the simpleton Calandro (from whom comes the title), so obtuse that he will swallow anything, a worthy companion to Ariosto's Camillo Pocosale, and a lesser brother to Messer Nicia Calfucci in the *Mandragola*, for all his doctorate 'the most simple and the most foolish man in Florence'. With him that lay humour which we have seen with Ariosto, the crossing of wooden swords without reference to time or place or individuality, finds bright expression: especially where Fessenio proposes to transport him in a chest to his love, taking him to pieces if necessary, or letting him die to bring him back to life again. Bright and superficial, without the *tempo* which Ariosto extracts from *I Suppositi*, and without the bite of Machiavelli into human gullibility, the *Calandria* remains a landmark but not a masterpiece. Here at least a step had been taken towards providing for the heroine something more romantic than merely waiting to be redeemed. Bibbiena's example was widely followed, notably in *Gl'Ingannati* (1531), the collective work of the Accademici Intronati of Siena. In Lelia who dresses as a manservant to be near her Flamminio, and who as such is sent on embassies to Isabella, only to inspire passion in the latter, Shakespeare's *Twelfth Night* is clearly, if palely, foreshadowed. And apart from direct imitations and translations this play, turned to a *novella* by Bandello, begot other offspring, as with the stories of Barnabe

Riche (1581) and a Scottish play which stems from them. Nor was this all Siena's contribution, and authors such as Alessandro Piccolomini, of the same academy, continue the tradition. But more life, if less form, and certainly less connexion with the Plautus-Terence pedigree, has the anonymous *La Venexiana*, which has only recently been printed. Its action is only anecdotal, a young Milanese in Venice between two Venetian women, both enamoured of him, and in the competition for his favours the one left waiting vainly in the end. Here dialect predominates, and is part of the frank immediacy of the effect. *La Venexiana* is slight in its development, but fresher and more real than most of its contemporaries outside the *Mandragola*.

It is often said that the poetry of Machiavelli is written all in prose: which is not to say that in the *Decennali*, the *Asino* or in the *Capitoli* (as in the admirable *Opportunity*) one cannot find his energy. The prologue to the *Mandragola* is of this category, written, as Ridolfi has said, with the same bitter ink that wrote the dedication to the *Discorsi*: the date, 1518, when the *Prince* had failed its purpose of attracting the attention of the Medici. It is this latent passion pulsating through the play that gives it a quality unique among its congeners. Called first *Messer Nicia*, or *Commedia di Callimaco e di Lucrezia*, it is better known as the *Mandragola*, from the root used for the decoction on whose employ the plot hinges. Callimaco has come back from Paris to see Lucrezia, wife to Nicia. Since she is more beautiful than he thought, he aims to win her. Though she is honesty itself, his task is made more easy by the simpleness of Nicia, anxious to have a child. Fra Timoteo lends his offices to the coaxing of Lucrezia, while Nicia consents to the potion of mandragola, and its incidental consequences: the chief of which is that the first to lie with Lucrezia afterwards will die within a week. If this is so, well let it be the first casual passer-by who can be pressed to service. Naturally, it is Callimaco in disguise who profits, and soon convinces Lucrezia of his prowess, as of the simplicity of her husband, who deserves what he will get. In this the acrid taste of the *beffa*, lingering in popular literature from the medieval story, mingles with the mood of Machiavelli after the rejection of his services; and with Fra Timoteo we tremble on the brink of satire of the sharpest kind. This is a play that might have been a *novella*; and with it we have *Belfagor*, the short story that might have been a play, where we have something of the same sharpness of tone. By the side of these the other plays of Machiavelli are of lesser interest: the *Andria* a free translation out of Terence, *Clizia* a hybrid between Plautus and a contemporary situation.

Once the way is opened the followers are legion. One of the most unconfined is the notorious Pietro Aretino (1492–1556), whose five comedies acknowledge no conventions, and are no longer fettered to the chariot of Plautus and Terence through his ignorance of Latin. This is not all gain, for though he is capable in snatches of the most comic *trouvailles*, especially in verbal coruscation, he cannot construct with any sense of unity or cohesion. *L'Ipocrito* has been seen as a distant presentiment of Tartuffe, but Aretino has not the power to generate deep characters, and here, as also in the *Marescalco*, the *Cortegiana*, *La Talanta*, and *Il Filosofo*, the real merit is in the evocation of contemporary life by vivid dialogue. Here is low life in vertiginous movement, but without the worser look which has made the *Ragionamenti* one of the clandestine books. More copious than Aretino is Giammaria Cecchi (1518–87), a Florentine notary and wool-merchant, but of half a hundred plays, in several styles, and a reputation in his time of some importance, little now remains. Of his comedies perhaps the best is *L'Assiuolo*, with a contemporary plot. More verve, with a little tincture of magic clinging to his name, and some of the exuberance of the south, distinguished Giambattista della Porta (1535–1615), author of the *Magia naturalis* as of many comedies, among the best of which are *L'Astrologo* and *La Fantesca*. Here Plautus, close to the surface, is overlaid with a touch of fantasy. Of greater power as dramatist, Angelo Beolco (Il Ruzzante, 1502?–42) is halfway into dialect, that of his native Padua. Half peasant by birth, an actor by profession, Ruzzante brings a wider range of emotions, including tragic ones which have suggested a parallel with Verga, and a feeling for humble life giving a less literary kinship with Plautus. For the rest, the transition to the *commedia dell'arte*, with its stock characters crystallized as masks and its tradition of improvisation, comes as a relief from the stagnant literary tradition. This will flourish with its *lazzi* until Goldoni attempts reform. Of other authors it may be enough to mention the fertile Antonfrancesco Grazzini (Il Lasca, 1503–84), whose many prolix comedies make abundant use of his predecessors, and bring the spirit of Boccaccio into view, and the single play of Giordano Bruno, *Il Candelaio* (1582). This is an exceptional work, not built on any model, rich in its own defects as a stage-play, and in its presentation of roguery in Naples fraught with a pathos and an implied criticism which points us towards Bruno's thought. So the sixteenth-century comedy ends, with more promise for Europe than actual validity in its own right.

Tragedy is not in much richer case, and we may take the comment of Voltaire as a guide, that regular tragedy begins in France as Italy with a tedious *Sofonisba*. Giangiorgio Trissino (1478–1550), whom we met as the unread author of *L'Italia Liberata*, and whom we might have met as author of an un-adventurous copy of the *Menaechmi*, *I Simillimi*, based his tragedy of *Sofonisba* on Livy, but his dramatic theory on Aristotle and the Greeks. Unity, then, of time and action, the chorus always present on the stage and breaking in to break the action, so that acts are unnecessary; the metre – a novelty of his own – the *endecasillabo sciolto*, without the disagreeable proparoxytons of Ariosto's comedies, but with the blank-ness of blank verse. Unfortunately, European dramatists were slow to learn the need for tragedy to be built upon the clash of characters and feelings, and here the action is set in a cold jelly which never wakes to movement. Even so, Trissino found imitators: as Giovanni Rucellai, whose *Rosmunda* mingles Sophocles with an episode from Paulus Diaconus, and who in his unfinished *Oreste* has direct recourse to Euri-pides. This road of imitation from the Greeks, unusual in the Italian Renascence, proves unprofitable, though the catalogue might continue with Alamanni, who rewrote the *Antigone*, or Giovanni Andrea Anguillara (author of one of the best verse translations of the *Metamorphoses*) who produced in 1556 an *Edippo* which was an attempt at copying Sophocles in *Oedipus Rex*.

Once more Ferrara leads the way, though this time it is a gory one. The theorist and main exemplar is Giambattista Giraldi (1504–73), who added to himself the romantic epithet Cinthio, because he sang of Cynthia. With him we come back to the Latin way, and this in tragedy means Seneca, set up by Giraldi as a conscious model, and imitated in essentials in the *Orbecche* of 1541. This is the *Titus Andronicus* of the Italian stage, and here we feel Seneca in the form, with its distribution into acts, the appearance of supernatural beings, the horror of the material echoing *Thyestes*, and the use of moral sententiousness. Orbecche as a child had informed her father of her mother's betrayal, and was the innocent cause of tragedy. Now she has married secretly one of less than royal rank, and her implacable father feigns reconciliation, only to kill upon the stage the husband Oronte and the two children of the marriage, sending the husband's head and hands as a gift to his daughter. She stabs her father, then herself. This must not be taken as the climax of the horror play in Italy. Sperone Speroni (1500–88) wrote a year later his *Canace* with its theme of incest, giving rise to one of the sharpest polemics of the century. But here the theme may seem horrible, without there being the same physical horrors on the stage. These will come in a spate with the *Marianna* (1565) of Lodovico Dolce, one of the untiring polygraphs. Here Herod has his captain drawn and quartered, Marianna's eyes put out before her heart is torn from her body and this thrown to the dogs, while his mother-in-law and his two sons are executed. As gruesome is the material of Luigi Groto's *Dalida* (1572) with its feast of slaughtered babies, poison, and the axe. And more so still is the *Acripanda* (1591) of Antonio Decio, who threw in all the ingredients of this poisoned chalice to make his horror-play. All these, and Giraldi who begets them, had their influence for us, and for our assessment of the Italian world. *Orbecche* is certainly better than her progeny, and just occasionally we might find in its bitter desolation a pessimistic vision pointing to a modern attitude:

> Come corrente rio sempre discorre
> Et non è mai una medesma l'onda,
> Cosí fuggendo la prima, la seconda
> Succiede, e un'altra a questa:
> Cosí il viver mortal nostro trascorre
> Et non siamo hoggi quelli,
> C'hieri eravamo, et presta
> Piú che saetta da nascosto viene
> La debole vecchiezza, e i bianchi velli
> Accompagnata da dolenti pene.

Here we might see a hint of Pirandello or of T. S. Eliot. But this is a glimpse only, and in the sadness of the material hardly seems enough.

Orbecche does not bound Giraldi's horizon, and having launched the horror-tragedy, and written in the *Discorso sulle comedie e sulle tragedie* the theory of tragedy, he turned towards an intermediate type, the tragedy with a happy ending, satisfying the spectator with the punishment of villainy and the simultaneous liberation of the righteous. While *Cleopatra* and *Didone* continue the line of tragedy, Giraldi's other plays, posthumously published by his son in 1583, move towards tragi-comedy, and are at the most *tragedie miste*. The fundamental elements of sixteenth-century tragedy were, a heroic world in which 'great and terrible' actions can take place, then unity, moral aims, catharsis, an elevated style and language. But with Giraldi (and this is the legacy of Ferrara) there comes the influence, palpable in patches all through his work, of Ariosto and the *Furioso*; and in the *Antivalomeni* and *Arrenopia* we can feel the echoes of this chivalrous world. They bring Giraldi from tragedy proper towards the tone of tragi-comedy, and from the exceptional atmosphere of royal beings in the glare of Grecian tragedy towards a more bourgeois world where the modern play, as distinct from ritual tragedy, is born. Out of these plays many of our English dramatists took hints, and Giraldi may count (without gaining greatly in substance as a writer) as one of the main innovators of the theatre. Here the prologue to *Altile* (1543) reverses the doctrine of the *Discorso* on tragedy, and looks towards the romantic play later to be known as *tragicomedy*, and with a happy ending. Forty years before Guarini's battle for his tragicomedy, the *Pastor Fido*, we have here the 'préface de Cromwell' of the Cinquecento.

Not for once so notorious as the *Canace* of Speroni, but still an exception in the multifarious work of Pietro Aretino is his one tragedy, *Orazia* (1546). Based on Livy, and on that killing of a sister by her zealously patriotic brother, this is the most cared-for plant in Aretino's careless garden. Here unity is given by the theme itself, and a dignity, even nobility of utterance, is at times attained which is outside the reach of Giraldi; while the innovation of the Roman mob as a direct actor on the stage was a bold move in the handling of a play. But it was Giraldi, and not Aretino, who made disciples, in spite of the true judgement of a modern critic on the essential defects of his work – weakness in erudition, in thought and artistry. Outside this uncomely tradition we may mention Pompeo Torelli (1539–1608) with an early *Merope* (1589), and this an attempt to revert from Senecan imitation to Hellenic models; and halting in between these and Giraldian tragedy the *Torrismondo* (1587) of Torquato Tasso. The date of this marks it off from the earlier happy mood of both *Gerusalemme Liberata* and *Aminta*. The night of doubt and of imprisonment has settled on him, and the dreams, omens, and forebodings with which *Torrismondo* opens, conventional as they are, may seem symptomatic of the change in Tasso. As a play it might have gained had Tasso concentrated on its opening theme, which is that of Torrismondo false against his will to his loyalty for his friend Germondo. Germondo loves Alvida, but cannot come forward directly as her suitor since he killed her brother in battle; and Torrismondo goes to ask her hand, ready to cede her to his brother-in-arms. But on the voyage home a storm drives them ashore, and Alvida with Torrismondo, like Aeneas and Dido, find shelter in one tent, where Torrismondo yields to the unquestioning embraces of Alvida, who thinks herself his bride. But this theme of loyalty would

have been enough for Racine, yet at this stage seems too little
for a play; and Tasso tacks to this an imitation of *Oedipus
Rex*, whereby, when he had offered his own sister Rosmunda
as a substitute-bride for Germondo, it proves that Rosmunda
is no sister, but a changeling; and still worse, that by a train
of circumstances Alvida cannot belong to Torrismondo
because she is his sister. So that his crime is not just dis-
loyalty, but incest, and after the dramatic irony of the old
queen welcoming the two marriages which are pending, that
of Torrismondo–Alvida and of Germondo–Rosmunda, we
have (as reported action) the suicide of both Torrismondo
and Alvida. All this has the dignity which Tasso is capable of
giving to it, without it actually coming to poetic life. But
even within the *Gerusalemme Liberata* Tasso has a line which
commemorates

> L'aspra tragedia dello stato umano,

and here suddenly the final chorus, with its Leopardian mixture of *settenari* and *endecasillabi*, comes to the purest poetry of
Tasso.

> Che piú giova amicizia, o giova amore?
> Ahi lagrime, ahi dolore!

The theme of tragedy has taken us forwards, beyond the
main contribution of Tasso to the dramatic literature of his
time: this is the *Aminta*, and we must go slightly back to see
the germination of the pastoral play. The pastoral element is at
times traced back as far as the *Ameto* of Boccaccio, and
through the eclogues of the Quattrocento (where Leon
Battista Alberti has recently been shown as head of the
vernacular tradition). Certainly, here also Ferrara can claim
some precedence, for in 1487 Niccolò da Correggio produced
there a *Cefalo* in five acts, based like Politian's *Orfeo* on a
classical myth. But this belongs to the prehistory of the genre,
and has no immediate influence. In the sixteenth century also
there are forerunners, as Tansillo with *I Due Pellegrini* (1526–
7), Marcantonio Epicuro with *La Cecaria* (1523), and especially G. B. Casalio with the *Amaranta* (1538), sometimes

thought of as the first conscious pastoral play. But here also Giraldi offers the first theory, and writes what we may regard as the decisive play, his *Egle*, of 1545. In his *Discorso sopra il comporre le Satire atte alle scene* Giraldi found a precedent in antiquity, in the *Cyclops* of Euripides, for the satyr play with a *scena boschereccia*, quite separate from the eclogue. The *Egle* is his attempt at this, and as in other departments Tasso received the imprint of Giraldi's ideas, adding the superiority of his genius in execution. So that we may not make the mistake of thinking the *Aminta* and the *Pastor Fido* as taking us downhill into a seductive, but degenerate, world, it is well to recall that here in *Egle* we have a flush of satyrs, with Egle herself, the *petite amie* of Silenus, on their side in finding pleasure only in the company of Bacchus or of Venus. The whole action is the hesitation of the Satyrs on the verge of using force, persuasion being of no avail, upon the nymphs of Diana, and there is at times an intemperance of language to remind us that the *Aminta* is a corrective as well as a concentration, not the exaggeration of a trend, but its purification. With the *Egle* we must couple also the *Sacrificio* (1554) of Agostino Beccari, another Ferrarese. Here in the wake of Giraldi we have hints for both the *Aminta* and the *Pastor Fido*: hints in abundance, but raw material only, without the touch of poetry.

As a consummation there comes in 1573, although not printed till 1581, the *Aminta* of Torquato Tasso, where the theory is sublimated. In the *Gerusalemme Liberata* Tasso spoke, as we have seen, with a divided voice. But here to the assertion

> Perduto è tutto il tempo
> Che in amar non si spende

there is no contradiction. Moreover, all the apparatus of shepherd-dom which had weighted the *Arcadia* of Sannazaro (crooks and flocks, lost *brebis*, and the like) is absent from the picture, which concentrates on feelings and emotions. And these are reduced to an essential simplicity. Aminta loves, Silvia not yet, and all the action is her conversion via pity to the world of Love, preached to her by Dafne in the first scene of the play. Here Love is the world's soul, and the poetry is of fulfilment, without regard to social obligations, or complications; but to heighten the poetry, and to deepen the sense of fulfilment, there is sounded in its fullest form the note of the brevity of human love:

> Amiam, che non ha tregua
> Cogli anni umana vita, e si dilegua:
> Amiam, che'l Sol si muore e poi rinasce:
> A noi sua breve luce
> S'asconde, e'l sonno eterna notte adduce.

And in this the eclecticism of Tasso, over-visible in the *Gerusalemme*, succeeds in fusing all the elements to one new surface, which is the purest and the strongest poetry of the Italian Renascence.

The *Aminta* is lyric rather than dramatic, and although it generates the spate of pastoral plays which follow, it seemed overshadowed for a long time by its first successor, the *Pastor Fido* of Battista Guarini (1538–1612). Since the *Aminta* concentrated the theme of the pastoral play to a pure element it was inimitable on its own terms; what remained was for someone to find the formula which made it assimilable for the generality, and this someone was Guarini. Here all the apparatus which had been expunged is reinstated, and a mere comparison of bulk will show to what extent this restitution has been carried: the *Pastor Fido* is over three and a half times as long as the *Aminta*. To its basic themes – Diana versus Love; the Satyr (representing natural instincts in their more brutal form); pity that becomes love – he has invented a background and a habitat. And since he found it in the orbit of the Greek theatre and of the rules for the theatre, his success was all the more assured. Here we have the wrath of the gods with destiny impending for Arcadia, oracles, dreams, and omens; a child, as in *Oedipus Rex*, swept off in its cradle in a flood of twenty years before, and yet preserved for an agnition and a peripety. We have a judgement and a sacrifice, with all the panoply of priesthood, and this implies a network round the sentiment of love, no longer isolated, as in Tasso, for its own sake and its own fulfilment, but here enmeshed with the welfare of the state, and the rights of parents. But lest we think too easily in terms of those old judgements of De Sanctis on the downward slope of the Renascence into hedonism, just as the *Aminta* was chaster than the *Egle*, so the *Pastor Fido* moralizes the *Aminta*: as has always been notorious from the echoing chorus of the Golden Age, where Guarini rewrites the law that governed bliss. No longer, *S'ei piace, ei lice* (All that pleases lawful is), but instead, *Piaccia se lice* (If it's lawful, let it please). Certainly, with the portrait of Corisca, whose machinations are the touchstone for the honesty of Amarillis and the faithfulness of Mirtillo, and with the general softness of the poetic surface, there is something here for all tastes; and the conception of the *Pastor Fido* as entertainment, more than literature, comes from this easiness of touch which made it the quarry for the European dramatist, and something known by heart as far afield as Russia or Sweden, and as late as the eighteenth century. It is only very slowly that the balance has been righted, and the name of Tasso left to reassert itself in the golden light of the *Aminta*. But even so, it still remains apparent that the *Pastor Fido* was a needed crucible, and that this 'faithful shepherd' (whom we half own in English, in one of the most brilliant of poetic translations, that by Sir Richard Fanshawe in 1647) is the link between the *Aminta* and the *Astrée* of Honoré d'Urfé, a necessary step to the ideals of the seventeenth century in France, at a moment, that is, when France was becoming the cynosure of Europe.

With the *Aminta* and the *Pastor Fido* the floodgates open for the pastoral play, and not in Italy only. But oddly, or significantly, when the tide recedes, and the fashion dies, it will be the foundation members of the school which still remain within the European consciousness. Out of the scores of Italian pastoral plays one or two remain subordinately in print, as the *Alceo* of Antonio Ongaro, which won the slighting epithet of '*Aminta* bagnato': and chief of these also-rans is certainly *Filli di Sciro* (1607) of Guidobaldo Bonarelli, still reprinted to the end of the eighteenth century as the third of the three best pastoral plays: the two first being invariably the *Pastor Fido* and the *Aminta*, most often in this order which ranks the technical achievement of Guarini above the simplicity of the *Aminta*. But this survival in such company of the *Filli di Sciro* is a historic accident which should not mislead us now about its quality. When even the *Pastor Fido* sinks, Bonarelli cannot remain, and as a beacon there still shines, uncommitted to one fashion of literature, the clear light of the *Aminta*.

CHAPTER 9

Figures and Trends within the Cinquecento

WE have been carried forward by various channels, and have
only seen obliquely one of the foundation-figures: Pietro
Bembo (1470–1547), patrician of Venice, Cardinal, legislator
for linguistic usage, and reformer of lyric poetry. It may be
his father Bernardo's contact with the Medici, and his own
residence as a child in Florence, which led to his adoption of
the Tuscan speech as the ideal norm. This did not mean
deficiency in classical knowledge, and his going to Messina
to study Greek with Costantino Lascaris is typical of Bembo's
thoroughness. But for the first time the study of the Tuscan
models, especially Petrarch and Boccaccio, and of the Tuscan
language, appears as an equal preoccupation with Greek and
Latin. The fruit is the *Prose della Volgar Lingua* (1525), the
first coordination for Italy of the rules of speaking and writing. If past writers were best there is no choice except to
follow them, leaving present usage; and since there is no
doubt about the excellence of Petrarch and Bocacccio they
emerge, for a century which is going to look for models and
for rules, as worthy of imitation in their respective spheres of
verse and prose. Bembo is the non-Tuscan codifier of Tuscan
speech for literary use. Here with gravity and lucidity Italian
is finally put forward as preferable to Latin, and the difficulty
of dialects removed by pointing to Florentine as the norm.
This, when reinforced by the practice of Ariosto in his revision of the *Furioso*, determines the linguistic development of
the century, and makes the language of the *Rime* and the
Decameron the patrimony of all Italy.

By comparison Bembo's creative writing seems a little pale,
more form than content. Even in the recently published
Carteggio d'amore with Maria Savorgnan the spontaneous flame
seems hers. Perhaps the *Stanze* beginning *Ne l'odorato e lucido*

oriente, which elaborate the Horatian *Carpe diem*, may be taken as the most genuine of his poetry. By comparison the *Canzoniere*, fruit of his leisure after his retirement from the post of papal secretary in 1521, is of formal rather than of substantial interest. At the end of the Quattrocento there had appeared a strain of petrarchism, frivolous in content and alambicated in form. Its representatives, such as Serafino d'Aquila, Tebaldeo, Cariteo, were noted then, and are forgotten now, though they may be, in a way, more interesting than their conqueror Pietro Bembo. But instead of the waywardness of a distorting tradition he reasserts the purity of the Petrarchan formula. As with the linguistic theory in the *Prose della Volgar Lingua*, here there is one god, Petrarch, and Bembo is his prophet. And here the traces of dialect which obtrude in Boiardo, Sannazaro, or Cariteo are all purged out in the meticulous revision which Bembo gives to his compositions. This is, of course, an exercise not corresponding to an experience, and more interesting now are the *Asolani* (1505), the book which first made Bembo's reputation. Since it is prose, Bembo looks already to Boccaccio as a model, and the complications of its periods make it a worthy contemporary of the *Arcadia*, printed first the year before. The first book is Petrarch, sophisticated, with Perottino discoursing on the bitterness of Love; but the second has Boccaccio for its sponsor, and Gismondo (whose name is an echo from the *Decameron*) as its spokesman. It is of course combated by the surface of both the first and third day, but that does not prevent it having a persuasiveness of its own. Gismondo's theme is of Love as the principle of the universe, and here Bembo as a prelude to Tasso and the *Aminta* is neither uninteresting nor unimportant. This, of course, is love in a cold climate, and there are passages which lead us onwards to the thesis of the third book, to what is better than the senses. This is the best-known portion of the *Asolani*, and it has been reinforced for posterity by the closing passages of the *Cortegiano*, where the doctrine of platonic love is eloquently voiced by Bembo in person. Youth is a fever, and we are born for immortal pleasures. If we go for the present reality, we shall only grasp the shadow, we shall be like one who is hungry and who dreams he eats. So with Lavinello we have expression given to the neoplatonism which had negated the arguments and the direction of the first half of the fifteenth century. But on the whole Bembo succeeds by his eclecticism in the *Asolani*, and there is not only the eloquent third book. In the polish and moderation of Bembo's skill as a writer the *Asolani* float on several tides.

The rest of Bembo's work, the Ciceronian letters as Leo's secretary, the equally Ciceronian history of Venice (turned by himself to Tuscan prose), is of less importance. His authority swelled with his age: made a cardinal in 1539, he was canvassed as the next pope at the moment of his death in 1547. In his own day the weight of his reputation could crush a would-be rebel like Antonio Brocardo, and in the eighteenth century Baretti saw *La Frusta Letteraria* suspended, himself exiled, for daring to call Bembo a *poor poet*. From this prestige came a new vogue for Petrarch, and a spate of petrarchism. Here are poetesses, as Veronica Gambara, Gaspara Stampa, and Vittoria Colonna (1492–1547), who put her mourning for her husband, Ferrante d'Avalos, into a *canzoniere* often moving in its sincerity, even if somewhat monotonous in its general effect. By her friendship with Michelangelo she brings us to the one great unprofessional poet of the Cinquecento. Michelangelo Buonarroti (1475–1564) brings to his verse something of the force that impresses us in the unfinished Slaves for the monument to Julius II. Uncertain in his search for a literary form, and often fragmentary or fugitive in expression, there may yet be a tempestuous energy pulsing in his broken or single lines:

L'amor mi prende, e la beltà mi lega,

and the twin themes of death and night are always lurking. And when he writes in a platonic vein, as in some of the sonnets for Tommaso Cavalieri, it is of Shakespeare rather than of Bembo that he reminds us (*Veggio nel tuo bel viso, Signor mio*).

We may balance Michelangelo, with his tumultuous content struggling to free itself from the shackles of this new medium (*Non ha l'ottimo artista alcun concetto*), against the formal perfection of Bembo, where content is imitative. And we might put Leonardo da Vinci (1452–1519) also as a contrast with Bembo. For Leonardo is in his own definition 'omo sanza lettere', and what prose he writes is the immediate expression of his scientific inquiries, coloured only by the passion of curiosity, and the sense of the beauty of the universe which transpires through those other scientific inquiries, his drawings and his painting. Leonardo's prose marches with Machiavelli's in its non-literary efficacy, and it is no insignificant paradox that in so academic a century these Florentines who stand outside the frontiers of literary theory (and who being Florentines do not need the tutorage of Bembo) should prove the strongest voices. Meanwhile, the path from Bembo leads forward to the *Dialogo delle Lingue* of Sperone Speroni, and to the *Ercolano* of Benedetto Varchi (1503–65). Here the Florentine nature of the literary language is canonized, just as Leonardo Salviati (1540–89) is on the point of establishing literary purism for several centuries with the machinery of the Accademia della Crusca (founded in 1583).

The deviation, with Michelangelo, into literary heterodoxy may not be inopportune as a hint, for the orthodox petrarchism of the century is copious and faded, and it is in the less compliant poets that we shall find most interest. Short and poignant are the life and the *canzoniere* of Galeazzo di Tarsia (d. 1553), and he first perhaps, lamenting on the plight of Italy, utters the cry of 'la fatal vostra beltate'. Of the south also is Luigi Tansillo (1510–68), who won notoriety in his early youth with his licentious *poemetto*, *Il Vendemmiatore*, soon placed upon the Index. In expiation he composed over a long period the *Lagrime di San Pietro*, remembered mostly because they inspired Malherbe to imitation. With the imaginative fervour of the south Tansillo allies an eye for Nature and for the scenes of rural life, as they are, outside Arcadia. And in an occasional sonnet, as in the two cited by Giordano Bruno in his *Heroici Furori* (especially *Poi che spiegate ho l'ale al bel desio*) he expressed under the symbolism of Icarus the daring

of the human mind. With such occasional heights Tansillo
is a more substantial poet than Francesco Maria Molza (1489–
1544), the famous author of *La Ninfa Tiberina*, whose elegant
stanzas move gracefully in a world of myths and idylls, and
of a petrarchan *canzoniere*. And both are preferable to those
who, like Claudio Tolomei, attempted direct imitation of
Latin metrics in the vernacular. Then there is that other sort
of academism, which is its reverse; and here Francesco Berni
(1497–1535), a little like Poggio a century before, the sharp-
witted Tuscan at the Roman Curia, gives his own name to
the bernesque (or burlesque) genre. Sometimes there is a
foundation of satire to his jesting, as in a famous sonnet on
the vacillations of Clement VII; but out of the spirit of
Burchiello there blossoms with Berni a poetry of trivial and
twisted things, told with gusto rather than with a satirical
intent. The height of this, and perhaps it pleased more then
than now, is the *capitolo Al Fracastoro*, with its account of a
night's lodging with the vicar of Povigliano. In all this the
raciest Tuscan is used to all its resources; nor does Berni
stand alone, and three volumes of bernesque poetry continued
to be reprinted for the amusement of Europe from the middle
of the sixteenth to the second half of the eighteenth century.

It is something of a relief to turn back to Tasso, the major
lyric poet of his century. In saying that, however, we must
not forget that his lyric powers are put forth at their best in
the *Aminta*, and in some passages of the *Gerusalemme*. By
the side of the first of those the *Rime* are too many, fed too
often by occasional compositions which Tasso's easy pen
turns out, and never, in spite of a project of 1591, ordered
by their author. But here, even more than in the *Letters*
(where Leopardi found the eloquence of Tasso's concern
with himself), we may find the pathos of his confinement
and his melancholy: as in the sonnet on the cats of St Anne.
And here finally the sensual note which had reappeared with
Pontanus in the neo-Latin lyric is absorbed into the petrarchan
stream to make a new amalgam. *Amore alma è del mondo* is the
one pole of Tasso's poetry (have we not seen it in the *Aminta*?),
the opposite one to that final chorus of *Torrismondo*, and it is

only natural that it should find strong expression here. And sometimes, as in the sonnet *Ne gli anni acerbi tuoi purpurea rosa*, we feel the full noontide of Renascence utterance. Nor does Tasso here, any more than in the *Aminta*, need to stoop to the metetricious devices which will soon be the stock-in-trade of the baroque age.

We have seen already the role given to the Bembo of the *Asolani* in the *Cortegiano* of Baldesar Castiglione (1478–1529). These dates show Castiglione, like others of a famous generation, with his roots in the Quattrocento; and the ideal date of the *Cortegiano*, set at Urbino in the period just before the death of Guidobaldo da Montefeltro in 1508, antedates the decadence that is to come. Over Urbino there hovers the aura of Federigo da Montefeltro, whose portrait by Piero della Francesca predisposes us, and whose personal prestige will not be lessened by inquiry into his life and character. Urbino also will lapse to the Papal State, and its noble palace become an empty shell, but its reputation in the golden moment of Federigo's reign remains undimmed, and Guidobaldo's was a noble twilight. It is no wonder that Castiglione draws from his connexion with Urbino this statement of contemporary ideals. True, his book echoes in form the *Orator* of Cicero, sets out in the same way, sometimes in the same terms, to depict the perfect courtier, as Cicero the perfect orator. True, Castiglione puts as first requirements noble birth and the profession of arms, and this will seem outmoded. But the courtier is not wedded to his cuirass, and the biting answer of the lady to the warrior who would not dance or hear music is very pertinent. She wittily suggested that he should get himself well greased and put away with arms and armour in a cupboard till need was, so that he might not rust more than he had. For war, or nobility, may be the starting-point, but they are not the centre of the *Cortegiano*. Castiglione's sturdy independence begins in the first book. Since Bembo is among the courtiers, it would be natural for him to adhere to Bembo's linguistic formulas (the *Prose della Volgar Lingua* appear three years before the *Cortegiano*, of 1528). But Castiglione plumps for use, not imitation, 'and it would be a foolish thing to love ancient speech for no other reason than to wish to speak rather as people spoke, than as they speak'. The language, and the ideals, of the *Courtier* have a contemporary flavour.

Since they are the fruition of the Quattrocento they partake of that goodness which Federigo inherited from Vittorino da Feltre. Here goodness precedes letters, which are the second ornament of the mind. Even the celebrated quality of *sprezzatura*, or easy grace of accomplishment, can best be thought of in an Albertian context. And Castiglione, beside his friendship with Bembo and Sadoleto, is a close friend of Raphael, a collector of many sorts of works of art. Duke Frederick, when he passed through Urbino and saw a house a-building, would stop to inquire, encouraging its owner 'to beautify' it. And the courtier in consequence does not remain indifferent to what is so patently the current of the century. In the Platonic climax to the *Cortegiano* goodness and beauty are equated; and in the earlier pages we shall find that the friend, and adviser, of Raphael has added requirements for the courtier other than nobility and skill at arms. To know how to draw, to be familiar with painting; nor is music, with the knowledge of various instruments, left out. In the eighteenth century Rousseau persuaded a Spanish gentleman, who had accomplished an artistic tour of Europe and was going home, to stay on in Paris, and learn *sciences*. So he introduced him to a world of which he had been ignorant, the world of Mme de Warens with its new atmosphere of test-tubes and alambics. It is the moment when the spirit of Galileo and of Newton penetrates to the general consciousness of Europe, starting humanity upon the track, which, for better or for worse, it is still following. But from Castiglione down to that Spanish gentleman it is the arts which dominate the civilization of Europe, and Castiglione's statement of the preoccupations of the gentleman marks an epoch in the history of the West. Here finally the medieval knightly virtues (*cortesia e valore, valore e cortesia*, the twin virtues of the purse and of the sword, which are Dante's ideal for society) are replaced by the interests of a gentleman.

Nor is that the end of Castiglione's innovations, or of his assertion of a Renascence as against a medieval ideal. Indeed, perhaps the third book of the *Courtier*, with its plan to put the *donna di palazzo* beside the perfect courtier is more novel, and more surprising than the rest. For here not only is the old ideal of courtly love cast aside (where we might have imagined it to triumph), but the Quattrocento picture of Alberti in the *Della Famiglia* of woman as the materfamilias absorbed in her small household circle, leaving her husband to look outward to the world, is equally superseded. In medieval theory (let Dante or Petrarch be our exemplars) *The fact of marriage is no good excuse from love*. But in the world of Urbino (and our exemplars this time are Federigo da Montefeltro and Battista Sforza, or Guidobaldo and Elisabetta Gonzaga – or Castiglione himself), marriage is the proper goal of love, and other sorts bring remorse as an accompaniment. In this new climate it is logical that the *donna di palazzo* should share the cultural interests of her masculine counterpart, and that the tributes to her as a softening and civilizing influence should ring with a lyric intensity. The theme is actually more revolutionary, and alongside the equality of woman there is suggested in the *Cortegiano* her superiority to man:

but, returning to the praise of women, I say that Sig. Gasparo will find me no remarkable man to whom I cannot find you his wife, daughter, or sister equal in merit and at times superior: besides the fact that many women have been the cause of infinite good to their husbands, and have at times corrected many of their errors.

The sixteenth century sees the *querelle des femmes*, and in Italy there is an outcrop of feminist literature, notable in bulk if repetitive and insignificant in quality. But for a living ideal we do not need to look further than the *Cortegiano*, and to that contemporary which we have already seen beginning, *Le donne, i cavalier, l'arme, gli amori*. For that order is not a casual matter, and there is in Ariosto too a streak of civilizing feminism (with which perhaps Alessandra Benucci is not wholly unconnected) which marks his kinship with Castiglione, and is not the least valuable of Renascence attitudes.

In Book IV we may think of Castiglione's political ideals as being overshadowed by the *Prince* and the *Discorsi*; and of course he must come forward as the partisan of a princely form of government. How else could the *Cortegiano* reflect Urbino? But even so, the political ideals of Castiglione are mild and humane. Nor can he remain out of earshot of the unanimous movement pointing to a *governo misto*. His prince is to elect a council of his nobles, and a popular one as well, so that the state takes its shape from a combination of three good forms of government. Here *leggi ed ordini*, the staple of Machiavelli's *Discorsi*, are the framework of the state, and the prince who can what he wills will will what he should not. The firmest anti-fascist passages can be found in this Fourth Book of the *Cortegiano*; and behind the condemnation of princes puffed up with their own esteem, thinking they cannot go wrong, and nursing up their subjects in an atmosphere of aggression against their neighbouring territories, we have the conduct of Duke Federigo, with his care for civilizing even war, his concern for keeping faith, and his paternal care for the administration of Urbino. And though Guidobaldo was prevented by the circumstances of his physique from equalling the fame of his father, yet with him Urbino still keeps its honest fame. To all this, and to much else as well, the tombstone is supplied by that remark of Charles V, when he heard in 1529 of Castiglione's death in Spain, 'Yo os digo que es muerto uno de los mejores caballeros del mundo.' But he had left to western Europe, published only the year before, one of the most influential books of the Renascence.

By its side the other courtesy books have only a limited importance; this is true even of the celebrated *Galateo* (which has given a name to good breeding, so that *sapere il galateo* is to know the arts of polite society) of Giovanni della Casa (1503–56). In Castiglione there is an attitude which forms a general directive for society, in della Casa's *Galateo* there is, in the purest and liveliest Florentine, the detail of civilized behaviour. That puts it on a lower shelf for us, though in its surface it is one of the most attractive books of its century: an attraction by no means lessened for the English reader in

the naïve translation made by Robert Peterson in 1576. With
the *Galateo* also we may remember – a reminder of the fertility
of the Cinquecento – the occasional excellence of della Casa
as a lyric poet (especially in the sonnets *O Sonno, o della queta,
umida, ombrosa* and *Questa vita mortal, che'n una o'n due*), in his
Orations, or in his *Letters* – this last a genre most copious in
this century.

No letter-writer was more voluminous than the most
notorious of them all, Pietro Aretino (1492–1556), the self-
appointed 'Scourge of Princes' – a somewhat misleading
appellation, since he used his pen rather to flatter the great
(by whose presents, as with those great gold chains which
hang about his portrait's neck, he maintained his state) and
to vituperate the lesser fry. Protected by Agostino Chigi,
and by the future Clement VII, Aretino fled from Rome after
the election of Adrian VI, whom he derided savagely; and
round his final departure from Rome in 1526 there hovered
the aura of his lascivious sonnets on the series of postures
engraved by Marcantonio Raimondi. From then on Aretino
finds a haven in inviolate Venice, lives by his venal pen, and
adds in half a dozen different genres – including religious
works – to the vast production of the century. Full of verve
even where most scurrilous, as in the *Ragionamenti*, opening
shafts of light on to the low life of his times, but also, as friend
of Titian and boon companion of artists of the Venetian
Cinquecento, a valuable witness for his age. In older views
of the Renascence Aretino stood with others in the dock as
the symbol of a corrupt society, and the Elizabethans made a
composite monster of Mach-Aretino which summed up in a
word the worst that could be brought from Italy. But time
has sorted these authors better, and the effrontery of Aretino
is something unmatched elsewhere: enormously successful
in his own time, remembered afterwards as a warning and a
phenomenon. What is alive principally in Aretino is the rapid
gusto with which he writes, unhampered by any of Bembo's
scruples on the vehicle to be used, the chief representative of
the unacademic side of his century, in revolt against the for-
malities of petrarchism, untutored by classicism (in spite of

Orazia), pouring out all that he writes in a natural torrent, treacherous often in its surface, but with the force at times of Nature herself.

Aretino and Machiavelli made a natural couple for the Elizabethan view of Italy, but we may see Benvenuto Cellini (1500–71) as pairing better in some ways with Aretino: not least in the untutored freedom of his prose, or the artistic insouciance of his waywardness. When Angelo Cocchi first published Cellini's *Vita* in 1730 he prefaced it with a remark on the utility of becoming experienced early in human vices no less than in human worth. Perhaps that couples him too much with Aretino, for it is the endearing qualities of Cellini that we may remember most, and all the flaws may seem like specks upon the surface of good metal, giving life and interest for the eye. And this is true especially of the form in this most famous of all artists' autobiographies. Knowing that he had no tincture of literature, Latin or Italian, Cellini applied to Benedetto Varchi for a revision of his work. This Varchi, to his credit, refused to supply, preferring the immediacy of impression of Benvenuto's vivid and spontaneous Tuscan: which has delighted a host of readers since, as one of the most richly succulent books of all the Cinquecento. Here Cellini appears not so much as he saw himself, for that would imply some process of auto-criticism which is absent from the book, but rather as he was in life itself. Perhaps Baretti summed this portrait up in terms which do not need revision either: here Benvenuto depicted himself 'bold as a French grenadier, revengeful as a viper, superstitious to the highest degree, full of *bizzarria* and caprices, gallant in a knot of friends, but not susceptible to tender friendship, lascivious rather than chaste, a little of treachery without acknowledging it, somewhat envious and malignant, vain and a boaster without suspecting it, without affectation, with no small dose of madness accompanied by a firm belief that he was very wise, circumspect and prudent.' His family descent traced from a captain of Julius Caesar sets the key for Cellini's own performance as an artist, as for the valour with which he meets all the haps and hazards that beset him, where he is always ready to leap out with drawn sword, against any numbers, with a loud shout: 'Tutti siete morti.' In 1527, in the Sack of Rome, he claims not only to have been instrumental in saving Clement VII and his cardinals, but to have shot with his own arquebus, at what must have been near the limit of its range, the Conné- table de Bourbon himself. As for his prowess as an artist, we may think of it in terms of a conversation with Clement VII, when the latter had thrown down other artists' sketches in favour of Benvenuto's model. One hesitation only, 'Ben- venuto mio, wax is easy to work, but making it in gold is everything.' 'Beatissimo Padre, if I do not make it ten times better than the model, let it be stipulated that you do not pay me for it.' In this rumbustious chronicle nothing is better than the famous account of his imprisonment and romantic escape. In the same episode of 1527 Cellini had dismounted all the papal jewels, and melted down their settings; and that ugly card Pierluigi Farnese, bastard of Paul III, suddenly accused him of having sequestered for himself some 80,000 ducats' worth, so had him taken up secretly, to be conveyed to Castel Sant'Angelo, where he suffered long and loathsome incarceration, with risk of death from poison, or from the mere conditions of dungeon life. Amongst the hazards of this was finding powdered diamond in all the dishes, and it was a matter for relief to find that the gaoler had substituted out of avarice a soft stone for the valuable diamond given for the purpose, so that Cellini escaped this trial with no more than passing inconvenience. A graphic commentary to the decorous official accounts of Paul III is Benvenuto's story of the Cardinal of Ferrara waiting the right moment to ingratiate himself and beg the release of Cellini (prevented normally by the obstinacy of Pierluigi, even after his accusation had proved utterly false). For the Farnese pope used once a week to have a copious binge, and the Cardinal waited till the moment when the wine was about to take effect, and the Pope ready to rise to go and vomit, so that with a great laugh he gave the Cardinal permission to act, which he did in haste, before Pierluigi could know and counteract it. So Benvenuto, after the false start of his own escape by ropes of knotted sheets from the tower-top, dragging himself with his leg broken because they were too short, found his freedom; and after convalescence passed to the service of Francis I, and to one of the richest periods of his production.

Benvenuto takes for granted his own equality as artist with other Florentines, as with Michelangelo, or with Leonardo da Vinci, when Francis I gives him a provision equal to what Leonardo himself had had. It is to another writer that we must turn to see the lives of artists in general, and the development of art set in perspective. As with *Letters* so with *Lives*, the sixteenth century sees a spate of them: but no collection of the latter has achieved the fame of that compiled by Giorgio Vasari (1511–74) as the *Vite de' più eccellenti pittori, scultori e architetti* (first published 1551, with a second, definitive, edition in 1568). Vasari was an omnivorous collector of the anecdotal, whether true or suppositious, and as a guide to facts for any individual artist it is always prudent to make reference to the critical edition by Gaetano Milanesi (1878–85). And, of course, since he could not anticipate our emphasis on what we take as major artists, we may always be surprised at the scant space given to some (let us say Alberti, or Piero della Francesca) who seem to us giants in their time, and yet get only the few brief pages which Vasari gives to many another whom time has shaken out through the bottom of the bag. But in spite of such obvious snags, here for the first time is an overall picture of the development of the arts from their horizon when the debased manner of the Middle Ages was first sloughed off to their zenith with Raphael and Michelangelo. Vasari looks back to ancient art, and traces with Pliny as his guide its rise, perfection, and decline. The age of Constantine was for him the boundary between the *antico* (which was valuable) and the merely *vecchio* (which was to be eschewed). The causes of decay were obvious, its momentum an increasing one, and only with the generation of 1250 did awakening come again, and Tuscany become the author of a *rinascita*. Giotto, Masaccio, Brunelleschi – we know the tally, because the lines which Vasari suggested for this history in the mid sixteenth century have remained little changed in their essentials through the art-history of nearly four centuries. That achievement has perhaps credited him too much with the invention of this fertile word, *renascence*, which acquiring a capital letter, and as often as not a frenchified spelling, has become the symbol of a period. Yet of course the concept of rebirth is one that Vasari inherits from the fifteenth century, quite as conscious as Vasari was himself of the gap that had been opened between the gothic world of the Middle Ages and the new principles of humanism. Nor was the concept of rebirth limited then to this one field of art. But by virtue of this focus in the vast corpus of Vasari's *Lives* he has often seemed inventor of one of the most fortunate of terms, and the word Renascence one that applied first to art, and only later was converted to a literary application for which it had more doubtful appropriateness. We need really look no further than to the closing page of Machiavelli's *Art of War* to see that the prehistory of this idea is a different one. For there he wrote the famous words on Italy seeming 'born to resuscitate what had been dead, as has been seen with Poetry, with Painting, and with Sculpture'. And as for painting itself, Politian's epigram on Giotto,

Ille ego sum, per quem pictura extincta revixit,

shows that Vasari could not at his stage invent what was already a commonplace of criticism. But the filling in of graphic detail, and the elaboration of the outlines, is the merit of Vasari, and his *Lives* remain as the living monument to one of the most momentous periods of artistic creation.

A monument equal in bulk, and sometimes claimed as equally a chronicle of contemporary life in Italy, is the vast *Novelliere* of Matteo Bandello (1485–1561), the first three parts of which appeared at Lucca in 1554, only a few years after Vasari's *Lives*, and the last one posthumously at Lyon in 1573. No one more than Bandello had the sense of all the changes that had taken place in the political scene of Europe from the fifteenth to the sixteenth century, from the time of independent states via the war of Cambrai and the Sack of Rome to the monarchy of Charles V; and no one aspires more humbly to be a recorder of real events. As a result perhaps of this very fact the artist is often drowned by the chronicler, and the tale of unhappy or even monstrous incidents does not always have the attraction for us which we may find in his account of the tragic love of Romeo and Juliet (II, 9). And even here, we may feel that Bandello, in his slow unfolding of the tale, misses the dramatic effects, and the heartbeat, which will be Shakespeare's contribution to the story. Elsewhere we may find his retailing of horrible particulars cold and nauseating. Bandello listened to too much, wrote with too little sorting of material: *vaste et ondoyant* as Montaigne himself, he is much less attractive and rewarding. But in his descriptions, as of the various cities of Italy, and in his circumstantial accounts of Italian life in all its sectors – with the accent on tragedy of events, set in a realism of particulars – Bandello had no equal among the *novellieri* of his time. These indeed are many, and others than Bandello have the distinction of having handed a *scenario* on to Shakespeare. But the sixteenth century does not quite rise to a *Decameron*, and many of its collections we know better by their names than by their contents. This is true of Lasca with his *Cene*, who had as his main merit a Tuscan liveliness of language and of detail; of Straparola with the *Piacevoli Notti*, set on the island of Murano, then less depressed in circumstance than now, where for the first time the *conte bleu* enters the pages of literature (with fables such as *L'Augellin bel verde* or *Re Porco*) alongside other stories from the traditional material. It is true also of one of the most bulky of the collections, *Gli Ecatommiti* of G.B. Giraldi (the author of *Orbecche*, here in his last guise), which appeared in two fat volumes in 1565, swapping the plague of 1349 for the Sack of Rome as a framework to the story-telling. A moralist who sees to it always that virtue triumphs over vice, Giraldi lacks all the powers that should belong to a good *novelliere*, and we have only to put his story (III, 7) which is the basis of Shakespeare's *Othello* alongside Bandello's version of *Romeo and Juliet* to see his artistic inferiority. More skilful as a writer is Angelo Firenzuola (1493–1543), author of an uncompleted imitation of the

Decameron, the *Ragionamenti d'Amore* (1525), with a licentious quality about it, as of a free version of both the *Panciatantra*, via its Spanish derivative, and of the *Golden Ass* of Apuleius. The first becomes the *Prima veste dei discorsi degli animali*, keeping fairly faithfully to the general texture of its original, with minor changes on the surface. The *Asino d'oro* has Firenzuola himself as its protagonist, with a consequent attempt to adapt the invention of Apuleius to the conditions of his own time: which, after all, Machiavelli had already done in that other *Asino* from which the gilt has just been taken, as being a title Machiavelli never meant. Nor from this list of *novellieri* can we omit Luigi da Porto (1485–1529), author of the useful *Lettere Storiche* which portray the background to the war of the League of Cambrai, but first author also of the story of *Giulietta e Romeo*, before it came to the collection of Bandello. No professional writer, da Porto nevertheless seized more strongly than Bandello on the dramatic qualities of the tragic story. In a minor key we may find confirmed with him what we have seen elsewhere, that it is the least academic side of the Cinquecento which has the most vitality. And on the other side we might still put with writers like Firenzuola others like Annibale Caro (1507–66), one of the most elegant of the professional *letterati* of his time, author of acceptable comedies, of the pattern collection of *Familiar Letters*, of a small and careful *canzoniere*, and last, but not least, of that verse translation of the *Aeneid* which was to be the staple of Italian usage even in the nineteenth century. Like Bembo, Caro was for long an authoritative figure; but for us he cannot have the life which we see pulsing in the less regular writers of his century.

CHAPTER 10

The Seventeenth Century

It is natural for us to look first to Giambattista Marino (1569–1625) as symptomatic of a tendency. Born in Naples, knighted in Turin, but – so unsure is court life – twice imprisoned also, he reached his apogee in Paris, where Maria de'Medici had brought Italian fashions, and where in 1623 his poem *L'Adone* found its sumptuous publication. Not only the form was noble: in the front there came the certificate, subscribed by M. Chapelain, that this was a poem without reproach, new, according to the rules, and 'le meilleur en son genre qui puisse iamais sortir en public'. The climax, that is to say, of the long poem. These words read oddly when we set them against Tiraboschi, coming in his last volume to the decadence of the Italian tradition, and seeing in Marino 'the most contagious corruptor of good taste in Italy'. We now have seen some seventeenth-century names step up again to high honour (as that of Bernini, or even better, of Caravaggio). But it is significant that in the volume *Marino e i Marinisti* (in the Ricciardi series) the editor makes his claim for revision half-heartedly, and leaves the poem itself as irretrievable: one single page responding to a real experience, and this the last part of Canto VIII, which expresses the orgasm of amorous possession. It is scant salvage from so long a poem, and whatever claim is made for *marinismo* elsewhere it leaves us nearer to Tiraboschi than might have been expected.

In one thing at least Chapelain was right about the novelty of the *Adone*: the epic before Marino had been uniformly (and however much an Ariosto formalizes the fighting this is still true of him) a poem of war. What Marino invented was the poem of peace, and to Chapelain this meant that it was unalloyed: the gold of Pleasure in its *pure purity*. Now when

Marino began the *Adone* he had only three books in mind:
that was before 1605, and in the long period of its elaboration
it grew to twenty books, and more than 5,000 octaves. For
the meeting of Venus and Adonis, the consummation of their
passion, and the death of Adonis, contrived by the jealousy
of Mars, it is too lavish a world of words. On to it Marino
proposed to tack an allegory, 'that immoderate pleasure ends
in pain', but he did not scruple to belie this moral intention in
explicit statements, as in the general temper of the poem.
Here all the motifs of preceding poetry are turned to decorative account in an atmosphere where only one law is remembered, that of Tasso's Golden Age, the lawfulness of all that
pleases. As a formula, this is the superfetation of previous
poetry, galvanized from time to time to new life by the
firework of conceits. As Venus gazes on the sleeping Adonis,
the colour of his cheeks, the scent of his breath, conquers the
Rose and puts the Lily to shame, so that the one turns pale,
the other crimson. And Venus turns to these closed eyes with
a whole stanza of hyperbole, which ends by their becoming

> Finestre de l'Aurora, usci del die,
> Possenti a rischiarar le notti mie. (III, 86)

Here the conceits have become the central stuff of poetry;
and Marino, as he pillages those who have preceded him,
must needs attempt to outdo them. Otherwise he is doomed
to fall into a fatal flatness. Paradoxically, the *Adone* has
perhaps too little of hyperbole and verbal fire to levitate the
mass, and if the conscientious reader retires from the effort
to reach the boar which wounds Adonis it is more likely to
be from boredom than from shock.

The *Adone* had been preceded by a copious lyric production.
La Lira (1602–14) sang already the pleasures of the senses,
and took, for instance, the kiss from the *Pastor Fido* to give it
independent and extended treatment. *La Galleria* (1619) with
its descriptions of paintings and statues, foreshadows the
Adone; while *La Sampogna* (1620), with its reworkings of old
myths, as Orpheus and Europa, leaves the lyric for such
narrative as Marino can muster. This prodigal world, in

which Marino spends the treasure which others have stored up, is typical of one side of the Seicento, and has given us its pejorative, *secentismo*. As Italy's political significance dwindled the spate of literature had not grown less, and now it proliferates on the basis of past literature. There is no historian who does not shrink at some point in the chronicle: it may be from the pastoral play, written by the hundred on the model of the *Pastor Fido*; it may be from the heroic poem, living on the achievement of the *Gerusalemme*. From this a little half-hearted salvage is normally attempted: as of Francesco Bracciolini (1566–1645), whose *Croce Racquistata* appeared at Paris in 1605, though the copy exaggerates the weaknesses of the model. Or it may be the *Conquisto di Granata* of Girolamo Graziani (1604–75), with the new subject of Ferdinand of Spain against the Moors. Even Leopardi, who looked bleakly on the seventeenth century, read this poem, and gave it the rare approval of his imitation, taking from it the names of Consalvo and Elvira, while the situation in his *Consalvo* echoes that of Osmino and Silvera in Canto XVII.

The world of lyric poetry is not in different case. From the tribe of *marinisti*, bent on spending words extravagently, we may remember one notorious line. This is Claudio Achillini in his sonnet laudatory of Louis XIII, *Sudate o fuochi a preparar metalli*. Alongside these, or better, preceding them, is Gabriello Chiabrera of Savona (1552–1638), creator of a different type of verse, which includes the *canzonetta*, a form that will be kept in store for the eighteenth century. He inherits from the Pléiade a dose of *mignardise*, which he imprisons in new and sprightly metres, based on short lines of anacreontic lightness.

> Del mio Sol son ricciutegli
> I capegli
> Non biondetti, ma brunetti;
> Son due rose vermigliuzze
> Le gotuzze,
> Le due labbra rubinetti.

His production covers all the fields of poetry; applauded in his time, he has a historic interest now as one who links the dying Cinquecento with Arcadia. What is lacking is the ability to limit himself: often, in spite of the shortness of the metre there is a feeling of longness in the composition, an opaqueness which Arcadia, at its best, will shed.

By Chiabrera's side there stands one with more ambition to give new life to the lyric: Fulvio Testi (1593–1646), a Ferrarese who has the success we might have wished for Ariosto. He begins with patriotic fervour for the cause of Charles Emanuel of Savoy against the Spaniards, but under Este pressure was prepared to change the tune. As Secretary of State for Alfonso III he had a crowded diplomatic life, from which he writes of the desire for rustic ease. Echoing Marino or Chiabrera at first, he swells to imitate Pindar and Horace, and shares with Graziani the honour of having caught the eye of the youthful Leopardi:

> Ben molt'archi e colonne in più d'un segno
> serban del valor prisco alta memoria;
> ma non si vede già per propria gloria
> chi d'archi e di colonne ora sia degno.

How evidently this is the base from which the opening lines of Leopardi's *All'Italia* spring: and how different are the two passages in their poetic statement! And it is Leopardi, in the *Zibaldone*, who places Testi: 'If he had lived in a less barbarous age, and had had the leisure to cultivate his mind more than he did, he would have been undoubtedly our Horace, and perhaps warmer, more vehement and sublime than the original.' As an appendage, we may place two other lyric poets whose reputation stood in their own time very high: Vincenzo da Filicaia (1642–1707), a Florentine, made senator by Cosimo III, and Alessandro Guidi (of Pavia, 1650–1712), who lived a courtier in Parma under Ranuccio II Farnese. Guidi had most pretensions, the self-appointed rival of Pindar: but his airy bubble has long blown. For Filicaia, who shares with Guidi a passion for sonority at the expense of substance, there are redeeming features; and while the odes upon the siege and liberation of Vienna may have gone the way of all flesh his sonnets to Italy have not lost their point:

Italia, Italia, o tu cui feo la sorte
Dono infelice di bellezza, ond'hai
Funesta dote d'infiniti guai ...
Deh fossi tu men bella, o almen piú forte ...

It is a small survival, and in fairness it should be said that Marino also left one sonnet worth remembering, *Apre l'uomo infelice, allor che nasce*, with a strong closing line, 'Dalla cuna alla tomba è un breve passo'. With Filicaia and with Guidi we have overlapped into Arcadia, and others of their generation share this moment of transition, as Francesco di Lemene (1634–1704), or Carlo Maria Maggi (1630–99).

It is to the rebels that we must look for vitality, and two of these appear as pointers at the end of the Cinquecento, one of them marking by his martyrdom the threshold of the new century. They are Tommaso Campanella (1568–1639) and Giordano Bruno (1548–1600), both coming from the south, and having in common a vehement regard for truth, a wayward surface to their works, and a history of persecution by authority. Behind Bruno we may sense the experience of Pietro Pomponazzi (1462–1524), with his speculations on the human soul, of Girolamo Cardano (1501–76), full of oddity, but pointing philosophy towards the study of Nature, and especially of Bernardino Telesio (1509–88), a fellow-southerner, who fought against the stifling authority of Plato and Aristotle, and based the study of mankind firmly on that of Nature. Avowedly *dormitantium animorum excubitor, praesumptiosae et recalcitrantis ignorantiae domitor*, Bruno took the path of exile, and strewed his writings, Latin and Italian, over the northern countries, including England. Going back at last, he ended at the hands of the Inquisition in a bonfire on the Campo dei Fiori in Rome in 1600. His worthiness of such a death seemed proved by his having roughly turned his eyes away from the crucifix, presented to him as he was led to the stake. But may not his aversion have been for those who did not blush to offer the symbol of martyrdom when they were ready not to suffer, but to inflict it? Bruno died for the freedom of the human mind to follow truth: it is perhaps the strongest and clearest of his doctrines. In fact, the scarcity of the original editions, and the difficulties of his writing, left him long forgotten. Bayle found him more obscure than the scholastics, Tiraboschi called him verbose and unintelligible. But struggling through this uneven surface are glimpses of the future course of thought. Bruno turns his back upon the *ipse dixit* of the past, sees knowledge and experience as growing and expanding, so that it is the moderns already who hold all the cards, able to outstrip their predecessors. And after a century's exploration of the rules of poetry he dismisses Aristotle's *Poetics* as defining what had been in Homer, not legislating for poetry to be. 'Sono e possono essere tante sorti di poeti, quante possono essere e sono maniere de sentimenti et invenzioni umane.' This battle for the freedom of the human mind implies an equal vigour of polemic against the pedants and the aristotelians, as with Manfurio in the comedy *Il Candelaio*. Written in Paris, perhaps for the Italian comedians, it looks back to the low life of Naples, richly presented in a gallery of characters outside the normal formulas of comedy. To it he put a famous motto, which has seemed to stand for himself, *In tristitia hilaris: in hilaritate tristis*. *Il Candelaio* used to be Giordano Bruno's entrance-ticket into literature, but his importance as a thinker depends upon his other works, especially the *Cena de le Ceneri*, the *Spaccio della Bestia Trionfante*, and *De gli Heroici Furori*. Here in a pantheistic conception of the universe Bruno fights for the new ideas of Copernicanism against the old orthodoxy, sees an infinity of similar, inhabited worlds, and rejects the dead hand of the past for the free investigation of the future. Instead of Tasso's nostalgic idyll of the Golden Age Bruno spurns the primitive as beast-like. We are on the verge of the discoveries of Giambattista Vico; and in between others, as Descartes, Leibniz, or Spinoza, will inherit some of his ideas.

Campanella has perhaps less philosophical importance, and a greater fringe of unacceptable oddity than Bruno, while being in himself a more endearing figure. The utopia of the *Città del Sole*, with its well-ordered communism, is of historic interest now; and it is the same with the plot to establish a utopia, with Fra Tommaso Campanella at its head at Stilo in Calabria – the cause of his imprisonment, for the most part in the castles of Naples, but for the last two years in the dungeons of the Holy Office in Rome. Twenty-seven years in Neapolitan dungeons, and the sharpest tortures, with madness feigned to escape death itself, then a few years of liberty. It is no wonder Campanella thought, like Tasso, of familiar spirits with whom he held converse. But from his dungeon he retains his sense of the superiority of the sufferer over those who inflict suffering. Witness the sonnet which he wrote for himself and all those imprisoned like him (xcii). Here we might take as touchstone a line of Petrarch's which Tasso also repeats, *Che ben può nulla chi non può morire.* But its metal has been tempered under this fire to give one of those new sorts of poetry of which Bruno wrote. It is the merit of Campanella's *Poesie* that their rough facets speak with this genuine utterance in a way unknown before. Sometimes he looks the way of Bruno and of Galileo,

> Il mondo è il libro, dove il senno eterno
> Scrisse i proprii concetti.   (vi)

And born to fight against the evils men have made in the world (especially the three extremes, tyranny, sophistry, hypocrisy), Campanella can burst out at times into the most powerful of utterance, as in that sonnet on the People, in which is epitomized so much of human history, with a presentiment of the predicament which will face mankind when the People waken to their strength:

> Il popolo è una bestia varia e grossa,
> Ch'ignora le sue forze ...   (xxxi)

Here is a grasp on the political realities which Machiavelli could not have attained to, and which shows, by comparison, how much a theorist Machiavelli was. But it is, of course, theory which leads to improvement, while realism exhausts itself in the vision of what is.

Tiraboschi turned with relief from the inextricable labyrinth of Campanella's thought to Galileo, who passed with a bold step into the unknown world of Nature. Here we might be leaving literature altogether: but Galileo is not conscious of the parting of the ways, and his first biographer Vincenzo Viviani says that he knew by heart a great part of Virgil, Ovid, Horace, Seneca, as well as almost all Petrarch, Berni, and little less than all the poem of Ariosto. The more Galileo read the *Furioso*, the more perfections he found in it. Nor was he limited to poetry, but knew the theory of music, and took delight in all the arts. The founder of a tradition, that of scientific discovery, which will for many replace that of culture, Galileo looks back over Renascence culture with an appreciating eye; and the clarity of his own expositions owes something to the strength of his literary nurture.

Born at Pisa Galileo Galilei (1564–1642) is the last great master in the line which had begun with Dante. Inheriting the passion of Leonardo for experiment as the 'mother of all certainty' he turns decisively from theory based on Aristotle to observation, and looks to mathematics as the key to Nature's book. It is now not Cleopatra's nose that alters the course of history, but in anticipation of Watt's kettle we have Galileo's observations (1582) on the movement of the pendulum. As Reader in Mathematics at Pisa he published in 1590 his *De motu gravium* to open the door into a world as new as that of Columbus. But round him the alarm of the Aristotelians brought trouble from the granducal court, and Galileo passed to Padua in 1592, where the rich hand of Venice fed him well for eighteen years, and where, without the lure of the Florentine court, he might have remained as safe as Paolo Sarpi. Having laid the basis for dynamics Galileo shows the width of his interests: from military fortifications via mechanics and hydraulics to cosmography. But it is his invention of the telescope (his 'occhiale'), of 1609, which strikes the imagination, opening the heavens to observation. His *Sidereus nuncius* announces the mountains in the moon, the nature of the Milky Way, the myriads of fixed stars, the satellites of Jupiter. No more than Campanella does Galileo think this exploration an attack on the Creator. What there is to find is what He has made, and Galileo, in a letter of 1610, gives infinite thanks to God for choosing him as first observer of things hidden through all the centuries. This seems the moment of triumph, with Kepler's *Vicisti Galilaee*, the spots in the sun, the phases of Venus, the ring of Saturn. Galileo returns to Florence as a celebrity, and reaches his apogee in 1611 with a triumphal journey to Rome, where a Jesuit acclaims the truth of his discoveries and cardinals handle his telescope in a demonstration at the Quirinal. Paul V, so hostile to the Venetians, is benevolent, and the Accademia dei Lincei, founded at Rome in 1603 for the study of natural phenomena, enrols him as the most illustrious of its members.

But the immutable heaven of the Aristotelians was incompatible with Galileo's discoveries. When *Sidereus nuncius* met with applause he went on in 1613 to take his stand with Copernicus, whose *De Revolutionibus Orbium Celestium* dates from 1543. So he brought the theologians hastening to defend the Scriptures, in reinforcement of the peripateticians. In vain Galileo protested against the use of scriptural readings in the context of natural experiment. In 1616 the doctrine of the mobility of the earth was condemned, and Galileo ordered to renounce it. For seven years he kept submissive silence, and then was tempted into the open by a dispute between a pupil and the Jesuit Father Orazio Grassi. Galileo wrote *Il Saggiatore* (1623), with an inexorable demolition of Grassi's arguments, earning the hatred of the Jesuit order. But the advent of the Barberini Pope, Urban VIII, brought hope of tolerance, and permission to print one of his major works, the *Dialogo de' Massimi Sistemi* (1632). This put the movement of the earth as a mere hypothesis, but made it seem more probable than any other. In 1633 its author was summoned to Rome by the Holy Office, and though confident in the rightness of his cause he was old and unable to endure the long interrogations or the threat of torture. On 22 June 1633 he made submission, his book was banned, and he condemned to imprisonment and penitential psalms. For nine years he lived on, reduced like Milton to blindness, and pursued by unremitting zeal. True, at the end of the year he received permission to live in his own villa at Arcetri, out of the movement of the world. Even so, he still produced the *Dialoghi delle*

Nuove Scienze (1638), harking back to the principles of dynamics; and round him he saw his pupils carrying on, ensuring the triumph of his ideas: Evangelista Torricelli (1608–47), inventor of the barometer, Vincenzo Viviani (1622–1703), his first biographer, Padre Benedetto Castelli (1577–1644), one of the most important of his correspondents. And the year which begins with Galileo's death (8 January 1642) sees in December the birth of Isaac Newton.

Galileo writes with the clarity and simplicity of style which Bruno and Campanella lacked. Not only the warmth of conviction, but a rigorous order and a logical enunciation of discoveries which might have been left unintelligible to the layman. Science now is esoteric to the non-adept, but Galileo looks both ways, and does not know that one will wither as the other opens up. And here the dialogue-form, so frequently misused within the Cinquecento, comes to maturity, and serves to expose his antagonists to Galileo's festive irony. To mark the opening of his career we have seen the founding of the Accademia dei Lincei; to mark his final triumph, *malgré tout*, we have the founding of that other notable Academy (in a period of silly ones), the Accademia del Cimento by Leopoldo de'Medici at Florence in 1657, with its motto, *Provando e riprovando*. Above the dubious elements which we have seen there will always shine the clear beacon of Galileo's prose.

There was another contemporary struggle, hardly less decisive, and again with one man as its hero. Since Spain owed extreme allegiance to the Holy See, papal authority waxed strong in Italy, in compensation also for the parts of Europe now outside its grip. But to curb papal intrusions into the temporal affairs of catholic states there comes the insuccess of Paul V to force his will on Venice in 1606. The causes of conflict were slight, but symptomatic: the right of Venice to control ecclesiastical acquisition of property, and its right to jurisdiction over criminal offences of ecclesiastics. Against this independence Paul V launched his Interdict, but Venice expelled the Jesuits, and ordered her clergy to ignore the ban. Fra Paolo Sarpi was appointed as theological consultant, and the Venetian case published to Europe. When the Interdict was lifted they had won a victory of which other catholic states were quick to take advantage: after this there is a limit to papal interference in their internal business. That this was so was mainly the merit of Paolo Sarpi (1552–1623). Entering the Servites at thirteen, Sarpi remains, like Galileo, a fervent son of the Church. His early interests included medicine and mathematics, and in both he might have reached distinction, and has, even so, been credited with discoveries of no small importance. But he passes to his major sphere with his resistance to the unjust claims of Rome in 1606. Summoned to justify himself, he prudently refused to leave the safety of Venice. And when even there he was pursued by the assassin's knife he made, in an age of vicious play on words, one of the notable puns of all time, *Agnosco stylum Romanae Curiae*. So moderate, self-possessed, inflexible was this antagonist whom Rome found amongst her own sons. The writings on the Interdict, on the right of asylum, the Inquisition in Venice, or the Index of Prohibited Books (set up in 1559 to gag the printing-press) are the minor side of his work. The major one is the *Storia del Concilio di Trento*, to which he gave his life, and which puts his name among the great historians of Italy. Published in London without Sarpi's knowledge by the Protestant convert the Archbishop of Spalato (1619), retouched linguistically to its disadvantage, it took its place at once as one of the classics of its time, and was read eagerly by the whole of Europe. This case against the Council of Trent led to the commissioning of Cardinal Sforza Pallavicino to rewrite its history from the official point of view: that the omnipotence of the papacy was right, and rightly reached. But this counterblast of 1656 by one who had not lived through the atmosphere of the Council made no impact against Sarpi's work. In his *Storia* there is everpresent the thesis of papal absolutism sanctioned by the Council by less than divine methods; and perhaps the 'blasphemous proverb' which he quotes as in common currency is best indicative of his own attitude: *That the Synod of Trent was guided by the Holy Spirit sent to it from Rome from time to time in the (papal) bags.* Whether one takes it that this conviction (based on an intimate knowledge of the copious material) is tantamount to bias will depend perhaps on personal attitudes. But few readers will be able to withhold their admiration for the calm temper of his writing. Unlike the friars who disputed on Transubstantiation to the tedium of all through their incomprehensibility, Sarpi is in full command of all the intricate theological web; and his tendency to statement without comment can be most damaging. As with the sermon of the Bishop of Ventimiglia, with its simile of the body: how monstrous without a head! 'Con quattro parole soggionse, che Christo era il Capo della Chiesa invisible; ma, con molte, che il Papa era il visibile' (Bk v). To which we may add the General of the Jesuits, enlarging on the charge, *Feed my sheep,* by insisting on the nature of this animal 'che non ha parte né arbitrio alcuno nella propria condotta'. Here from the tortuous processes of the Council comes a wealth of attitudes, authentic and memorable, down to that acceptance by a hesitant Pope, convinced finally that if interpretation was reserved no one could appeal to the authority of the Council against that of the Roman Curia: hence the conclusion to the long-drawn-out Council of Trent, by which its decisions were confirmed *in toto,* but no one had the right to interpret them. Sarpi, no doubt, looked for support against papal usurpation from the protestant north; and the latter looked to Venice as a likely field of proselytism. But Sarpi remains within the pattern set by Dante, who also had consigned popes to hell without a protestant intention. And he remains constant in his vision of religion based on inner consciousness and not on outward pomp and ceremonies, as in his desire for a return to the simplicity of the primitive Church. Here is the root of his resistance to the claims of Rome.

While Sarpi and Galileo fight decisive battles, others look with ineffectual hostility to the yoke of Spain. The best representative of this anti-Spanish feeling is Traiano Boccalini (1556–1613). After Machiavelli political theory had shrunk rather than advanced: and already in the Cinquecento there comes the new voice of monarchy as the right order of the world. Its representative is Giovanni Botero (1533–1617), author of a book with a notorious title, *Ragion di Stato* (1589). It is to Botero's credit that here he looks, as also in the *Relazioni Universali* and the *Cause della Grandezza delle Città*, to the new province of economics. It is to his discredit that he acquiesces in political servitude. It is here that Boccalini takes his place with Sarpi in the aspiration for freedom. Having had various employment in Rome, he went to Venice as the best asylum for one who hated Spain, and there published his major work, the *Ragguagli di Parnaso* (1612). This created a literary journalism, with Boccalini as reporter from the imaginary realm of Parnassus, governed by Apollo with the aid of *virtuosi* of all times and races. Into it Boccalini put the full range of his good sense with a sparkling irony for the foibles and abuses of his time. Through the book there runs his admiration for the political freedom of Venice in terms often reminiscent of the political vocabulary of Machiavelli. And since this is Parnassus, the defects of contemporary literature have much attention. The defect of the *Ragguagli* is that they are too scattered to make a full impact at any point. Even Boccalini's hatred of Spain can be seen more clearly in the *Pietra del Paragone Politico* and in the *Commentaries* to Tacitus (printed posthumously in 1678 as the *Bilancia Politica*) in which he has the merit of having sensed, under the swell of Spanish power, the fatal seeds of Spain's decay.

Others also look outside the Italian peninsula, and two were for a long time the representatives of right thinking and authors of historical works of the first repute. These are Enrico Caterino Davila (1576–1634) and Cardinal Guido Bentivoglio (1579–1644). There is a remarkable parallelism about their histories: both had been actors, Bentivoglio as Papal Nuncio, Davila as a combatant, in the countries which they chose as subjects. And the two themes, the Civil Wars of France from 1559 to 1598 and the rising of the Low Countries against Spain (1559–1607), are closely linked in character, and often in the actors. Nor is the texture of their narrative a very different one. Free from the vices of *secentismo* they both offer proof that Italian, rather than just Tuscan, exists as the

literary vehicle for the future; and for the stirring chronicle
of faction and intrigue which leads past the Massacre of St
Bartholomew there is still no more fascinating reading than
the crowded pages of Davila. It may be that here the actors
are more noble and numerous, but certainly life and movement are more notable in the *Istoria delle Guerre Civili di
Francia* than in the *Guerre di Fiandra*. It is rather that Davila
is more engaged in the struggle he relates than Bentivoglio.
Now in the eighteenth century the British critic Blair could
equate this pair with Machiavelli, Guicciardini, Sarpi; and for
us there is a scission. We may see the gap in a remark of
Bentivoglio in his *Memorie* on that same Night of St Bartholomew, 'che bastò bene a raffrenare in alcuna parte, ma non già
quanto bisognava, l'audacia e la rabbia degli Ugonotti'.
That is all, on a massacre which took the lives of 40,000
people in cold blood: it was enough, and not enough. *Causa
regis, causa Dei:* on the one side, all right and the necessary
recourse to sharp measures, always excusable; on the other
talents maybe, as with the Prince of Orange, but ready to
degenerate when turned to 'ambitious and corrupt designs'.
And these equate with opposition to legitimate power (to
the right of Philip II to rule in Flanders as he ruled in Spain).
Here the Duke of Alva echoes the Jesuit General on the
nature of sheep: 'The disobedience of peoples strikes equally at
all Princes ... Your empire embraces several worlds together,
and God has placed you in it even more for the increase of
His glory than for yours ... Governments are doubtless
various. But they cannot vary in the obligation of obedience which is owed by peoples to their Princes. With this law
are subjects born, and if they wish to break it then they come
to do violence not to receive it.' With that voice there speaks
already the Holy Alliance of Metternich. And if we look
backwards we can see how limiting is this one-sided attitude.
With Machiavelli the struggle is seen whole, none of the
actors lifted artificially beyond the reach of censure: in point
of fact, the criticism of ambition goes rather to the ruler
than the ruled. Here one half is paralysed, wrong however
right it may be, while the other is right however wrong it

may be. In this way we are detached from the narrative by a gulf which mere dexterity in presentation of events cannot fill up. Davila, I think, still shows up here more favourably, for though monarchy is right, and orthodoxy too, yet this is less heavily marked than with Bentivoglio. Nor can the tortuous policy of Catherine de'Medici or the foolishness of her brood show up as *ipso facto* right in any narrative. Even so, this pair so long established may yet be eclipsed by one who has not yet slipped into the record. This is Nicolò Contarini (1553–1632), the Doge who laid the foundation-stone of Santa Maria della Salute. But he also succeeded Andrea Morosini in the notable series of official historians of Venice. These, beginning with Sabellicus, Bembo, Paruta, and Morosini, continuing with Battista Nani, Michele Foscarini, and Pietro Garzoni, present in varying forms the impressive stretch of Venice's long independence. They suffer from a common defect, that of looking outwards in a fragmentary way to the farflung interests of Venice. This is true of Contarini, whose *Historie Venetiane* (covering only 1597–1604) were kept for consultation only by decree of the Senate, and so never published. That he stopped short of the Interdict is a matter for regret, for as a friend of Sarpi his testimony would have been welcome. But with Contarini, one of the most noble and likeable of characters, in whom all the patrician responsibility of Venice still shows at its most manly and creditable, we do not feel that decline from the front rank of European States which is all too soon to show itself with Venice. And where his history has concinnity, as in the long and brilliant analysis, seen with the eye of an interested neighbour, of the devolution of the Dukedom of Ferrara to the Holy See in 1598, we may still mention his name in the same bracket as his friend Paolo Sarpi.

We have narrowed down the field, and may legitimately be more brief. Indeed, some names, as that of Daniello Bartoli (1608–85), the author of the *Istoria della Compagnia di Gesú*, with its rich descriptions of the Jesuit world, interest us now by a reflected light: because Leopardi thought him one of the portents of Italian prose. Otherwise, with Paolo

Segneri (1624–94), that other master of sacred eloquence, in an age when all *eloquence* is dubious, he has vanished out of sight. Nor am I tempted to deal much more optimistically with the jocose authors. When the heroic poem lay dying of a surfeit, mockery might well seem the best by-pass. It is Alessandro Tassoni (1565–1635) who invented the mixture of burlesque and grave together which gave piquancy to *La Secchia Rapita*, published like the *Adonis* in Paris, and a year before it; and as the anonymous author of the *Filippiche contro Spagna* (1614–15) he had breathed a patriotism similar to that of Boccalini. In his mock-heroic poem the conversion of Helen to a Bucket may seem amusing, but there is too little of such sauce to keep the poem going; and burlesque enumeration of long armies is as tedious as any serious one. Nor are we likely to be amused now by the fact that some of these poltroons – with the Conte di Culagna at their head – are portraits. It is a short long poem, and has some quips; but is not really vital. And this goes also for *Lo Scherno degli Dei* (1618) of Francesco Bracciolini, for the *Malmantile Racquistato* of Lorenzo Lippi, or for the later *Ricciardetto* of Niccolò Forteguerri (1674–1735), to whom it fell to smother the chivalrous epic finally in mockery of its spirit. Indeed, it may be better to look to explicit satire, with the painter-poet Salvator Rosa (1615–73). Placed by our eighteenth century aloft with Claude, Rosa has climbed from the abyss into which Ruskin sank him. But as he has shed the legend of a patriot's part in Masaniello's revolt of 1647, so he has left his seven satires, in Ariostesque *capitoli*, on a lower shelf. There is a certain rough-and-readiness about Rosa's manner, and in verse this lack of quality is accentuated. The three first *Satire*, on music, poetry, and painting, with their rude good sense employed against the lascivious votaries of the first, the extravagancies of *secentismo* in the second, and against mere daubers in his own high art, are the best nourished and most permanent. In the others some contemporary vices, or the perennial corruption of the Roman Curia, are roughly lashed, but Rosa is too slipshod for more than single lines to be memorable.

There is one poetic composition which cannot be called mediocre, though in the best sense of the word it may not be poetic: this is the once-famous dithyramb of Francesco Redi (1626–98), *Bacco in Toscana*. This is a *tour de force* which astonished his contemporaries when after twenty years' work it was printed in 1685; and Browning still quoted from it the snatch of song in *Strafford*. Here the cue is in a line which became proverbial, MONTEPULCIANO D'OGNI VINO È IL RE; and the poem staggers through a variety of metres as Bacchus drains his way to rapture. That was only relaxation for Redi, who follows the tradition of Galileo in experimental science with his *Osservazioni intorno alle Vipere* (1664) and the *Esperienze intorno alla Germinazione degli Insetti* (1668), away from the old legends of frogs out of mud. Others follow the same road, as Lorenzo Magalotti (1637–1712), who also by his encyclopedic culture and his contacts with northern countries suggests the flavour of the next century. In sympathy with his geographical interests we may quote his edition of the travels of Francesco Carletti (1671). Carletti (*c.* 1573–1636) was a Florentine merchant looking west, not east, and writing out of his experiences his *Ragionamenti sopra le cose vedute nei viaggi dell'Indie occidentali e d'altri paesi*. Here with the sense of the anthropologist Carletti records the world of new and primitive peoples: chopsticks, breadfruit, chocolate and the banana, the slave-trade, Polynesian boats or oriental justice – all comes within the scope of one who had circled the globe.

A rival to Carletti is Pietro della Valle (1586–1652). A Roman patrician, travelling after disappointment in love, and touring the East, if not in comfort, at least in affluence with many camels, Pietro has many endearing traits. For twelve years he gave a keen eye to the new sights, and carries with him also a substantial culture from the ancient past. Before Schliemann he stands upon the ruins which he takes for Troy, before Howard Carter he penetrates into the Valley of the Kings. In Constantinople he looks to Santa Sophia under the mosque it seems; in Jerusalem he seeks out the Holy Places. On the Pyramids he writes his name, and where he goes an

Italian painter in his train records costumes and scenes, while he himself looks avidly for ancient books in learned oriental tongues, and makes progress in Turkish, Arabic, or Persian. Those who think the Seicento a mere arid tract in the long annals of Italian literature might do well to start with the robust and unaffected prose of Pietro della Valle, or sip with him the first coffee at Constantinople in 1614.

Nor have we finished with good things, for with Giambattista Basile (*c.* 1573–1632) we have a book which is in its kind a fundamental milestone, and unsurpassed for its happy tone. For with the *Pentamerone* (or *Lo Cunto de li Cunti*), out of the world of popular fantasy a new dimension, a new element, opens for literature. This is the land of Cinderella and the Sleeping Beauty, peopled with all the types which will occupy the people down to Grimm and Andrew Lang, and going by way of Perrault in the *Contes des Fées*. But to this canvas, rich and taking in its novelty, Basile brings as rich a gallop of Neapolitan verve to make a book difficult for the mere northerner, but full of brio. Here the baroque cannot offend, being tempered by a festive spirit which does not lose sight of honest earth; and in the timeless atmosphere of the fairy story we feel all the expressiveness of the Neapolitan temperament, and the serenity of the unmatched Bay of Naples.

In this abbreviated account of the vast field of Seicento literature there is one author who might have gone at the beginning, and has been left to last because a score of years ago he would not have been on the list at all, and so is, like Contarini, a token of what may be discovered. This is Federico della Valle (1560?–1628), a rather unrewarded follower of the court of Charles Emanuel of Savoy. For us he has a special interest, as being the first Italian to turn into a tragedy the subject of Mary Queen of Scots. His first redaction of this dates from 1591, only four years from her death, though the final version belongs to 1628. The original editions of his works had been reduced to one or two copies, and it is Benedetto Croce who discovered him again. Since then he has been made accessible, and high claims put forward for his poetic quality. Tasso (as closest predecessor) and Leopardi (as sometimes striking the same note) have been introduced as sponsors. They are perhaps misleading, inappropriate or too ambitious, though the actual language and metre doubtless derive from Tasso. But what is reassuring about della Valle is that at the moment of Marino he writes with a quiet dignity, unforced, unfeigned, and with a sincere religious conviction which can find its focus in the martyrdom of Mary Queen of Scots as in the scriptural world of Judith or of Esther. In his poetry we find muted to an elegiac note that sense of tragedy which floods the final chorus of Tasso's *Torrismondo*. Needless to say, the most ambitious of his plays, the tragi-comedy *Adelonda di Frigia*, is also the least successful, and his qualities show best in the simple mood of biblical fervour which stirs *Iudit* to the destruction of Holophernes or *Ester* to the rescue of Mordecai. Of *La Reina di Scozia* we may say that the mere subject brings a bonus, and that though the quality of these three plays is surprisingly even, this last will still remain what we shall look to first, or most. Naturally, it shares with other sixteenth-century tragedy – with, say, Robert Garnier in *Les Juives* – a lack of dramatic handling. For this Europe has to wait for Corneille with *Le Cid*. In the meantime the action of *La Reina di Scozia* consists rather of the lament over the inevitable from the central character, and in the mistaken hopes of her attendants, who see liberation coming with the mandate for her execution. This is Jhon Bocchas on the Fall of Princes, announced unambiguously in the first soliloquy of the Queen, with its strong note of the lability of greatness. And here also we may feel the absence of those arts of literary cookery which in the same lapse of time were to make the name Marino notorious in Europe. Compared with the great names of Italian poetry Federico della Valle is a modest addition to the roll; but he represents a strength and healthiness which had been thought entirely lost in the period when he wrote, and we can take him finally as proving that the Seicento, though it may not have the splendour belonging to its predecessors among the centuries, has much to offer the explorer, and may still have more to come.

CHAPTER 11

In and Out of Arcadia

THE sixteenth century had seen with Palestrina (1524–94) the return of human emotions into music, but polyphony had to be replaced before musical drama was possible, and the death of Palestrina coincides with this new departure. Halting on the edge is the *Amfiparnaso* of Orazio Vecchi (1597), where the singing is still choral, and the action disjointed; or the *Combattimento di Tancredi e Clorinda*, where Claudio Monteverdi takes Tasso as a basis for music. It is Ottavio Rinuccini (1562–1621), a Florentine who passes with Maria de'Medici to Paris, who finds the new form of the *melodramma*. His *Dafne* dates from 1594, the theme indicative of the well-tried reservoir, and the slightness of the treatment proof of a tentative start. The *Favola di Dafne* begins too with a spectacle loosely attached, Apollo descending by machine from the clouds to shoot the Pythian monster. It is a reminder that soon the machinery, that is the spectacle, will swamp the boat of poetry. Here it is a fringe, the essence of the play in the pursuit of Dafne, and in her reported metamorphosis (in terms which just suggest Bernini's group). The successors, *Euridice* (1600) and *Arianna* (1608), add development, though this is not pure gain. And the ending of *Euridice* is revised, as too tragic for court entertainment. Nevertheless, it is perhaps superior by the greater articulation of its sentiments. And here for the musicians (Peri, Caccini, and then their chief, Claudio Monteverdi) are clear characters, and the first opportunity for monody to replace the polyphony of the sixteenth century. The apparatus, and the rules, of tragedy are not abandoned, though they are clarified: a Messenger may still relate the most important parts; prologues, monologues, and moral sentences remain. But all is ready to be taken over by music, not as a round, but in the clear singing of individual parts. Perhaps the third play, *Arianna*, while it contains the most celebrated morceau (*Lasciatemi morire*), shows most the dangers of tampering with established material. How make a play of Ariadne on an empty beach? Rinuccini garbles palpably, and we are on our way to the first success of Metastasio, *Didone Abbandonata*, in which Virgil is as much abandoned as the heroine. In between had come the abandonment also of the simplicity of Rinuccini: for when the *melodramma* left the cultured company of Florence it was ready to forget the literary nature of its origins. Brought to Venice in 1637, where the first opera-house with seats to be paid for is opened, opera turns to the provision of the spectacular, with the showy music of Francesco Cavalli matching the new lavishness of apparatus. Sometimes it will do better in a foreign clime, as with the Florentine Giambattista Lulli, who filled the court of Louis XIV with his music. But in Italy it is only with the close of the century that Apostolo Zeno (1668–1750) makes the first attempt to bring opera back towards literature. His intentions were honourable: to look back towards classical tragedy, so to respect the unities, with special emphasis on that of action, care for what the Italians call *costume*, and sobriety in the disposition of the arias. Zeno was 'poet and historian' to the Emperor in Vienna (1718–28), and this is the prelude to Metastasio. But well-meaning was not enough, and the nearly seventy *melodrammi* of Zeno are lacking in artistic life.

The merit of reform belongs to Metastasio, whose age spans all the heyday of the eighteenth century, down to the threshold of the Revolution. Even in his dates (1698–1782) Pietro Trapassi was born lucky, and in nothing more than in the change of name to the euphonious Greek equivalent to his name. Lucky in his sponsors, too, with first Gian Vincenzo Gravina (author of tragedies meant to be exemplars, and of *La Ragion Poetica*, a forerunner of Muratori's *Perfetta Poesia*), who adopted him, intending a nurture in the sternest classicism. Lucky then in the timely death of Gravina (1718) which left him as his independent heir. Now Ovid, Guarini, and

Marino meet his eye, the middle one of these being specially important in his development. Then in Naples his diversion, *Gli Orti Esperidi* (1721) for the Spanish Viceroy, brought a new protector in Marianna Bulgarelli. In 1724 *Didone Abbandonata* sets him upon a triumphal course, which soon leads him – *sulle ali del canto* – to be Imperial Poet in Vienna (1730). From now on he basks in all success, and the birthdays of the Imperial family receive the due tribute of his *melodrammi*. In these, as notably in *Regolo*, the Roman hero who returns upon parole from Carthage, only to persuade the Senate to send him back to torture, Metastasio puts into verse the sentiments of patriotism, needing none himself. And when Austria enters the war-years he keeps silence. This gap between the surface of his *melodramma* and the real interests of Metastasio suggests the shamness of the heroic world he stages. And if we look to the Neapolitan diversions we can see him everywhere lifting from Guarini's *Pastor Fido* motifs which belong to him more genuinely. Thus in *La Primavera* we find Metastasio reworking the rich lament of Mirtillo, *O primavera gioventú dell'anno* (III, i), and in the change catch a revealing glimpse of the way that Metastasio is going. Mirtillo's lament was poetry in its own right, individual and satisfying. With Metastasio it has lost all superfluous flesh, to be reduced to a general statement in its simplest form. As such it is immediately apprehensible to all, and as an *arietta* fluid and communicable: to become (it is Flora's formula for Metastasio) the poetry of the common-place (to which I leave a hyphen, lest it should seem only the commonplace in poetry). To this we must add a phenomenon which need not surprise us in court entertainments. Thus in the *Orti Esperidi* Mars is roused to jealousy, and when lulled he sings his *arietta*:

> Di due bell'anime,
> Che amor piagò,
> Gli affetti teneri
> Turbar non vuò,
> Godete placidi
> Nel dolce ardor.

Oh se fedele
   Fosse così,
   Quella crudele,
   Che mi ferì,
   Meco men barbaro
   Saresti amor.

And the Cyclops Polyphemus (in *Galatea*) coos you as softly
as any turtle-dove in the same deft and simple language. And
in the more ambitious plays the heroism is still one of *ariette*
at the end of scenes, sung by characters whom we might not
by ourselves have associated with such prettiness of sentiments. And though the eighteenth century was carried away
by his accomplishment to inscribe his tomb *To the Italian
Sophocles*, we can only rate him as a clever purveyor of genera-
lities, wrapped in the small neat packet of the *arietta*, com-
mitting no one, and least of all himself, to any personal
experience, but enshrining in an often beguiling form many
of the sentiments and much of the traditional wisdom of
mankind. Sometimes, in the long series of successes in Vienna,
we feel he comes nearest to firmness and dignity of handling,
as with *La Clemenza di Tito*, with *Temistocle* or *Regolo*; but it
is difficult to forget for long that this is a pasteboard world.
When Queen Christina of Sweden sponsored the Academy of
Arcadia (in 1690) its banner was simplicity and good taste.
But the world of the new Arcadia was different from that of
Tasso in the *Aminta*, where feelings were concentrated by the
omission of what was irrelevant. And the simple, unless it is
also the true and real, is likely to be attractive, but brittle and
ephemeral. Metastasio is the incarnation of Arcadia, and we
can only find his sophistication artificial, his *ariette* toys.

With him there triumph those short metres of Chiabrera,
and appropriately, no ancient poet has a greater vogue now
than Anacreon, translated and imitated. We may see the
authentic note of the Arcadian *canzonetta* in *Si m'è caro un fido
Amore* of Paolo Rolli (1687–1765), a Roman who came to
London, and even translated Milton in his graver moments,
but who was most at home in the lighter world of Arcadian
verse. Even Metastasio, author of countless *ariette* of artless

neatness, wrote nothing neater than this trifle with its simple play of thesis, antithesis, and synthesis (the words too ponderous for the process). Here even the pains of Love are painless, and human experience reduced to a pretty formula to which we can consent without commitment. And this trifling is the better side of Arcadia, the other being that endless production of all the ritual forms of verse for the host of petty occasions to which life gives rise. Here the great artificer is Carlo Innocenzo Frugoni (1692–1768) – one of those eighteenth-century *abati* uncommitted to a clerical environment – who poured forth an endless flood of verse of every kind, and as court poet at Parma from 1749 seemed to rival in Italy the position at Vienna of Metastasio.

Et in Arcadia ... the Venice of the eighteenth century partakes of this carefree atmosphere, but as befits the only independent state in Italy, with more vitality. Look at the roll-call, Piazzetta, Tiepolo, Canaletto, Guardi, Piranesi, Canova – the best-known artists are all Venetians in their origin. And in literature the Venetian counterpart to Metastasio is one often thought of as unconnected with Arcadia. But Carlo Goldoni (1707–93) is the mirror and epitome of the Venice of his time, shrunk from the Lion of the Adriatic to be in temperament the Serenissima, no longer preoccupied with high policy, or the trade-routes and possessions of the Levant, concerned only with the pleasures of living against the eternal background of the Venetian scene. And in Goldoni's plays there is no urgency of satire, no sense of a tragedy in life, only the amiable, and sometimes careless, presentation of the contemporary scene. And this, of course, is in itself a novelty, and the basis of his reform. But it is a picture of the old society, not a preparation for the new. Nor does this destroy the importance of Goldoni. The *commedia dell'arte*, both in and out of Italy, had now flourished since the sixteenth century, with its masks and situations, its magnification of the actor and its minimization of the author. As it grew old it had replaced verve by vulgarity, inspiration by exaggeration. It owed Nature a death, and it was Goldoni's hand that struck the mortal blow. At four he was enraptured by his father's puppets, as a boy he played the *prima donna* at Perugia and ran away from legal studies to follow a company of comedians to Chioggia. That is predestination, and though Goldoni cheats a little in his *Memorie* by making reform of the theatre an early and consistent aim (whereas it came to him gradually), the way opens naturally to his vast production. In 1738 *Momolo Cortesan*, with one part written, and a canvas (or *intreccio*) for the other actors; then a whole comedy written, the *Donna di Garbo* (1742–3); then for the theatre of San Luca a spate of sixty comedies in a ten years' run. And now he was strong enough to write them all *in toto*, and to base them as comedies of character on the portrayal of the contemporary world. Creative when he keeps to the dialect of Venice (so that his best plays are often those least known here, as *I Rusteghi* or *Le Barufe Chiozzote*), Goldoni is insipid in his use of literary Italian. Infinitely amiable is the surface of Venetian society, so that his plays are likeable, as pictures by Pietro Longhi. From the Italian point of view he has always been the Italian Molière, but he is a Molière without a cutting-edge, and without *Tartuffe*. The comedies by which he is best known in England, as *La Locandiera*, *La Vedova Scaltra*, or *La Bottega del Caffè*, have an innocent appeal and a never-failing gentle humour; what they lack is bite. Even so, Goldoni found enemies, with as ringleaders the tireless polygraph Pietro Chiari (1711–85) and the more respectable Carlo Gozzi (1720–86). Before them Goldoni retired to Paris in 1762, where he found it difficult to reform the Italian comedians, but achieved the feat of writing *Le Bourru Bienfaisant* in French; in which language he wrote the *Mémoires* which record, not always quite faithfully, the gentle life of their author. And here he died in 1793, a few years before the fall of Venice herself at the tender hands of Bonaparte.

The very abundance of Goldoni's production militates against him – some 250 compositions of the most varied kind, and with all the discount, still over a hundred comedies based on his observation of society. Their tendency is to replace the *imbroglio* which had done duty as a plot with simple and natural events which spring from character. The action is of the stuff of everyday life, seen in a spirit of festive gaiety. That one so placid should have enemies may seem unnecessary, but Chiari disliked his success, and Gozzi could not bear to see the old *commedia dell'arte* snuffed out. From his boutade that any silly novelty would have as much success comes the fairy-story play, *L'Amore delle Tre Melarance*, its substance from Basile, with an infusion of fresh satire. Fired by its success Gozzi went on to write nine *fiabe* between 1761 and 1765. At first they were acclaimed, but Sismondi's comment on their seeming the work of a northern imagination accounts for their scant lasting success in Italy, and it was Schiller who paid Gozzi the compliment of imitating *Turandot*, his Chinese fairy-story. But here is a laughter which is near to tears, and themes which run beneath the shallow surface of contemporary society into the emotions of mankind. Gozzi is at times more vital and more universal than Goldoni, though Italian posterity has chosen to see rather the unruly fantasy than the flashes of profundity.

Before we come to the renewal we have one of the most substantial names of the century, who yet belongs by himself, Giambattista Vico (1668–1744). His attitudes are prophetic for later time, and he might take the place of Rousseau as the discoverer of the primitive to replace the sophisticated. For Vico points backwards to the beginnings of mankind with a feeling for historic, and prehistoric, depth which had not been known before. He did so in conscious reaction against Descartes. By placing the emphasis on the process of thought and on mathematical certainties, Descartes had seemed to sweep the past out of view; and Malebranche could talk of the libraries to be burnt as lumber. But for Vico what God has made is for God to understand, for man there is supremely what he has made himself, that is, human history. So he looks back across the centuries to the long upward, and downward, path of man. All this he puts into the rugged structure of his *Scienza Nuova* (1725). And by its second edition in 1730 Vico has the main lines clear, with the history of the human race from the age of the gods through that of heroes down to ordinary men. First fierce as Polyphemus, then magnanimous as Achilles, next just as Aristides or Scipio, then with great virtues and great vices, as with Caesar or Alexander, then deliberately wicked, as Tiberius. Here for the first time we have a sequence in the rise and fall of peoples, and the *degnità* (or fundamental maxims) light up the dark places: so that even the theme of Gibbon seems parochial compared with this pattern for the whole of human experience. By the side of this poetic picture of mankind Vico left a short *Autobiografia*: the sickly child who fractured his skull at seven, and became one of the great autodidacts, unappreciated Professor of Rhetoric at a beggarly salary, to die unrecognized. If poetry consists, as Croce thought, of pictures, none more of a poet than Vico, although his verse is occasional and not valuable: but he lights up with his *degnità* the processes of man's development, and with his images he gives a life and body to the mythical past.

While Vico looks to the principles governing the course of history, the great erudites assemble its materials. We may take as symbol the *Verona Illustrata* (1731) of Scipione Maffei, so much more a monument than the *Merope* which seemed the foundation for eighteenth-century tragedy. Or the *Storia Universale* (1697) of Francesco Bianchini which already looked to archaeology as an aid to finding the first strata of history. And then with Lodovico Antonio Muratori (1672–1750) we come to the great pattern of the tireless scholar, his splendid series of *Rerum Italicarum Scriptores* till then unrivalled in the world. Here the documents and the chronicles of the Dark and Middle Ages come to light, two thousand of them for the first time of printing. Nor was that all of Muratori's activity, and to it we may add the *Antiquitates Italicae Medii Aevi*, in six quarto volumes, and the vast *Annali d'Italia* based on his omnivorous sifting of the records. And others emulate his diligence with different material, as Girolamo Tiraboschi (1731–94), who produces the first monumental *Storia della Letteratura Italiana* (in 14 volumes, 1772–81, and still a mine of information, principally for the lives of writers); or Luigi Lanzi whose *Storia Pittorica dell'Italia* (1796) covered the long ascendancy of Italy in the realm of art, and marked its close. And what Lanzi did for painting, Leopoldo Cicognara did for sculpture (*Storia della Sculptura*), beginning with the same rebirth, and ending proudly with Canova.

All this is proof that the century of Arcadia has its serious side. And there are other proofs, as with Pietro Giannone (1676–1748), whose *Istoria Civile del Regno di Napoli* (1723) stands as firmly for the independence of the lay state as had the voice of Sarpi a century before. Less lucky though than Sarpi, Giannone left his asylum of Vienna, and arrested by trickery in Savoy spent twelve years in prison till his death at the hands of the ecclesiastical authorities. The ideas of the *Istoria Civile* he elaborated in the *Triregno*, tracing the degeneracy of religion from the primitive Church, down to the wealth of external ceremonies and the assumption of power over individuals. In Naples there were others working for enlightenment; and from Milan we have the epoch-making *Dei Delitti e delle Pene* (1761) of Cesare Beccaria, with its persuasive polemic against judicial torture and capital punishment; or Pietro Verri's journal, *Il Caffè* (1764), alive to the currents of French thought and anxious for social improvement. In the same years Carlo Gozzi's brother Gasparo is amongst the initiators of Italian journalism with *La Gazzetta Veneta* (1760) and the *Osservatore* (1761); while from an earlier date Francesco Algarotti (1712–64) brings from his northern travels the fashions of European thought, turning the new world of scientific discovery to a discourse for the world of fashion, as in his *Newtonianismo per le Dame* (1737). Algarotti writes elegantly as one of the first conscious vulgarizers, while another northern traveller wields a heavy lash against all belonging to the stuffy past, or the Arcadian present. This is Giuseppe Baretti (1719–89), friend of Dr Johnson, author (as Aristarco Scannabue) of *La Frusta Letteraria* (1763–5). This is the blunderbuss rather than the rapier, and Baretti made the mistake of crying up Metastasio, and decrying Dante; but in general the robustness of his good faith and good will is valuable, and he fights valiantly for the enlightenment of his century against the fetish of the past, against Arcadian pastorals and stale academies, for good sense. Opposite Baretti (whose Letters and accounts of travel – including the reply to Samuel Sharp, the *Account of the manners and customs of Italy* – contain much of the best of his writing) we may put that other traveller, Giacomo Casanova, whose celebrity is notoriety, and whose prolix *Mémoires* are only a *succès de scandale*. Or with Baretti we may note one who travels in imagination into the north, to mingle all the influences of the eighteenth century. This is Melchiorre Cesarotti (1730–1808), who translates Ossian, very freely, and ranks him with Homer among the heights of poetry. And does not this suit with the century of Vico and of Rousseau, with the recognition of poetry as being the primitive voice of man, and not the artefact of cultured centuries?

But there is one who chose a harder course, and yet brings us back to the main line of creative literature. This is Giuseppe Parini (1729–99), who may have been the first poet of the new order, but whose poetic form is dictated by his allegiance to Latin models, the first of whom is Horace. Parini is the peasant introduced into the urban society of Milan; employed by noble families, the Borromini or the Serbelloni, as tutor to their children, he suffers the humiliations which menials of this sort received, looking in return with the disapproval of an austere nature on the frivolities of rank and station. Instead of a poetry which goes with the grain of the century, mirroring its flippancy, here is one which goes against it: worked also by one who was tireless in self-criticism, using incessantly the file of Horace. Thus is born *Il Giorno*, its first part (*Il Mattino*) in 1763, its last posthumous and uncompleted. Naturally, it is a satire, bringing an Italian to the company of Pope and Boileau. But it has a new surface, setting out in gravity to give the precepts for the day of the Giovin Signore, the young fop whose worthlessness is exposed by the seriousness with which his empty world is anatomized, and extolled. The irony of Parini's intention is underlined from time to time by the contrasts he introduces, with the peasant and the artisan; and at times, as when the common herd must scatter before the gilded coach, we feel a scarcely

contained resentment which points on to 1789. But we must
not do Parini the injustice of thinking him a revolutionary,
and there is a famous anecdote of his last days, when called
to join in the cry, *Death to the aristocrats*, he answered both
vehemently and temperately, *Viva la repubblica, morte a
nessuno*. And in those turbulent days he was wont to ask, 'Are
you as good as you were yesterday?' It is a measure of the
firmness of his temperament. But his formula means a lack of
opportunity for the overt satirical wit of Pope or Boileau, and
with the difficulties of his expression – not as angular as
Alfieri, but outside the range of any spoken Italian – leaves
him tied particularly to his own time. Here we can only
harvest a few memorable lines, and they are welded (as with
the *leitmotiv* of his burden against *cicisbeismo*, *La pudica
d'altrui sposa a te cara*) to an extinct surface of society.

We may enjoy Parini better in his minor verse. Here too
he looks to Horace as a model, and without following that
master to his more worthless attitudes is free to give a lightness to the touch which would be out of place in the uniform
solemnity of *Il Giorno*. In a world of anacreontic trifling the
Odes of Parini have a firmness of content and direction, combined with a sprightliness of manner. And here he gives the
measure of himself as man and poet,

> Colui cui diede il ciel placido senso
> e puri affetti e semplice costume ...

Nowhere in Italian has the mood of Horace been more
felicitously caught, or transposed to a more simple dignity
than here. At the head of his verse there is the ode *La Vita
Rustica*, and it is from this haven that Parini writes. Yet he
does not deny the possibilities of a worthy use of station, only
the fatuity which makes a mockery of it. Hence the old-
world gallantry of *Il Messaggio*, with its response to the flattering interest of 'l'inclita Nice'; and hence also the robustness
of his sentiments in *L'Educazione*, where he puts before his
noble pupil a programme which Rousseau might have
approved, with at its centre an insistence on moral values.
Parini died as modestly as he had lived, and though he did

not boast with Horace that he had built his monument already, yet he wished none. 'Voglio, ordino, comando, che le spese funebri mi siano fatte nel piú semplice e mero necessario, ed all'uso che si costuma per *il piú infimo dei cittadini.*' It is a fitting epitaph for the most estimable poet of the eighteenth century.

Parini's successor is his opposite in this matter of restraint. For Vittorio Alfieri (1749–1803), the Piedmontese noble converted to the cause of freedom, brings with him all the excessive ardour of the neophyte. No word rings more insistently in the *Vita di Vittorio Alfieri scritta da esso* – than *bollore*, the boiling of his temperament, whether in love for Penelope Pitt, in the passion for horseflesh, for liberty in a servile world, or in the overmastering desire to escape from the ignorance of ordinary nobility and write his name in the book of Italian poetry. Naturally, in the *Vita* it is the record of the earlier part which captures most our interest. Here the tempo is a compelling one, in spite of Alfieri's *noia* or frustrations. Desperately travelling – to Prussia, even Russia, Sweden, Denmark, Germany, four times in England, whence he returned with a string of fourteen horses over the passes of the Alps – Alfieri charges us with some of his own energy. And here his temperament seems at its most preromantic. Yet when he turns to writing, it is the past and not the future which has claim on him. Like Parini he looks backward to the models, and as part of a necessary linguistic training (for one nurtured in the French tradition of Turin) to the Trecento texts of the Crusca tradition. At the same time he desires vehemently to flee the singsong and effeminacy of Arcadia, and in one or two famous epigrams expressed the need to be hard, obscure, intricate, but thought, and not sung. His lines he revises from a natural form to one that is rugged and independent. His tragedies he squeezes of all inessentials, not only to plunge *in medias res* with a few main characters, but to reduce speech to its most pregnant use. The classic case is in a scene from *Filippo*, the tragedy of the King of Spain whose jealous tyranny prompts death for his own son, Don Carlos, where twenty-two words make nine speeches, and one whole scene (II, v). To this concision there is an amusing commentary: Alfieri may have found its model in Metastasio, who by mere economy can be as brief (and in *Temistocle* there is the clash of this Udisti? – Udii ...). But the urgency is Alfieri's own. We might take a motto for him out of Spenser,

> But O! the greedy Thirst of royal Crown,
> That knows no Kindred, nor regards no right.

Here all is black, against all white: on the one side Filippo, with his refusal to admit anything but silent acceptance of his absolute power; on the other, the noble spirits, Don Carlos, the loyal Perez, doomed before the play begins.

From the restlessness of his life Alfieri turned in 1775 to the settled purpose of writing tragedies, at one time to be fourteen, like his English horses. But his *bollore* forced his hand, and they crept to nineteen. Nor should we regret this, for Alfieri's style matured, and some of the best are in the later ones. Even then, he added an afterthought, his late coming to Greek studies bringing a reworking of Euripides' *Alceste*. Then there are the prose-works which throw a necessary light on his ideas, *Della Tirannide* (1777), *Del Principe e delle Lettere* (1778, completed 1786). Here the stark contrast is set out in its development. The paradox – of the brilliant ages under an absolute ruler, Pericles, Augustus, Leo X, or Louis XIV – is examined and dismissed: literature may have polish under despotism, it will have force only in freedom. And Tiberius will have no friend but Sejanus. Alfieri subscribes to Montesquieu's theory of the separation of powers (the legislative from the executive); and naturally, not only his native ruler of Savoy and Piedmont finds condemnation, but also and especially the ecclesiastical despotism of Rome. For Alfieri the Protestant nations alone are truly free, and he enumerates the six links in the chain that binds the catholic ones (the pope, the Inquisition, Purgatory, Confession, marriage as an indissoluble sacrament, the celibacy of the religious). Fear, military force, religion are the bases of despotic power. These ideas, interesting and symptomatic rather than original (often the language reveals his dependence on Machiavelli, or on Montesquieu), light up the processes behind the tragedies. Nor are we surprised to find that the polite tyrannies of the eighteenth century do not find favour with him: if despotism were harsher, the reaction against it, the liberation from it, would come more violently, more readily.

Something of Alfieri's dynamic pulses in the *Rime* which he wrote from 1775 on, not so much in the sonnets for the Countess of Albany, the *degno amore* who fulfilled his life, as in those which depict his own portrait, or look (as with a famous sonnet on Rome) to the conditions round him. Then after that bespattering with French with which he began there is Alfieri's gallophobia. Paris was the least attractive capital for him, and the Revolution, after a first welcome to the fall of the Bastille, the rise of plebeian tyrants in the plural. In short, the liberty he dreamed of, or applauded in the English constitution, was different from the Terror. But Alfieri, whose indictments are so strong in the pages he wrote, has no urge left over to action; and in the face of the oncoming French he merely thinks of removing valuables, and shunning unwelcome contacts (as with poor Ginguené, whose friendship for Italy deserved a better reception). His action was limited to having made a dozen copies of the splenetic *Misogallo*, to secure the survival of his contempt for the French. This does not do its author much credit, though it has a prophetic closing sonnet on future recognition for the poet; and we must turn back to the tragedies, written between 1775 and 1787, for Alfieri's real stature. In *Saul*, where Greek fatality broods over Israel's king, and Saul is torn between his jealousy of David and his love for his daughter's husband, he has put something of himself; and the picture that Saul paints of his moods,

> Fero,
>
> Impaziente, torbido, adirato
> Sempre; a me stesso incresco ognora, e altrui;
> Bramo in pace far guerra, in guerra pace,

has often been taken as modelled on Alfieri. And here, though the theme of tyrannous power, with Abner as the poison-counsellor, is obviously not absent, we do not feel it reduced to a theorem, as in *Filippo*, or *Antigone*. In *Mirra* that theme is lacking, and the play of emotions runs unmixed with theory to its tragic close. In both of these plays Alfieri attains to a dignity of expression which seemed beyond his reach in the first seeking for harshness. But strong as are the qualities which he brings to his self-chosen task, Alfieri is a rallying-point for Italy more than a peak in European drama. And even one might say that his most interesting play lies outside the record. For in his last years he turned to comedy, breaking the moulds for tragic diction. Here all will be as colloquial as may be, with a press of Alfierian neologisms. The first four comedies have a political basis, their titles binding them into one play with twenty acts (*L'Uno, I Pochi, I Troppi*, and *L'Antidoto*). Machiavelli would have caught their drift, and may well have inspired it. But the sixth is the luckiest hit: *Il Divorzio* (*Commedia VI, ed ultima ultimissima di tutte le invenzioni mie. Moderna tutta, e non tradotta*). This satirizes *cicisbeismo* with a gusto and a vigour which Goldoni did not find for castigation. Indeed, we may say that Alfieri's satire sparkles more in the *Divorzio* than in the *Satire* which he added to his other verse.

Neither Parini nor Alfieri quite attains the status of a major poet, yet their significance is sufficient to cancel from our view most of the versifiers who saw the century out. Perhaps it is not really fair to take Ludovico Savioli (1729–1804) as an example, since his *Amori* appeared in 1758. But they are still reprinted by Bodoni in a noble format in the early nineteenth century, with an Ovidian motto on the title-page, *Me Venus artificem tenero praefecit amori*. Here simplicity and elegance are brought to verse purified of Ovid's more flagrant attitudes. Others continue their production longer, as the Arcadian Giovanni Fantoni (1755–1807), whose poetry, reprinted even into the age of Leopardi, sometimes suggests by a title or a hint the coming of a more substantial world than the old shadows of Parnassus. Sometimes, naturally, the new influences of European literature are felt: with Cesarotti's version of Ossian we have Aurelio Bertola (1753–98) initiating the discovery of German literature, and translating the *Idylls* of Gessner as a first sample of new pleasures. And Klopstock's *Messia* had preceded them by a few years, while soon the anguish of Goethe's *Werther* will provide a model and an attitude. At the same time, in a century shot with anglomania, the impact of Gray and Young and of sepulchral poetry is felt. In a little while Foscolo will heed these influences, and *en attendant* we have one of the most fortunate books of the closing century, the *Notti Romane* of Alessandro Verri (1705-88), in which the air of gloom and nebulosity has been exploited. Meanwhile some have followed the scientific trends, allying these with a glance at the most classic of scientific poetry, as with the *Coltivazione del Riso* of G. B. Spolverini (1695-1762), modelled on the *Georgics*. The most happy marriage of poetry and science was made by Lorenzo Mascheroni (1750-1800), whose *Invito a Lesbia Cidonia* to tour the University of Pavia brings together the desire to please and the need to inform. This is the poetic answer to Algarotti's *Newtonianismo per le Dame*, and may serve to remind us that the perfumed world of Arcadia was still a period of Italian contribution to the world of science: as witness, to look no further, Volta and Galvani. Or sometimes, as notoriously with the 'non casto abate Casti' a careless and often unseemly production sprawls over half a dozen different spheres. Giambattista Casti (1724-1803) wrote nothing more amusing than an occasional *novella* in *ottava rima*. Yet the reader who looks for such a pretty trifle as *L'Anticristo* will find himself ingurgitating a lot of stale stuff with the rest of the *Novelle*. Of his copious works we may remember the *Poema Tartaro*, which Gladstone rated with Byron's *Don Juan*, and which controverted the adulation for Catherine II, and the *Animali Parlanti*, a vast poem, written just at the dawn of the nineteenth century, in which under the guise of animals, the policy of monarchical Europe is roundly and prolixly condemned. It supplied a quotation for Leopardi in the *Operette Morali*, and may account also for Leopardi's clinging to the animalesque satire, down to the *Paralipomeni*. But more typical of the century's end is the gentle Ippolito Pindemonte (1753-1828).

He travelled abroad between 1778 and 1796, and his stay in London made him, if not friendly to the tyrant of the seas, preventer of the new millennium, at least familiar with the new breezes from the north. His novel *Abaritte* (1790) models itself on Samuel Johnson, his tragedy *Arminio* (1797–1804) has Alfieri as progenitor on one side, and William Shakespeare in the offing on the other. From the *Poesie Campestri* (1785) we may note the dying fall of the eighteenth century, the gentle prelude to the *mal du siècle*, with the title and the content of *La Melanconia*. And this also is derivative from Gray. In another direction one of Pindemonte's major accomplishments is the blank verse translation of the *Odyssey* (1809–22), which stands only a little lower than that of the *Iliad* by Monti.

With Monti, and for Monti, comes the revaluation of Dante. Baretti had tilted against his poem, and Saverio Bettinelli (1718–1808) had poured ridicule on the *Divina Commedia* in his *Lettere Virgiliane*, salvaging – long before Croce – only a few cantos (as Francesca, Ugolino …). As for all of Dante's time, to the fire or to the Crusca with them. What Bettinelli wished was to move forward with the times, and his interesting *Risorgimento d'Italia negli Studi e nei Costumi dopo il Mille* (1773) shows that he looked to the Renascence as a bringer of light and progress. But just as Bettinelli was denigrating Dante, the pious Varano (1705–88) was bringing back the genus of the vision, based on Dante and the Bible. That was a turning-point, and so we come to Vincenzo Monti (1754–1828), who could seem to his contemporaries not only the major poet of their time, but also a new Dante sprung to life, only better than the first one, a *Dante ingentilito*. For us, it may seem best to say frankly as a preliminary, Monti is placed in a difficult position by his successive changes of front. He mirrors the passing show over too wide an arc: coming to Rome at twenty-four, the protégé of a cardinal, he basks in the favours of the papal court, and as a dutiful Arcadian writes elegantly and copiously. The symbol of this papal facet is the *Bassvilliana* (1793), where the *Divine Comedy* is laid under contribution as a formula to deplore the excesses of the French Revolution. But in 1797 Monti left Rome without ceremony, in the company of the French general Marmont, and before long his voice was raised into a paean for the rise of Napoleon. *Il Beneficio* (1805) celebrates the crowning of an Emperor, and the *Bardo della Selva Nera* – a pot pourri of poetic influences – recounts the progress of Napoleon over the battlefields. Alas, Napoleon also had his day, and Monti survived to see a better era coming after him. As soon as May 1815 he was ready with his *Mistico Omaggio* to an Austrian Archduke, while the *Ritorno d'Astrea* (1816) opens with a stage direction of 'Horrible devastation, cities burnt etc.', to offer a godhead as a remedy: Francis I of Austria, the new Titus for the world to adore now that the horror had gone.

It cannot be disguised, then, that in some ways Monti is not sterling gold. And perhaps in some other ways the prospectuses that have been written for him are not really valid. Thus, the *Bellezza dell'Universo* (1781) has been put forward as his masterpiece, with his sensitivity to beauty, his plastic images for all the objects falling under the survey of sense. But this cannot disguise the hollow subject-matter. *Candide* is barely before him, where the world is shown as not so jolly good a show, and Leopardi is following after, with whom the haunting beauty of the universe underlies and underlines the tragedy of man. How in such a sandwich can a simple poem on the Beauty of the Universe seem other than the prize essay or the Poet Laureate's exercise? In poetry, although it is the music which matters, music without sense is not the genuine article. What, then, can we still say for Monti? First, we may take as keynote his most celebrated anthology-piece, the ode on his return to Italy after an uneasy interlude in Paris, *Bella Italia, amate sponde*. Here is a note that rings whole and sincere, where the love of beauty coincides with *italianità*. Monti may have had no political conscience, but is not devoid of patriotism of his own kind, and in the list of invocations, beginning with that of Petrarch, this is not the least eloquent, or affecting. And in some of his transitions perhaps Monti could find excuse, or attenuation. Did not Alfieri himself shift his ideas as the Revolution passed near him? And Monti has his value as a barometer, with as a redeeming feature his genuine commotion at the name of Italy. And he is one of the first to spread and popularize the idea of a united, and non-stagnant, Italy. A passage from his Roman tragedy, *Caio Gracco*, reinforces *Bella Italia* with a new, specific, note. It is when Caio demands of the assembled citizens if liberty for Italy is to be thought a crime, and the suggestion becomes an acclamation:

> LO CITTADINO: No, Itali siam tutti, un popol solo,
> Una sola famiglia.
> POPOLO: Italiani
> Tutti, e fratelli.

Italy, said Metternich contemptuously, was a geographical expression; and Carducci answered that it was a literary expression: in this the voice of Monti is an important novelty, a pointer towards the coming age of the Risorgimento.

In spite also of the understandable hesitation over the Terror there is in *Caio Gracco* (begun in 1778, completed in 1800, played at Milan in 1802) more than a hint of the new mood of Europe. 200,000 privileged, but 25 millions unprivileged: it is the moment of the dictum, 'Le tiers état n'avait été *rien* dans l'ordre politique, il devait être *tout*'. The moment when the new word NATION begins to have a content. And Monti catches the drift, with Caio standing for the people, against Opimio, who stands for the patricians as oppressors. The moments, then, of Monti are better than the whole; or than the machinery of eighteenth-century poetry. For Monti is the natural neo-classic, who sees poetry as the scaffolding built on simple foundations by the use of well-tried formulas and traditional apparatus. Even this is not quite enough, and the very title, *Il Bardo della Selva Nera*, will have shown how even Monti listened to the northern sirens, imitating incongruously *The Bard* of Gray. Indeed, as with Pindemonte, it may be the timeless, rather than the dated, which appeals most now in Monti's work. Not for nothing has his translation of the *Iliad* seemed his most enduring monument. The work of one unversed in the original Greek, this version nevertheless catches something of the essential spirit of Homer while giving Monti full scope for his ability in handling words. But we must also add his plays as being of more permanent interest than such period pieces as the *Bassvilliana*. *Aristodemo* (1786) belongs to the classic theatre as revived by Alfieri, and its principal character carries the weight of guilt with the burden of the crown. But though there may be too obvious an echo of *Oedipus* (for this is not a pre-revolutionary theme) the play is more harmoniously handled than are any of Alfieri. For *Galeotto Manfredi*, following hard on *Aristodemo*, Monti has come to recent happenings; and besides, the impact of Shakespeare stands out apparent. Manfredi soliloquizes as Macbeth upon the dread of night, and in this tragedy of jealousy Zambrino is most clearly the Iago of the piece, dragging the noble Manfredi downwards. With this awareness a new cutting-edge is introduced, felt most strongly in Monti's third play, *Caio Gracco*, which has inherited from his reading of the Roman plays of Shakespeare. Firm, clear, and simple in its language, just occasionally echoing Alfieri in its compression, but without his harsh inversions, as without the complicated *style noble* of the eighteenth century, this is the straightforward tragedy of the great protagonist of Roman liberty, doomed to perish by his own magnanimity. And here especially the English reader will note the recurrent intrusion of the voice of Shakespeare, with the People as actor, and Opimio bringing on the stage the murdered body of Emiliano, to re-enact the speech of Antony. And all the while the echoes answer us:

Il fato
Credi, è tremendo, perché l'uomo è vile ...

The fault, dear Brutus, lies not in our stars,
But in ourselves, that we are underlings.

And for *Caio Gracco*, looking forward even more than Monti may have meant to the rise of national consciousness, we may venture to modify a famous judgement of Leopardi, that Monti *was a poet of the ear and the imagination but in no manner of the heart*. For that is just, without quite doing all justice, and there is something to be added on the plus side of Monti's account after all the debits have been reckoned. With him we may say the eighteenth century fairly ends, for Foscolo, who is born within its orbit, looks out consciously towards the age that is to come, and writes moreover his major poem within the new era of the nineteenth century. To this, and to the travail of the Risorgimento, we must now pass.

CHAPTER 12

The Trilogy of the Opening Nineteenth Century

IN the chain of events which swept on Italy from 1796 to 1815 there were some – and we may take as sample Luigi Lamberti (Membro della Legione d'Onore, Cavaliere dell'Ordine della Corona di Ferro etc.) – who like Monti used their talents in the service of regnant authority. And there is the historian, Carlo Botta (1776–1837), who wrote perhaps too many works, and used a somewhat antiquated style, but who thought in a manly way. His *Storia della Guerra dell' Indipendenza degli Stati Uniti d'America* (1809) opens the sights, and shows the colour of his liberalism. His *Storia d'Italia dal 1789 al 1814* (1824) surveys in full and memorable detail the turmoil of those years, without acrimony, and with a final recognition of the solvent quality of French rule to the old fettered state of Italy. Compared to Botta Pietro Colletta (1775–1831) is a fiery partisan, and his *Storia del Reame di Napoli* (for 1734–1825) pulses with a hatred for all the feudal abuses of the South, for the cruelty and perjury of the Bourbons and the obscurantism of the Church. And Vincenzo Cuoco (1770–1823) gives the close-up picture in his *Saggio storico Sulla Rivoluzione di Napoli*, the first-hand account of the reversal, in 1799, of the Parthenopean Republic, set up by the noblest spirits there the year before, now pitilessly hounded by King Ferdinand.

Meanwhile others found high seriousness in a formal reaction against the careless gallicizing of Italian. There is something heroic in the quality of Basilio Puoti or Antonio Cesari (1760–1828), who can head in 1824 an anthology of *Novelle* in the language of the Trecento. And even with Pietro Giordani (1774–1848), though he looked forward to liberty and civil progress, stylistic preoccupation proved a sterilizing influence. Acclaimed in his day as the first prose-writer of Italy, and important to us as a factor in the life of

Leopardi, Giordani has disappeared from view for want of any major work with which to connect him. And sometimes, as with Cesare Arici (1782–1836), what seemed to have lasting quality in verse proved equally ephemeral. Arici continued, in the cataclysms of the Napoleonic era, the didactic strand of poetry. In 1805, the year of Trafalgar and Austerlitz, he put forth *La Coltivazione degli Ulivi: invita Minerva*, and the spirit of the times. *La Pastorizia* follows in 1814, with all the rural dallying we can find in Dyer's *Fleece*. It is salutary to turn to Foscolo.

Ugo Foscolo (1778–1827) was young enough, in the first flush of revolutionary ideas, to welcome the liberating Bonaparte in 1796. Born in Zante, of a Greek mother and a doctor father of Venetian origin, he came as a young man to Venice after his father's death. His *Ode a Buonaparte Liberatore* (1797) was dedicated to the citizens of Reggio in flamboyant terms, the emphasis all on the idea of *freedom* and the *free*. It was inevitable that the ensuing Treaty of Campoformio, with Venice handed in a parcel to the Emperor, should seem the betrayal of all Foscolo wished to stand for. Thrust out as a wanderer, and finding – in a life full of short or longer loves – a bitter disappointment in Florence, where Isabella Roncioni was affianced to another, Foscolo subsumed his despair in the autobiographical novel, *Le Ultime Lettere di Jacopo Ortis*, written on the turn of the century. But to Napoleon he was ready to raise the voice of freedom, and free criticism, and the *Orazione a Bonaparte* (1802), on the occasion of the conventions in Lyons which were to elect Napoleon Perpetual President of the Italian Republic, is the first open manifesto, even though it is limited to the prophecy of woe for tyrannous courses. The *Sepolcri* (1807), the short-long poem which is Foscolo's most permanent claim to fame, is still inexplicit as a political statement: but the references to Nelson, and the use of Marathon as an inspiration (against what barbarian?) are transparent. When the Napoleonic system ended Foscolo might have stayed, *choyé* as was Monti by the Austrians. But he trod the path of exile, lived, like a lord when he could, like a hack when he could not, in London from 1816 to 1827, and died there in distressful anonymity with a background of debts. In this last period Foscolo managed to become the first Italian critic to concentrate upon the essential question of the quality and character of an author's work; and he had in hand, unfinished and unordered at his death, a longer poem called *Le Grazie*. Unpublished till the middle of the century, *Le Grazie* remained a respectable monument, but not a vital sector of his *œuvre*. Recent Italian criticism has claimed it as the culminating point for Foscolo, and even as the highest point of lyric poetry in the Italian nineteenth century.

To those essentials there is much else to add. A handful of sonnets give that old form a concentrated energy, with themes of self and personal relationships, or of his native island; and two Odes (*A Luigia Pallavicini, All'amica risanata*), with their appreciation of feminine beauty, echo the theme of *Le Grazie*. But his three tragedies add little to his credit. *Tieste*, written at nineteen, was an offering to Alfieri, with a shrill note and the darkest Theban aura to the ruler and his palace. *Aiace* too (1811), with its suggestion of Napoleon under the guise of Agamemnon – still the Alfieri–Montian stage-tyrant – was long, rambling, and tedious, with little of the atmosphere of Troy or Greece or poetry. It was laughed off the stage in Milan when in Act V the dialogue produced the comic invocation, *O Salamini* ... *Ricciarda* also (1812–13), though the subject, presumably is medieval, yet keeps the atmosphere of the juvenile *Tieste*, with Guelfo thirsting for blood, especially for kindred blood. These are the last death-throes of the old manner, and we may excise them from our consideration of Foscolo.

He dissolved his name to *phos* and *chole*, *light* and *spleen*: and we may think of his two most prominent works as the malady and the antidote. The *Ultime Lettere* were begotten out of the unhappiness of their author and the literary habits of the time. The Voice of Nature, crying from the tomb, derives from Rousseau in the *Nouvelle Héloïse*, so does the epistolary sequence. From *Werther* comes the theme of suicide, and the background includes the *Night Thoughts* of Edward

Young, with all that stream of tomb-poetry in the wake of Gray. Since despair is at its climax when the book begins, its theme is a meditation on the unhappiness of man. *Jacopo Ortis* is thus a book shot through with Leopardian hints, which yet do not add up to Leopardi. Here already virtue is an empty name, Nature a stepmother to us all, men enemies amongst themselves and all illusion, and when the illusions break, what is left is *nulla*. And Foscolo looks back, as Leopardi will in *Alla Primavera*, to the good fortune of the ancients, who sacrificed to Beauty and the Graces, *e che trovavano il BELLO ed il VERO*. As in the celebrated line of Keats, Beauty and Truth are interchangeable. This is to be the centre of *Le Grazie*, even if it is inhibited in *Ortis* by the bitterness of the moment, and the gloom of Foscolo's youth. This, with the long-foreshadowed suicide of Jacopo, made the book a dangerous one, tinged with a morbidity which brought others to the point where Jacopo succumbed, and Ugo Foscolo survived.

For, naturally, the book was cathartic, a consolation for the unhappiness of life, pointing Foscolo toward the one true consolation, the power of poetry itself. Here his often-quoted invocation (*O Italiani, io vi esorto alle storie*) from his prolusion *Dell' Origine e dell'Uffizio della Letteratura* (1809) lives in this context: springing from an acceptance of Vico's vision of the ages of mankind. The tomb which gave the epigraph for *Ortis* is still the centre of *I Sepolcri*. But here, with Vico, the tomb is the first symbol of the civilization of mankind; and with it there is that voice of poetry (which calls from the tomb as much as Nature does) which records, and so keeps alive, and finally is, the finest achievement of Man. The poetry of Homer illumes the desert which was Troy and the deserted grave which is the tomb of Ilus; and if the Italians wish inspiration, they must go to Santa Croce with its monuments commemorating the highwater mark of Italy, caught in the verse of Foscolo. Personal survival has vanished from the account, and the piety of the living to the dead is repaid in the continuity of a tradition thus created, and sublimated into poetry. *I Sepolcri* may not always be quite logical in its transitions, but it is swelled by a dynamic which does not fall away, and it represents a firmer and more personal statement than had been achieved by Foscolo's own predecessors, Alfieri or Parini. What, then, of *Le Grazie*? In my view, the attempts to put the *Grazie* into the highest place are doomed to disappointment. The very concept is one that Foscolo has already used, and he has nothing to add here but a decorative treatment; and he is looking back to the scenes and the mythology of the ancient world, so that here for the last time the classical allusions form the substance of the line. It is a formula which has lost communicative power. We may legitimately extend the sphere of Foscolo's importance, to his biography, so rich, especially in its English phase; to the *Epistolario* in which so much of his personality is revealed; to such critical essays as the *Discorso Storico sul Testo del Decameron*, or the *Essays on Petrarch*, which point forward fertilely and unmistakably to De Sanctis. But to attempt to resurrect the *Grazie* for anything but specialist consumption is impossible. And since the *Ultime Lettere* is by now a period piece which can never repeat its European success, Foscolo for the mere foreigner looms less large a figure than for the Italian critics: in many ways of great importance, exercising great influence, but without a holding of his own to which we can give extensive, or unconditional, allegiance.

The first publisher of *Le Grazie* added a footnote at one point on Foscolo giving a hard knock 'at the northern school'. But Goethe had said that literatures get bored with themselves, and Mme de Staël had written *De l'Allemagne*, and the ideas of Schlegel, Schiller, Herder – and of Rousseau – were filtered through to Italy. The *Grazie*, dedicated to Canova, were still in the cupboard when the *préface de Cromwell* of Italian Romanticism appeared, the *Lettera Semiseria di Grisostomo* of Giovanni Berchet (1783–1851). Mme de Staël's views had been summarized in an article of 1816, and the protagonists of romanticism (as Lodovico di Breme, 1781–1820), soon to group themselves round the *Conciliatore*, defended the new idea of literature as an image of society. Berchet's letter accompanies a prose translation of Bürger's ballads, and follows the lead towards a popular front in poetry. Imitation is most harmful, particularly (shades of Foscolo!) if of the ancients. Poetry must be spontaneous, spring from individual sentiment, and from a quickening of the imagination. The poet must be in spiritual communion with the people, understand their griefs and hopes. It follows that it must now be a Christian poetry, repudiating pagan mythology; educative, and on occasion stirring the people to warlike spirits, invigorating the national conscience. The *Biblioteca Italiana*, which had printed the article of Mme de Staël, shrank from the battle; and the *Conciliatore* (September 1818–October 1819) was founded to advance the new liberal, and liberating, ideas, with foremost among the editors Silvio Pellico (1789-1854). Quickly falling suspect to the Austrian authorities the main collaborators tasted martyrdom, and Pellico himself spent ten years in imprisonment, the last and major part in the infamous dungeons of the Spielberg. And Pellico exemplifies what Berchet meant: converted, during his imprisonment, to a warm and simple faith, he wrote *Le Mie Prigioni* (1832) in no vindictive spirit, but in a style accessible to all. Its popularity – in all senses of the word – which made it like a battle won – puts it unmistakably on the side of Berchet and Romanticism. Others will be carried in their impetus towards a new mythology coming from the North, but Pellico, if in a humble way, shares the balance and the Christian moderation which will belong to Alessandro Manzoni. His plays (including *Francesca da Rimini*, based on Dante) have lost attention; as have those more numerous of Giambattista Niccolini (1782–1861). Niccolini saw the literary revolution in, passing from early orthodox tragedies to others with a romantic bias, or a patriotic intent. It is these which are best remembered, as with *Giovanni da Procida* (1830) and *Arnaldo da Brescia* (1843), where the patriot aims his attack against that old sore of Italy, the temporal power of the papacy.

Meanwhile Alessandro Manzoni (1785–1873) has laid one half of the foundations of Italian nineteenth-century literature. He too was born soon enough to welcome the new idealism, and opens his poetic score with *Il Trionfo della Libertà*, tied to the apparatus of the vision, and flushed with a young man's rhetoric. But Manzoni never loses contact with this youthful belief in liberty. What he loses is his first inheritance, via his mother Giulia Beccaria, from the rationalistic ideas of the French encyclopedists. There is a youthful anecdote of Manzoni exclaiming against 'l'orribile figura d'un prete' at the bedside of a dying friend, and there are snatches in his youthful poetry against the Druids in their purple. But by 1810, with only a slight production behind him, Manzoni enters the Catholic fold, and is ready to dedicate his talents, and his whole conception of literature, to the service of belief. And once again it proves that he has not so far as might have seemed to return, for Manzoni had written his *profession de foi* in the best of his early poems, *In morte di Carlo Imbonati* (1805); and his programme there can still do duty for the *Promessi Sposi*. Nor was the anticlericalism of his youth irreligious in its substance: indeed, the anecdote quoted needs finishing, for the same Manzoni was convinced of reunion in another world.

The first fruits of conversion were the *Inni Sacri*, which should have covered the major festivals of the church year, and by a sluggishness in Manzoni remained at five. Here also Manzoni was moving with the spirit of the time, wishing to look from any *stile dotto*, towards the popular quality, the conversational tone and wide appeal of French verse. His solution was to adopt the short Arcadian metres in this attempt to express the highest meaning in the simplest words, and their aura of frivolity is one which even Manzoni's reverence finds difficult to defeat. In France the Catholic Reaction of the early nineteenth century led to reactionary views; but Manzoni does not desert his faith in the inspiring principles of the Revolution, and the compassion which we shall find for the humble in his novel here embraces all mankind. Stronger than the *Inni Sacri*, and with a more personal flavour, are the few occasional poems of Manzoni: his ode written for the hopes of 1821 (*Soffermati sull'arida sponda*), and the poem written for the death of Napoleon in that same year, *Cinque maggio*, with its echoes of the passions surrounding

Napoleon's name, and its succinct statement of his vicissitudes. And in the first of these the patriotic aspirations of Manzoni find expression:

> Non fia loco ove sorgan barriere
> tra l'Italia e l'Italia, mai piú!

> ... o compagni sul letto di morte,
> o fratelli su libero suol.

Manzoni, however, took no part in the actual struggle for independence; and the patriotism here, if unmistakable, is also subdued in tone. We may stop for a moment to contrast Manzoni with Berchet, who though no real poet expressed himself more vigorously in the call to arms, while his commotion for the plight of Italy was shown also in his best poem, the *Romito del Cenisio* (1823), in an atmosphere of slightly rhetorical exaggeration. But what Berchet has upon the surface Manzoni has in depth, and we may take these two poems of his, with the choruses which provided the lyrical element to his two plays, as the height of his achievement as a lyric poet.

Before the plays he wrote, rather unwillingly, since he abhorred controversy, an answer to the protestant Sismondi, in whose *History of the Italian Republics* (1807–18) the decadence of the Church was made the prime cause for the degeneration of Italy. Manzoni's *Osservazioni sulla Morale Cattolica* (1819) does not wriggle on historic counts: the Night of St Bartholomew, for instance, was *notte infame*. But these are the aberrations of men from the Sermon on the Mount: for the sake of which last Manzoni looks to the separation of Church from State, towards freedom of teaching, conscience, speech, and press. His title might have taken us towards de Maistre or Lamennais, but the substance of his arguments shows Manzoni still advancing on his own ground. And after the attempt to widen the canvas to embrace an epoch (as in *Cinque Maggio*), he comes to the historical play as offering the right opportunity for this. *Il Conte di Carmagnola* (1820) he worked on from 1816 to 1819, and the dates reveal the identity of inspiration with his lyrics. To this he adds the revolt against the conventions, with Goethe and Schiller, and Shakespeare's conception of tragic grief, as the new canon; while the unities are nothing but a target for attack, in the preface, or in his *Lettre à M. Chauvet*. Carmagnola is a fifteenth-century *condottiere*, seen through Manzonian spectacles, that is, idealized, to form the tragedy of a noble and innocent character, undone in a world of ignobility, and ending with a Shakespearian reminiscence, of the renunciatory mood of Richard II: so that Carmagnola in his downfall offers to his family the spectacle of Christian resignation. More Manzoni, in short, than history; and this repeats itself in *Adelchi*, despite the long study which produced a *Discorso sopra alcuni punti della storia longobardica in Italia*. In spite of, or rather, because of, this subjectivism *Adelchi* is better than its predecessor. Here we have gone further back in time, with Charlemagne's excursion against the Lombard King, and the tragedy of Italy exposed to the harsh winds of history as the essence of the subject. Under the disappointment of the rebuffs of 1821, when liberal hopes seemed permanently blunted, Manzoni writes in *Adelchi* as if there is no hope of a just settlement in this world, so that all hope must be transferred to the next one. The Christian resignation of Carmagnola is heightened with Adelchi, the character into whom – against all historical possibility – Manzoni projects himself, *l'alto infelice*, who dreams of a world of peace in one doomed to continual strife. For him, as for his sister Ermengarda, there is the better destiny of failure, for (as Eliot might put it) in a world where success attends brutality to fail is to succeed, a *provida Sventura*; and therefore there is more, and better, to come, but not here on earth. This pessimistic concept covers all human activity, and is a sharper statement of something that could be found in the poem to Carlo Imbonati. Here no room is left for a Dantesque rightness of society on earth: *non resta Che far torto, o patirlo.*

This pessimism, so unlike the sentiments of the ode *Marzo 1821*, is something from which Manzoni recovers in the period (1822–7) which sees the gradual evolution of his novel from *Fermo e Lucia* via *Gli Sposi Promessi* to *I Promessi Sposi*. The scale is again much wider, the subject remains the same: in the words of an early critic, *il grande secolare dolore della sua patria oppressa*. But now the end of martyrdom is not envisaged in a supernatural context, and Renzo sees the hope of justice in this world, and lives through the storm to find a happy marriage waiting. If it had not been for this change of mood it would have proved impossible for Manzoni to lighten his book with all those touches of shrewd humorism which have delighted his readers since the first publication of the greatest novel of the Italian tradition. For though Don Abbondio represents the Church in one of the aspects for which Manzoni, before and after his conversion, has the most distaste, yet his figure is drawn with indulgence, and without revulsion either on Manzoni's part, or ours. And this yeast of a gently playful spirit pervades the book, giving it surprising lightness in spite of its mere bulk. Here the revolution in literature has been consummated, and we have only to think again of Foscolo's *Grazie* to see how we have come to the opposite pole. Here the heroes are two humble peasants, and the world they live in, with its catastrophes, natural and human, scarcity, war, and pestilence, is not outside the range of comprehension of the general army of readers. Sometimes the press of public events, whether in the Bread Riots in Milan, or the incursion of the Imperial army for the War of Monferrat, threatens to swamp the story; and the plague at the end seems over-obliging in picking out the bad for burial, the good for recovery. But in spite of the tenuousness of the actual thread (Renzo and Lucia prevented from marrying on the appointed day, owing to Don Rodrigo's bet to have her and Don Abbondio's inability to stand his ground in face of intimidation from Don Rodrigo's *bravi*, their flight and separation, and after all their reunion in happier circumstances), the *Promessi Sposi* made an immediate appeal to the Italian public on a wider front than had been ever before achieved; and maintained itself through the century as the most popular book in modern Italian literature.

This did not move Manzoni to repeat his triumph. He had

approached his novel with the aims of his historical tragedies: to achieve the indissoluble union of an invented story with a period in its right perspective, studded with historical characters, presented as they had been; just as the invented characters were to be presented as they would have been. Was not the basis in the *grida* which he had read, of 15 October 1627, prescribing penalties for forcing or preventing marriages? And had he not plunged into the folios of Ripamonti's *Storia di Milano* to reconstruct the period? Were not the main opposing characters, the Cardinal Federigo Borromeo and the Innominato, taken from history? All this did not prevent Manzoni proving, in his *Discorso sul Romanzo Storico*, that the historical novel was a falsificatory hybrid having no right to exist. And Manzoni fell back into a silence which was to last for nearly fifty years. Not quite a silence, for the six years of composition of the *Promessi Sposi* had left him painfully aware of the *questione della lingua*. Born in the north, he had inherited the Lombard dialect, and thrust in contact mostly with French culture, he had struggled to find the right expression for his prose. Dissatisfied with the result, he went to Florence, in whose spoken language he convinced himself the norm for Italian usage should be found. Hence the *risciacquatura*, in a typically whimsical phrase, which ended finally with the definitive form of the *Promessi Sposi* in 1842. After which he only emerged in his old age to do battle in the same cause of linguistic unity. And the patriotic theme? The novel deals with events in Lombardy in the first half of the seventeenth century, when Spanish Viceroys in Milan governed in their own interests, without thought or comprehension for the common people. And the *Promessi Sposi* offered hope for the underdog. Renzo and Lucia stand both for themselves, and for all Italy oppressed by alien rule; not just that of Spain two hundred years before, but more immediately, that of Austria now. And to all those who waited it offered under a veiled outline the hope of deliverance. Like *Le Mie Prigioni* the *Promessi Sposi* spoke to everyone.

By a neat irony the *Promessi Sposi* were published in a year which saw another book on which its author built great hopes, which yet spoke to very few. This was the *Operette Morali* of Giacomo Leopardi (1798–1837). The good fortune that had smiled on Manzoni's birth was less evident with Giacomo. True, he came of a noble family, but he was born in an unfrequented corner of the Marches, to a father clinging to the vanishing world of eighteenth-century privilege, and threatened personally by the advancing French. Instead of that freedom of movement which launched Manzoni to Paris, and set him reading the modern literature of Europe, Giacomo was condemned to remain in Recanati, where his pabulum was the huge, and antiquated, library which his father Count Monaldo had put together out of the suppression of the local convents. With his prodigious talent Giacomo eats up what is set so copiously before him, looks as a child to fame as a philologist, and outstrips on the path to erudition not only the reeds whom his father finds as tutor, or his father himself, but even correspondents like Angelo Mai (soon to be Librarian of the Vatican). In these aspirations to fame his father eggs him on; and Giacomo's confidence survives his conversion (in a literary way of speaking) from philology to love of literature (1816–17). Instead of *studi grossi*, with grammars, Greek and Hebrew dictionaries, the scattered fragments of forgotten rhetoricians, Leopardi gives his enthusiasm to Virgil and to other authors; and follows his friend Giordani in seeing Greek as closer than Latin to Italian style, and out of this sees it as something to be turned to service in the regeneration of Italian poetry. Out of this dark corner comes the cry for *libri veramente nazionali*: a surprising desideratum in a boy till then immersed in erudite research. But it shows that Leopardi had sensed the *Zeitgeist* as much as Berchet or Manzoni, and he too will look to a sort of literature that has a wide appeal, and speaks a simple language. Where his *Canti* begin, with patriotic *canzoni* inspired by Foscolo and the sense of a poetic mission, Leopardi is still a little opaque, a little tied to earlier patterns of expression. But we have only to turn to the corresponding poems, the *Oda a Bonaparte*, the *Trionfo della Libertà*, to feel the strength of Leopardi's opening poetry. And if one perseveres one will feel after the initial difficulties the genuine pulse of Leopardi beating in *All'Italia*.

The opening poems of the *Canti* had been preceded by a poem Leopardi left out, *L'Appressamento della Morte* (1816). Here his apparent allegiance is to the orthodoxy of which his mother Adelaide was the most stalwart champion. And the year before in the *Orazione agli Italiani* and the *Saggio sopra gli errori popolari degli antichi* the family environment triumphs palpably. Here the sweet ways of legitimacy contrast with the abhorrent conduct of the French, or the fount of Truth lights up the aberrations of antiquity. But the illness which brings him to death's door, the prelude to a half-life for the rest of his career, tests and detaches Leopardi. He would have met it in the spirit of Adelaide, who saw safety in short-circuiting the dangers of the world, by early death, by un-attractive looks. If the next world is the everlasting treat, then hastening to it is no hardship. For four cantos Leopardi keeps this Christian countenance; but in the fifth his dis-appointment breaks out: all he had hoped of life cancelled before tasted. That is surprisingly different from the advertised purpose of the poem: but from now on he will retain the logical extremism of Adelaide's view of Christianity, to recoil from it. Henceforth he looks to this world only, and all the family dreams of a Giacomo using his prodigious talents in the service of the Church fade before the obstinate aversion of Leopardi's eyes.

The bitterness of this experience tinges even the ardour of Leopardi's patriotic poetry, and the third poem, *Ad Angelo Mai*, introduces us to the depths of his despair:

> Il certo e solo
> Veder che tutto è vano altro che il duolo.

Here all the Foscolian premonitions have come down to the ground floor of life, and affect us as substantial statements. This negative side will be soon enshrined in the *Operette Morali*, written in a period of poetic silence. In these satirical dialogues – which have at their best, as in the *Cantico del Gallo Silvestre* or the *Dialogo di un Venditore d'Almanacchi*, a supreme and desolating eloquence – we find the necessary unhappiness of human beings, with the stoic remedy of indifference. Man as he is in Nature is microscopic, and uncatered for. The larger part of his living is a shrivelling to death, and Nature herself is inexorably indifferent and unaware, of his presence as of his needs. And to this Leopardi adds the ultimatum of the *Zibaldone*, the commonplace book which could be franker than his published works: 'The human race, which has believed and will believe so many silly things, will never believe either that it knows nothing, or that it is nothing, or that it has nothing to hope for after death.' Here is the maximum expression of Leopardi's nihilism. Yet paradoxically it is not the truth, or not the whole truth, for Leopardi; and it has happened not infrequently in the European tradition that the most positive of writers have proved negative, and that the most negative may prove, as Leopardi, unexpectedly positive. Have we not seen all Adelaide's vision vanish, and Leopardi cling to what he hoped of this world? The positive poles of Leopardi are all in this world, and they are won not by the production of a *deus ex machina* to turn wrong into right against appearances, but by the revaluation of man as the protagonist of the tragedy.

It is here that, unconsciously in part, a whole side of Leopardi's explicit statements drops away. For it should follow, if all is *nulla*, and man a microscopic particle of this *solido nulla*, that there is no interest, or importance, to attach to his sentiments. And, logically enough, Leopardi, seeing sentience as suffering, demands of Fate to sink through the strata of sentient beings to the lowest margin. Yet this does not happen, and Leopardi's choice is the opposite of what he said. It is here that we can see the continuation of that spirit which, out of the benightedness of Recanati, looked to fame, or to the renewal of Italian literature. In spite of all the suffering which nails him down, Leopardi keeps his native superiority of spirit, and after he has spoken, often, of the end of his capacity to feel, he can still without a sense of any contradiction return to the essential note. Witness the scorn for ignobility in *Il Pensiero Dominante*, and the cry which follows it, *Maggior mi sento*. In reality, Leopardi's *Canti* are built, like Petrarch's *Rime*, on a set of contradictions; which here, as there, do not destroy, but are proof positive of vitality. Only, we may be better able to see that negative and positive are equally strong within his poetry. I say, equally, and it is a concession to that old tradition which sees him as the poet of *noia* and *nulla*; but it is clear as we read the *Canti* that the positives transcend the negatives. And it is as clear elsewhere. Leopardi looks back over a century and a half of nullity (akin to that of Spain); the breath of his criticism falls scornfully on a Bembo or a Monti; and one who longs for a culture which is live and national cannot be moving from a negative set of principles. Where Foscolo saw the supreme consolation in words, Leopardi looks to *activity* and *vitality*; and even in the desolate spaces of the *Operette Morali* the accent falls insistently on an unexpected side. We who have seen the development of the machine to a point Leopardi could not have dreamt of may still relish his satire of the machinists, with the demand for a steam-robot (or shall we say, an electronic one?) 'atto e ordinato a fare opere virtuose e magnanime'. The more ambitious the machine, the less it will fulfil so simple a condition. But why did Leopardi, crying for insentience, want magnanimity? The answer is conspicuous for those who read the underlines, that side of Leopardi which the nineteenth century found it hard to see: no one more than he stands champion and representative of the magnanimity of man.

If this transpires through the *Operette*, and in the *Zibaldone*, it is self-evident that it must pervade, and sweeten, all his poetry in the *Canti*. Here we have seen the magnanimous impulse which dictates the first poems. As this recedes, and Leopardi is faced with the stark issues, and with a universal tragedy which he is too honest, and too great, to refuse to see, he looks first to the appearance of the world: to this vast machine with its ineffable grandeur, the setting which seems to promise so much to man. Nature, as a spectacle, is something which Leopardi sees in the most tender terms: for a time, indeed, it can seem to him, as to Rousseau, that Nature had provided the rights and man the wrongs. But that fancy does not cheat Leopardi long, and Nature loses her crown of laudatory adjectives, to become the *brutto Poter* which rules to general hurt. But this must not blind us to the fact that Nature, in her other guise of appearances, remains to the end fair and beguiling. Leopardi's poetry is responsive throughout to the beauty of the quiet scene: the open vowels, the unobtrusive consonants, give their flavour to the scene itself, prepare us for that most caressing of all Leopardian touches,

> Sí dolce, sí gradita
> Quand è, com'or, la vita?

On this side there is something whose only relation to the often-quoted *nulla, noia*, is that of opposite. The one note throws the other into stronger salience; and if we listen, though advertisement, or the fierce resentments of youth, may make us first pay heed to the desperate utterances, it may well be the second note which lingers with us, and seems the authentic component of Leopardi's poetry. Alongside the sweetness, the magnanimity; and for those who do not wish to limit poetry to a verbal music, or the mere provision of pictorial contemplation, *La Ginestra* will assert again the claims of man; while the Leopardian Social Contract not only allows the positives, but credits them to man alone. In his system it is inevitable that man should appear at last, innocent as the broom, creative of what magnanimous sentiments there are. The negatives are burnt out, or thrown away, before the strongest affirmations made for man. It is these pulses, beating unabated through the *Canti*, that make them the most vital poetry of nineteenth-century Europe; while Leopardi offers, in the *Canti*, in the *Operette*, and in the *Zibaldone*, the vital touchstones for our own problems and attitudes in a world which has exaggerated the outlines of the one he knew.

The course of Leopardi's poetry is uphill, that of his life implacably descending. From Recanati he had his first brief respite in the winter of 1822–3, in his uncle's house at Rome. Here he looked for the recognition which eluded him at

Recanati, only to find that Roman antiquarianism was different from the sort he had cast off, and now needed to resurrect in order to have some countenance. The petty world of papal Rome offered no hope of employment, except based upon conformity, and made him almost welcome return to his 'bel Recanati'. Release came unexpectedly, in the offer of hackwork from the Milanese publisher, A. F. Stella, and Giacomo set out, rejoicing in freedom at the moment of submitting to servitude. When his powers succumbed, he went back to Recanati as to an endless night. Once more this was broken, by monetary assistance from the 'friends of Tuscany', as welcome as the dawn of day after the polar night. But this also failed, and Leopardi was left to the mercies of Antonio and Paolina Ranieri, who cared for his last years in Naples. For Recanati Leopardi had the bitterest aversion, and the tenderest affection, so that it dominates his poetry. Neither Florence, which he admired as mother of civilized living, nor Pisa, where in 1828 he found resurgence of health and feeling, find entry in the *Canti*. But *La Ginestra* sets a Leopardian seal on Naples and Vesuvius. Of his activity I have chronicled only the most significant parts. Despite the briefness of the *Canti*, and in the tragic briefness of his health, and life, his is a heroically productive career. To the not small corpus of the philological works we have to add the *Paralipomeni della Batracomiomachia*, a satirical poem in which there is more life, and more generosity, than has been generally admitted. And alongside his other work we have from Leopardi one of the richest *epistolari*. Indeed, if we leave Petrarch on one side (his letters all in Latin), there is no other *epistolario* of comparable richness in the range of Italian letters; and none, of course, charged with the same eloquence of pathos.

While Manzoni and Leopardi transcend the labels and the fashions it was natural for others to be bound by them. Who more representative of this than Manzoni's friend, Tommaso Grossi (1790–1853)? Grossi is one of the first practitioners of Romanticism, to which his little volume of *Novelle Romantiche* bears open witness. The less slight of these verse *novelle*, *Ildegonda* (1820), makes unstinted use of all the apparatus of the new dispensation. Ildegonda, uncompliant with her father's demand for instant marriage, is doomed to a nunnery, and we plunge into the atmosphere of the cell, the dungeon, the minstrel singing without, insidious traps, hair-shirts, and delirium. The climax comes with Ildegonda, half-dead, half-mad, pursued by scratching nuns down subterranean holes. This is of course, for us, a cautionary tale, not Grossi's best: nor is his epic, *I Lombardi alla Prima Crociata* (1826), mixing both Scott and Tasso without achieving a tone of its own. But under the impress of Manzoni Grossi wrote his most popular work, the historical novel *Marco Visconti* (1834). To get the atmosphere Grossi steeped himself in Muratori, but though he tried the fourteenth century, it is a Manzonian plot that comes to view, one that has long since failed to convince, as history, or novel. We might take it as a warning to all the tribe, with its mingling of the two masters, the Scott of *Ivanhoe* and Manzoni. But to it we must add some names. The first is Massimo D'Azeglio (1798–1866), who sees his novels as part of the political struggle. Thus in *Ettore Fieramosca* (1833) his intent is to arouse against the foreigner, in theme (with the challenge, and victory, of Barletta, of 1503), and in its treatment. More scrupulous in its handling of history is his second novel, *Niccolò de'Lapi* (1841), built round the heroic defence of Florence in the siege of 1530. Akin to *Ettore Fieramosca*, but vastly superior to it, this also has its lesson: the need for unity, the warning against faction. And superior to both, perhaps, are the memoirs published posthumously in 1867, though in *I Miei Ricordi* the continual, conscious, moralization chills the narrative.

For Tommaso Grossi, close friend of Manzoni, and D'Azeglio, Manzoni's son-in-law, it was right to steal space to put once-popular books on record. We may give scanter shrift to others, as Cesare Cantú (1804–95), who contributed *Margherita Pusterla* (1838) to the tribe of historical novels; or F. D. Guerrazzi (1804–73), whose turbulent spirit was expressed in a dozen novels where *amor patrio* found violent vent, and garbled history was often more than story. The best perhaps is the *Assedio di Firenze* (1836), with the same background as *Niccolò de' Lapi*. But the political energies of the Risorgimento are better expressed in works that are purely political in scope: as with D'Azeglio in the *Ultimi Casi di Romagna* (1846) or Cesare Balbo in *Le Speranze d'Italia* (1844); and in especial, with the work of Mazzini and Gioberti. Vincenzo Gioberti (1801–52), a priest fired with liberal dreams, produced in 1843 one of the inspiring books of the century, the *Primato Morale e Civile degli Italiani*. Its title might have come from Foscolo, its fervour brought a utopia into view, of an Italian Federation under the presidency of the Pope. For Gregory XVI this offered no attraction, but it became the gospel of Pius IX in 1846. But it is of Giuseppe Mazzini (1805–72) that we think specially, as of the one who dedicated himself to the cause of propaganda. Maybe that in spite of the multifarious nature of his writings he does not belong strictly to the history of creative literature. But where his ideas are focused rather than diffused we may admire the austere qualities which made him one of the main forces of his time. And if Italy could have listened more to Mazzini, the Mazzini of the *Doveri dell'Uomo*, the course of her history since might have been clearer.

Who should serve better as a punctuation-mark here than Giuseppe Giusti, whose dates – 1809–50 – leave us poised in mid-century. Giusti had a sense of what he wrote as being ephemeral; and this modesty sounds better than the self-assurance of Guerrazzi. He brings to patriotic poetry a new sense of satirical comicity; he jettisons the consecrated form of satire (which had done duty from Ariosto to Alfieri), and looks to popular forms and metres. Here a racy Tuscan comes back into currency, perhaps a trifle overdone: though Giusti's Tuscan is never a cryptogram like the seventeenth-century *Tancia* of Michelangelo Buonarroti the younger. But Giusti lacked organizing principles, and his poems are mainly negative, with titles like *Dies Irae*, *Delenda Carthago*, which show their burden. Yet he has, what Berchet lacked conspicuously, an edge and a bite, and his satire at its best has kept its savour, as in *L'Incoronazione* or *Lo Stivale*. And at least once alongside the satire there turns up a different note, as in what may well be his finest poem, *Sant' Ambrogio* (1846), where the initial distaste for the Croatian soldiery melts under the impact of their singing, and of Verdi's music, and Giusti finds himself coming involuntarily to think of them as pawns also of a tyranny, so that he can embrace them mentally in a new vision of *Kameradschaft*, which transcends the nationalism of the nineteenth century. In the normal way Giusti writes with a sprightly sharpness: in *Sant' Ambrogio* he achieves a commotion of which Manzoni himself might not have been ashamed, and gives a hint which offers, in the unceasing pattern of man's hostility to man, some vision for the future.

CHAPTER 13

From Carducci to D'Annunzio

As an appendix to the patriotic poetry of Berchet it is right to recall two poets, and two poems: Goffredo Mameli, who died in the defence of Rome in 1849, wrote the hymn *Fratelli d'Italia* which fired the minds of those who took part in the last struggles. The other poem is the *Spigolatrice di Sapri* of Luigi Mercantini (1821–72), commemorating one of the most pathetic episodes that lie on the hard path to Garibaldi's liberation of the south from the dead clutches of the Bourbons. And Mercantini also added a fighting line for the Garibaldians in 1859 and 1860. But in the mid-century there are not lacking others who wrote copiously, and scored a success with their contemporaries which time cannot maintain. Italy also has her Bérangers. Chief of these is Giovanni Prati (1815–84), one of the most abundant, and most applauded, romantic poets. *Fieno e fiori*, said Manzoni of him, and though he ranged through all the forms of verse (except the theatre) it was the lyric which flowed most naturally, and least revealed his lack of intellectual powers. In *Edmenegarda* (1841), his first success, he had fused Byron with Lamartine. Later in *Armando* (1866), a long poem, he intended to philosophize, and it is significant that from it only one inserted lyric has survived as an anthology-piece, the *Canto d'Igea*, with its burden that health and thought are opposites. Then the collections of his lyrics, *Psiche* (1876) and *Iside* (1878), show his facility and fluency. Carducci later will convince himself that a golden book can be made, selected out of Prati's poetry, and Croce find instead matter for ten poets without the work of one: with which ambiguous statement it may be best to leave him.

His competitor was Aleardo Aleardi (1812–78), he also the conventional figure – poet, romantic, patriot; and with two equal loves, for woman and for *patria*, so that he set down his sorrow from betrayals by the first and for the misfortunes of the second. Rather than lyric effusion, his line is that of historical evocation, looking vaguely back to the *Sepolcri* and faintly forward to Carducci. With him feeling is diluted too much in particulars; though he is less careless than Prati, and has more substance, his writing is marred by his tendency to lengthy circumlocution, and by the fixity of the pose adopted. With Aleardi and Prati we may put two who might not relish juxtaposition. First, Giacomo Zanella (1820–89), priest and professor, finally Rector of the University of Padua, who won fame in 1868 with the publication of his verse in volume form; and who looked to the new problems – politics, social questions, industry, applied science, materialism, and positivism – which Prati had meant to tackle in *Armando*. Zanella saw the conflict between the new science and the old religion, and was anxious to deny the worst of darwinism while praising the illuminating power of science. Part of his success was due to the pleasure of finding liberal sentiments in one who might have been obscurantist; part came from the practised skill of a professional latinist who could turn easily accessible ideas to acceptable verse. Perhaps his best poem is *Sopra una Conchiglia Fossile*, admitting man as a newcomer to this world with its recession into remote timelessness, but as its heir, and with a vast, if vague, future of progress still to come. It is this atmosphere of confidence in Man's divine destiny which makes juxtaposition with Emilio Praga (1839–75) piquant. For Praga from the first (his poetry collected as *Tavolozza*, 1862; *Penombre*, 1864; *Fiabe e Leggende*, 1867) aspires to draw upon himself the odium accruing to a wilful imitator of Baudelaire. Here is the macabre and the sensual (accompanied, for good measure, by personal excesses in women, absinthe, blasphemy). But Praga had too much the temperament of an Edmondo de Amicis, with its bourgeois interest in little things, to be wholly convincing in the role which he adopted; and this mixture of the spirit of the *Fleurs du Mal* with the lachrymosity of *Cuore* is less a bogy than a bore.

It is not only in verse that we can find the middle of the

century copious. Giuseppe Rovani (1818–74) derives in intention from Manzoni, and left as his monument a work whose title shows how he wished to extend and codify. *I Cento Anni* (1859–64) is founded on the desire for moral and political reflections, allied to educative intentions; but with an inevitably tenuous continuating thread it aspires to cover the whole pattern of society from 1749 to 1848. Is his character a tenor? – then the picture of Milan is extended through the realm of opera and music. Is he in love with a blue-stocking? – so we must pass to scientific interests and female education in the eighteenth century. As the book proceeds, in pages and in time, the narrative thread grows thinner; and in the end its mere bulk overwhelms the reader. Contrasting with Rovani, as Praga with Zanella, is Ippolito Nievo (1831–61), whose *Confessioni di un Ottuagenario* (published posthumously in 1867) belongs to the same lapse of time. In intention also he is not far removed, wishing to depict, as Rovani Lombardy, the state of Venice from the eighteenth century into the Risorgimento. But he chose a more natural method, using his own childhood in Friuli as the basis. Hence his canvas is restricted, but more genuine, and the first quarter of his work, portraying the decaying feudalism of Friuli, shown in the Conte di Fratta and his medieval castle, seen from the turnspit's corner, has a liveliness which has not evaporated. As the book proceeds, its inherent defects show more clearly. Carlino, who had observed the castle life, with La Pisana, who loves and torments him though the book, is involved in all the happenings of the nineteenth century. The link grows thinner and more arbitrary, and the reader is advised to limit appetite to the first 300 pages. We may think of Nievo thus as a bridge towards the memoirs proper, leading us away from Manzoni, and to the *Ricordanze della mia vita* of Luigi Settembrini (1813–77), which set a brand upon the Bourbons of Naples like that of Pellico upon the Austrian tyranny. And from the pseudo-history of Rovani and Nievo we may turn with relief to one who built his poetry quite largely on a sense of history, and who stands as the most substantial figure of the second half of the century.

Giosuè Carducci (1835–1907) comes as a reactionary against that *épanchement* of romantic poetry which had begun in France with Lamartine. The preface to the *Odi Barbare* speaks vigorously, and typically, and in it the essentially combative nature of Carducci is well seen. But in this turning back towards a more difficult expression, it is well to be clear that there is nothing of the reactionary about him. He is fiercely Mazzinian in his republicanism, not only anticlerical, but also anti-Christian; anti-romantic more by pugnacity than by rejection of the basic strands or atmosphere of the early nineteenth century. For Carducci, with his patriotic zeal, his sense of history as the stuff and content of lyric poetry, continues rather than refutes tradition. And his ambition, to be ITALICO VATE A LA NUOVA ETADE, makes him the heir of Alfieri, of Foscolo and Leopardi. Not, however, of the Leopardi of the Idylls: for Carducci has lost the impulse towards the spontaneous as the best. That preface to the *Odi Barbare* explains partly why, and Carducci spurs himself up the slopes of Parnassus with a banner on which is writ *Excelsior*. That has meant loss as well as gain; and the charge was early brought that he was too erudite, the professor rather than the poet. This is no light charge, and we all know how inferior the one article is to the other. As well, Carducci by the mere bristles to his brush raised enemies. It is a tribute to the strength of his achievement that from the time of the *Odi Barbare* he became almost officially *the* poet of modern Italy.

Carducci's *Juvenilia* date from 1850–60, his last verse collection was the *Rime e Ritmi* of 1898; and in between an incessant activity culminates in the *Odi Barbare* (1877–89). His childhood battles were built on Roman history and on the French Revoltuion, and when his father punished him by confinement with improving books (including Manzoni's *Morale Cattolica*) he turned on these a Catilinarian hate. And at the Scuola Normale of Pisa he burst out on a tormentor, reciting outside the door the *Natale* of Manzoni, with a fierce cry of *Viva Giove! abbasso il suo successore!* This revulsion echoes in the *Inno a Satana* of 1863. The title comes from

Baudelaire, but the poem is outside the line of Baudelaire or Praga, and Carducci's Satan stands for the sunshine of life in opposition to the must of asceticism. Amongst the symbols recurrent in his poetry are the train and the fulling-mill; and both stand graphically for adherence to a world of activity. Meanwhile, the *Juvenilia*, starting with a watchword of classicism, were largely imitative: their strength in what they avoided, and in precision as an aim replacing vagueness. Gradually the anger of Carducci at the conditions of his times comes uppermost, as the *Levia Gravia* (1861–71) lead on to the *Giambi ed Epodi* (1867–72). Here the metres of satire are the vehicle for an overflowing indignation, as in the *Meminisse horret* which expresses his feelings after the humiliation of Garibaldi at Mentana; or we have his abhorrence of the papal condemnation of Monti and Tognetti. The *Giambi ed Epodi* are immeasurably stronger than the *Juvenilia*, but political poetry has its limitations, and Carducci is now ready to transcend it. Does not the *Canto dell'Amore*, starting in Perugia with memories of the papal fortress, end with commiseration for the old Pope, now an unhappy prisoner in the Vatican? In the *Rime Nuove* (1861–87) Carducci comes to personal themes, with nostalgia for his childhood in the Versilia, or affection for his kin. And with the greater serenity of age Carducci turns from the irritants to what is positive for him, giving expression to his admiration for the classical world of Greece and Rome.

It was natural, even because of the title, that this should fill the *Odi Barbare*. Here Carducci abandons rhyme, and combines the existing verse-forms to imitate classic metres – the *barbarous* of the title being a judgement on this hybrid. But this new world of mainly Sapphics and Alcaics is classical in its intention, following the prelude which had come with *Primavere elleniche*. Out of that evocation of Sicily and Theocritus there comes the exclamation to the undying gods of Greece. Frozen into the purity of their marble at the approach of Christ, their youth still lives in poetry. Here the polemic still stays latent, yet we have shifted resolutely to a new surge of welcome: *Datemi i marmi e i carmi!* It was the sarcastic note of Heine which sounded in the *Giambi*, but here we have August von Platen as an epigraph.

Certainly, the author is the same, and Carducci too robust ever to give up polemic. *In una Chiesa Gotica* is from the same hand as the *Inno a Satana*. If anything, the attack on individuals has turned to a judgement on institutions. We may take the noble *Fonti di Clitumno* as a pattern. Here is the thesis which Carducci has in common with Foscolo, the sanity of classical thought and religion opposed to the servility of Christian asceticism. The pure fount with its one surviving temple sends him ranging back through history, to the mingling of races which form Italy, mother of corn and wine and laws, now stirring back to life as the train passes, replacing with a new activity the stagnation of papal Rome. And nothing is more typical of Carducci than this use of history, which gives an unforgettably different surface to his various poems. Here *Miramar* and *Napoleone Eugenio* are our examples, with a similar burden, but a wholly separate background. For Carducci poetry is still structural, and history is its nurse: it is only with his successors that we shall find poetry losing content and structure to express mood and feeling only. In this historical poetry, in the feeling for Nature and its pulsating life, and in the spectacle of Italy, lies the best poetry of the *Odi Barbare*. Nor should we be surprised to see a romantic note creeping in. Already in the *Rime Nuove* Carducci dreamt of what never was, and several pieces here echo this mood of the blue lagoon, as notably *Fantasia* and *Percy Bysshe Shelley*: in which last the Carducci of duty, work, reward in natural pleasures takes us towards something different:

> L'ora presente è in vano, non fa che percuotere e fugge;
> sol nel passato è il bello, sol ne la morte è il vero;

which might take us back to Foscolo and *Le Grazie*. There remain the *Rime e Ritmi*; and here one poem must come first, the *Chiesa di Polenta*. For stern as Carducci's attitudes were, they were modified, and he mollified, with advancing years.

Had he not accepted the House of Savoy in the regal presence of Queen Margherita at Bologna? And now the feudal age has gone, the robber-baron's castle frowns no longer, the *util plebe* has come into its own. In this mood (foreshadowed by the *Canto dell' Amore*) Carducci can feel piety towards the church where Dante may have knelt. He melts sufficiently to feel the music of the Ave Maria over the valley: it is the nearest that he comes to Christian sentiments. In spite of this mellowing, the *Rime e Ritmi* marks a hardening of his formulas, leading to a density of historical allusion which defeats itself. Thus poems like *La Città di Ferrara* are a last exaggeration of his mannerisms, the final reminder that he was professor as well as poet. His Chair of Italian Literature at Bologna (1860–1904) was the main incident of his life, and from it flowed continual work in illustration and exploration, especially of early Italian literature. His criticism ranges over the whole field, his work as editor is of prime importance; but he lacked the general ideas which gave crucial importance to the critical essays, and the *History of Italian Literature*, of Francesco De Sanctis (1818–83); and though Carducci disliked De Sanctis it is noticeable that sometimes (as for Ariosto or the *Decameron*) he borrowed his general concepts from the latter. Nor was De Sanctis's impact limited to Carducci: the pioneer of literary criticism, his ideas held the field unchallenged, though at times exaggerated to the point of distortion. For him the criticism of literature was a criticism of life, and since he saw his task as educator in the sense of moral renewal he interpreted the past in terms of the needs of the present. With De Sanctis it is the general judgement that is important, not the insistence on particulars; and Carducci, whose forte was particulars, thought of him as insufficiently scholarly. Doubtless clear general judgements were a novelty, and a gain; but where it was a wrong judgement, his very authority perpetuated a false point of view. Nowhere is this more apparent than with the Renascence, where De Sanctis started on the wrong foot, and got the general answer wrong. But after automatic following of his line (often given sanction by the criticism of Benedetto

Croce) there has come caution, and reaction. Carducci's criticism did not share in this prestige, and has sunk back to be the prose lining to his poetry.

Perhaps it is not really legitimate in a history of literature to give more than a moment's notice to Edmondo De Amicis (1846–1908); and it is certainly unkind to pin him next to Carducci. Yet he too wished to contribute to the unification of Italy, even if he found it hard to write a book which was all in one piece. His quality can be seen in *La Vita Militare* (1868), sketches of the new barrack-world, with ideas and pictures that all could understand. *Descrittore meraviglioso delle cose piccole*, with an abundance of easy sentimentality which led to popularity in every sense of the word. This is still true of *Cuore* (1886), based on the schooldays of his own two boys, and following Enrico Bottini through the whole school year, punctuated by stories which incite visibly to civic pride and juvenile heroism. In *Cuore* there is a whole set of actors who have the flavour of their time, and De Amicis's narrative is lively and efficacious. But over the book there hangs an odour of moral blackmail, with a harrowing of the feelings carried to unfeeling lengths, or a civic well-meaningness which grows priggish in its unction. And in the longest story, *Dagli Apennini alle Andi*, the agony is protracted more than with the death of Little Nell, only to end at long last with the mother's despairing shriek under the operator's knife, and the echoing shriek of Marco, who thinks her dead. And if the reader had not seen this tableau coming from the beginning of the fifty pages of the story he must have been more than usually short-sighted. Naturally, De Amicis went forward steadily with a growing list of books, often of travel-sketches, which have all the useful virtues of small change.

It is elsewhere that the weight lies, and with Verga we meet for the first time a novelist whose work stands comparison with Manzoni. Verga is the most substantial of the Italian *veristi*, but by his side is one who urged him in that direction. This is Luigi Capuana (1839–1915), a fellow-Sicilian, aware of the same world of rural backwardness. Capuana believed in realism as something essentially of his time, part of art's duty to submit to all the exigencies *del metodo positivo*. He demanded the impersonality of the writer, starting from human documents to reconstruct the psychological process that has taken place: as a doctor examining a patient to find out his disease from his symptoms. So Capuana evolves a 'realism' of his own, quite distinct from that of Verga. Here psychology and pathology make intrusion into literature for a clinical case-study which leaves ample room for an imaginative subjectivism. Capuana wished to see himself as the Dr Follini of his first novel *Giacinta* (1879), studying the heroine with the 'cold curiosity' of a scientist engaged on a *Fisiologia e Patologia delle Passioni*; and into the pot come the occult world, spiritualism and telepathy, elements we shall find in Fogazzaro. From this, via other books whose titles tell their story (*La Sfinge*, 1897; *Le Appassionate*, 1893), Capuana came to his best book, *Il Marchese di Roccaverdina* (1901). Here the study of social conditions in Sicily is impressive, with the detailed notation of the way the powerful landowner maintains himself. The pity is that this is the beginning, not the core of the book. Had it been written thirty years later it would have been a detective novel; as it is, the unsolved homicide (the Marchese's agent Rocco Criscione shot dead) leads to a psychological case which links this back with Capuana's earlier work more than with Verga.

With De Amicis we find the striving after unity, with Verga there comes the corollary which is near to its defeat. The old unified tradition of Italian literature is now not so much broken as denied. It is a reminder that the new Italy of the Risorgimento was the heir to the misrule of Bourbons and the old Papal State, with that *problema del mezzogiorno*, more than to the culture of the Renascence. After the facile idealism of one type of romanticism art now turns to look at brutal facts, at men below the level where ideals can subsist. From the upper we come to the lower classes, to a bourgeoisie with no concern for more than money, to peasants with the bleakest lot, to the dregs of society. Now we shall see the world of the peasant without Manzoni's rosier tinting: something harsh, yet maybe more acceptable, because more genuine.

Giovanni Verga (1840–1922) began in a wild and passionate mood, an addict to the French *scapigliatura* of the mid-century. His early novels have a common theme: sharp sensual appetite consumed in inner contrasts, or in the clash with social conditions outside. The first title, *Una Peccatrice* (1866), gives the flavour for all, and Pietro's words, 'Io amo nella donna i velluti, il profumo, la mezza luce, il lusso ... tutto ciò che seduce ed addormenta', put us at the opposite pole to *Nedda*. Of these early novels *Eva* (1873) was one of the most read, and in spite of the artificiality of the ingredients, one of the best handled; while in *La Storia di una Capinera* (1871) he achieved the most romanticized version of Diderot's *La Religieuse*. This story of the unwanted stepchild, destined to the convent, falling shyly in love (known only as sin), but taking the veil, and ending in pathetic death, is coherent and affecting, if a little overheightened for our taste. It is perhaps the easiest narrative work of Verga, and we have only to compare it with Grossi's *Ildegonda* to see that it has considerable virtues of sobriety that we might not have suspected if we looked at it only by itself.

But it is, of course, the mature Verga who matters; and of all his earlier production he wrote the epitaph, 'Ero falso nell'arte com'ero fuori del vero nella vita.' In 1874 he wrote, alongside his erotic novels, a *bozzetto siciliano*, a sketch of Sicilian life, *Nedda*. Here there are few details: peasants waiting for the evening *minestra*, then to lie huddled, waiting for dawn and hiring. Among them Nedda, who has left a distant village and a sick mother to scrape a little money. She returns to find her mother dead, her lot a little easier thereby. She loves, and gives herself, but her lover has malaria, persists at work, falls from a tree, and dies. It is more difficult to earn now she is pregnant, and she sells what she had put together for the marriage which had not come. A child is born she cannot feed, which wastes and dies, and Nedda blesses the dead who no longer suffer. Here is a stamp which we shall still find unmistakable in some of Pirandello's pictures from Sicily, in the *Novelle per un Anno*; and here the course is set for Verga's realism, for all his mature production, while we can sense the motto which he put to the series of novels he intended, *I Vinti*. And in this an abiding strand is to be seen, for are not Enrico Lanti in *Eva* or the nun of *La Storia di una Capinera* also conquered by life? It is a reminder, as with Flaubert, who also desired impersonality, that the objectivity of the historian is not quite in Verga's grasp.

Indeed, it may be argued that the recurrence of catastrophe within *I Malavoglia* (1881) is part of Verga's subjectivism, something that makes us wish at times for the patient economic analysis of a Balzac: and after all, this is part of the romantic streak, and will take us downwards till with Zola we look on the most abject side of life; as if nothing that was not bad is real. Here this fisher-family at Aci-Trezza start with a rough cohesion (the fingers of a hand, with the hierarchy which this implies), with a hard life, but an independent means of livelihood in the fishing-smack *Provvidenza*, and a rude plenty in the farmyard. Then one by one the hammer-blows of fate fall on them, shaking the structure of the family, ousting them from the 'casa del nespolo'; till gradually, and at the end, Alessi manages to buy back the house, but this is a new venture. In this series of calamities the emphasis might fall more strongly on zio Crocefisso, the usurer who exerts a stranglehold once the *Provvidenza* has been wrecked, and its unpaid-for cargo lost. But in Verga's handling there is no exposition from outside, with not so much a narration as an illustration by comment and dialogue from the participants, and the full light plays on the members of the Malavoglia family, while a crucial character like zio Crocefisso remains in the half-light. But in this elemental world the book acquires an epic quality, as far removed from Manzoni as Homer is from Ariosto.

The sister-work is *Mastro Don Gesualdo* (1889), both more ambitious, and less successful. Here the two prefixes sum up the life-span of Gesualdo, from bricklayer to the noble particle. He is a type which Verga studied in the *novelle*, the peasant who toils unremittingly to build up a patrimony, and who takes us over a wider social arc than *I Malavoglia*. His wife, the last consumptive daughter of a noble family (who could not marry the young man she loved), gives him one daughter (who may not be his own), whom he educates expensively at Palermo, whence she returns with a distaste for her father. She loves a penniless young man, and is married to a Duke, whose debts and *train de vie* eat up Gesualdo's money. And to the *palazzo* with its bristling ceremonial Gesualdo comes to die, relegated to an attic, while the ducal agent waits to inventory his estate. This is a situation worthy of Balzac; but the real life is in the lower reaches, in the relatives who sponge on Gesualdo and who pursue him, in the world which he dominates, rather than in that to which he climbs. Here length has dissipated some of the concentration of the earlier book. It is because of this that the short stories of Verga are more satisfactory: born of the mood of *Nedda* they have a unity and a simplicity of statement which adds to their effect. *Vita dei Campi* (1880), *Novelle Rusticane* (1883), take us into a world in which there is no sympathy, no neighbourly charity, no margin of life for any but those born *galantuomini*, or who give their whole life to build up a position, like the Mazzarò of *La Roba*, the spiritual kin of Gesualdo, and who curses the coming of death because it will rob him of all he has amassed. Or else we have the throb of primitive passions, as in *Cavalleria Rusticana*, a drama which survived transference from its original *novella* form, and which has carried Verga's name to the world at large. And with *Jeli il Pastore*, *Rosso Malpelo*, or *L'Amante di Gramigna* we feel a genuinely poetic notation of the background of Sicily. Verga's production continues to the end of the century, but without the supreme quality which gives its cachet to the work lying in between *Nedda* and *Mastro Don Gesualdo*.

With Verga and Carducci we feel a clarity and sanity of vision; with Gabriele d'Annunzio (1863–1938), who derives from both of them, we have passed to the sultry decadence of the *fin-de-siècle*. It is no accident that d'Annunzio's lifetime links the Risorgimento to the Fascist era, which ennobled him with an Edizione Nazionale. Born in the primitive Abruzzi, he shares with Verga a consciousness of the lower levels; but this shows in his work, as in the early *Novelle della*

Pescara (1884–6) or in the later plays, *Figlia di Jorio*, *La Fiaccola sotto il Moggio* (1904–5), with deep traces of barbaric atavism. His transfer to Rome covers this substratum with a veneer of elegance, and the background of the Roman centuries becomes the foil to debauchery. To add to this we have him as the man of action. He welcomes the Lybian War of 1912, and champions in 1915 the cause of Italian intervention. In the Great War his was a hero's role (with a first flight over Vienna); and after the war there came Fiume. In the meantime he poured out an unceasing stream of works, in a variety of genres, all highly charged with the same colourful individuality.

The d'Annunzio who first pops up out of the box in 1882, with the youthful verse of *Primo vere*, proclaims his identity unmistakably, and will do nothing later but to deepen and exaggerate the tints. From the date, Carducci is his mentor: to him one poem is dedicated, and in *A l'Etna* Carducci's historical procedure is closely imitated, with the *Fonti di Clitumno* offering the thesis. But already Venus is the keynote of the Prelude, and d'Annunzio springs forward with an appetite for all that can be taken, a desire

> di por le mani audaci e cupide
> su ogni dolce cosa tangibile.

Ready to replace the sanity, and to dissolve the technique, of Carducci there is here fully fashioned the riotous sensuality which is to stamp the hallmark of d'Annunzio over a sprawling *œuvre*. In the early *Novelle* the fascination of the senses, and a cold insistence on all the cruel torments of the flesh with its deformities, holds sway; and in the early verse collections we have the exuberance of physical strength in face of nature, an exultation in muscle and sinew, and the enjoyment of cruel spectacles. Is there not the sonnet of the shipwreck, with the octopi waiting on the seabed, till the twilight wreathes with tentacles and limbs? And other spectacles are savoured in the stories, as in *La Madia*, or *Il Martirio di Giallucca*. Here the analytical processes of realism are twisted to a savage barbarity, a seductive splendour where cruelty and wantonness are equal ingredients. It is a preparation for the orgy and the sadism which is to predominate in d'Annunzio's writing.

The title of his first novel, *Il Piacere* (1889), will hardly come as a surprise; nor will the search of its dannunzian hero, Andrea Sperelli, for *piaceri non mai provati*, or his desire to commit *orribili sacrilegi*. His is a *natura involontaria*, given to the exercise of the most refined sensuality. Naturally, there is a lot of d'Annunzio in Sperelli; but not all is his own work, and French literature, with Murger, the Goncourt brothers, and Zola, had pointed the way, while a close brother is the Fortunio of Gautier, also a connoisseur of horses, statues, pictures, women; and in Paul Bourget there had been already a similar reaction against the prevailing realism, a choice of exceptional subjects for moral anatomy, and an exaggerated claim for psychological study. Andrea Sperelli Conte d'Ugenta stands, like his begetter, above the grey democratic flood; and all d'Annunzio's art is to be a claim for this superiority, a desire for 'eletta cultura, eleganza ed arte'. Amidst the dissipations Andrea Sperelli practises the most difficult types of art. We have only to look over our shoulder to see whence the echo comes:

> Oui, l'œuvre sort plus belle
> D'une forme au travail
> Rebelle,
> Vers, marbre, onyx, émail.

And in the celebrated lines of Gautier we may note that he chose an easy little metre to talk of hardness in. There was a hint of falsity in that gap; and as we read *Il Piacere* the bogus side of this devotion to an *ars difficilior* is clear enough. The genuine Sperelli is another:

Each of these loves brought him to a new degradation; each inebriated him with an evil rapture, without contenting him; each taught him some particular and subtlety of vice still unknown to him. He had in him the seeds of all infections. He corrupted, and was corrupted.

The *facilis descensus* matches ill with the arduous Cult of Beauty; and if it is objected that d'Annunzio was speaking for himself, the answer is the same: d'Annunzio's work is not chastely chiselled to perfection, it is a torrent with the force of a tumultuous current, but with its turgidity and turbidity.

Il Piacere, being the first, is not the best of d'Annunzio's many novels: but it sets an inexorable course, and the heroes that follow are twins to Sperelli, as to d'Annunzio. Even in *Giovanni Episcopo* (1891), which forms an interlude in the Romanzi della Rosa, the spineless Episcopo offers the common programme:

> Ogni uomo alimenta in sé un sogno segreto che non è la bontà e non è l'amore, ma un desiderio sfrenato di piacere e d'egoismo.

Such was the *cursus vitae* of the most gifted, and the most applauded, writer of Italy at the turning of the century. In *L'Innocente* (1892) comes the logical claim, made for Tullio Hermil, but made by d'Annunzio: that of being an *elect*, a *rare* spirit, the rarity of whose sensations ennobled and distinguished all his actions. Nor does d'Annunzio see any oddity in the admission, thirty pages from that proem, that man has in his nature the horrid faculty of enjoying most acutely when he is conscious of hurting the creature from whom he draws enjoyment. 'Perché un germe della tanto esecrata perversione sadica è in ciascun uomo che ama e che desidera?' Where a drop taints, it is unnatural that the cupful makes up the rare, the elect, the *Übermensch*. Yet such is the formula of d'Annunzio, nor has the Russian influence which invaded Europe around 1890 done more than touch a few of his characters on the outside. The cold egoism of Tullio Hermil, given as a return to the boundless devotion of the women round him, makes one of the clearest, and the most revolting, books in the dannunzian list. I say *clear*, because his development as novelist is away from straightforward narrative. In the *Trionfo della Morte* (1894) Giorgio Aurispa (the Tullio Hermil of the piece) sees himself as the egoist-aesthete who likes to feel 'la sostanza della sua vita dissolversi in vapore di sogno'; nor can this happen without beginning to dissolve the structure of the novel. Here is an extension of psychological analysis; and in an occasional excursus, as in that of the festival at the sanctuary of Casalbordino, there is the triumph of d'Annunzio's cruel powers of description. With the *Vergini delle Rocce* action disappears, and then d'Annunzio bursts into flame with *Il Fuoco*, first of the Romanzi del Melograno, the red and flaming fruit (disappointingly seedy when it comes to eating it – I mean, the fruit), which should have been his sincerest novel, as being most his own, and has been judged his falsest – perhaps logically and *because it is* most his own. Here d'Annunzio has idealized himself, under the style of Stellio Effrena, for more than 500 pages: and the shape of what is to come is visible, for Stellio Effrena (how all these names cling to one pattern, emit one odour!) will create the Latin theatre. He has so far to his credit only speeches, impressions, artistic, historical, mythological memoirs. But he is the ARTEFICE IMAGINIFICO, with a daemon inside him. What he proposes for the future is fine tragedies, what he does in the present is to make a fine speech. It is either too little, or too much; and it leaves d'Annunzio as the artist of sensations. From De Amicis (no other!) he received with gratitude the advice to make the dictionary his favourite reading; and Gautier had tried the same trick, and arrived at the same virtuosity. Gautier also was the image-spinner. Out of this attitude come the celebrated descriptive pieces – the snowfall and the roses in *Il Piacere*, the song of the nightingale in *L'Innocente*, the fountain sleeping and reawakened in *Le Vergini delle Rocce*; and as a finale, or a furore, the elaborated descriptions of Venice which form a backcloth for *Il Fuoco*. And though in the *Vergini delle Rocce* the lack of movement stifles the reader, or in *Il Fuoco* the atmosphere seems too charged to be breathable, yet either of these novels is more palatable than *Forse che sì forse che no* (1910), which is the culmination of a tendency. For here we have the open proof of the vulgarity of d'Annunzio's Superman, of the Paolo Tarsis whose perfect friendship for Giulio Cambiaso has been tested in the desert (drinking the stale of horses from the gilded puddle) and in the submarine, and who thrills, in the world of 1910, to the speed and dust of racing motor-cars, and is the owner of the airplane Ardea, which stays aloft and wins the race when all the rest have crashed. Shades of Nietzsche! the Superman a racing motorist! Did not Sir Epicure Mammon know his business better? Here the thirst for action ends in the flying competition; but that is only the one side of the book. On the other we have inevitably the culmination of debauchery. With Paolo Tarsis there is Isabella Inghirami, and they and d'Annunzio are ready to take their revenge on Manzoni, who toned down the love element in the *Promessi Sposi* because there was enough of this dangerous passion in the world to ensure continuation of the species without fomenting it. 'L'amore, l'amore!' sighs Isabella as she abandons herself languidly and avidly, 'Se sapeste come amo l'amore, Paolo.' She has her fill of it by the end of the book, when she is left a crumpled rag; and by her side there is her sister Vana, and the brother Aldo, with that motif of love made piquant by incest which is endemic in d'Annunzio (cf. *L'Innocente* and, in the plays, *La Città Morta*). In this pulling out of all the stops of passion there may be in part an explanation why there is only left for later Italian writers the squalor of theme of Ugo Betti, or the squalor of treatment of Moravia.

With these qualities as artist it is natural that most praise should tend to go to d'Annunzio's poetry, to the *Laudi* (1903–12) and specially to *Alcione* (1903–4). It is a poetry of sensations, with the structure gone. Have we not arrived at that juncture when Croce was deciding that 'la poesia della struttura' was a bogus one, and that there was only 'la poesia della poesia'? This is the discovery also of the practitioners, so that all the logic and coherence to which Carducci felt bound has been thrown overboard. Sometimes, as in *La Morte del Cervo*, a moment of narrative helps, and we can feel the epitome of d'Annunzio's world in the violence of the struggle and the effluvia of wild beasts. And as a pointer in this sea of images we may look to the anthology piece which can best represent d'Annunzio in this notation of sensations without ulterior motives, the *Pioggia nel Pineto*; and other short poems, as *Le stirpi canore*, *Il nome*, or *L'onda* may be linked with it. These are fragments of a poetry which has worn somewhat thin, and more legible are the plays to which we know d'Annunzio turned (between 1897 and 1914). We do not need to be informed that *Francesca da Rimini* (1902) treats her in a different way from Pellico, or Dante: in d'Annunzio's words, it has become a 'poema di sangue e di lussuria': which is to say, it is the same d'Annunzio. And there is a similar pattern to the plays, starting clear and legible (as *La Gioconda*, *La Città Morta*), bursting into the major key with *La Figlia di Jorio* (1904) and *La Fiaccola sotto il Moggio* (1905) to end in the turgidity of *La Nave* (1908). The setting for the *Figlia di Jorio* is in the Abruzzi, the time long ago: and both particulars allow accentuation of the primitive and the passionate. Here there is a languor in the decorative repetitions of the dialogue (not belonging to the hard forms of poetry), and with the superstitions of the Abruzzi this is a legend rather than a play. Even Mila the Harlot feels it this way, and shares d'Annunzio's pleasure in the flames (which are to burn her at the stake): *Laus Deo*, adds d'Annunzio. But d'Annunzio's dream, of the clash of passions in an age and place knowing no restraint is not yet satisfied, and the next year sees the *Fiaccola sotto il Moggio*. Set in the vast and ruinous castle of the Sangro, its hundred rooms propped up with poles to stay the effects of mining in the valley, and with a greater decadence in the last representatives of a noble family, this is akin to *Hamlet* in its web. Tibaldo has married a serving-woman within a year of his first wife's death. Was she, or he, or both, the murderers of the wife? Is she the author of the sickness hanging over the young Simonetto? Gigliola broods over vengeance, while Tibaldo's half-brother enjoys Agnizia, the serving-woman, and insults Tibaldo, and an old grandam keeps watch over the ugly family. In the end blood flows to match the fire of *La Figlia di Jorio*.

In a little tract entitled *L'Armata d'Italia* d'Annunzio gave an exultant picture of the torpedo-boat at work, killing the great battleship, as new David to an old Goliath. It was a premonition of that thesis of 1939 by which the new, and economical, factor of aircraft would cut the Mediterranean in two, and break the power of the British Fleet. And there was in these calculations something of the bogus quality which we have seen in Andrea Sperelli's devotion to the difficult forms of art. If we look back finally to the hero of *Il Fuoco*, with his advertised inability to speak of anything except himself, we shall find a picture soon destined to have fulfilment in real life. Stellio Effrena affects 'a limitless ambition, an insufferance of mediocrity, a claim to the privilege of princes, an urge to action which drives him towards the masses as to a prey' etc. And is not d'Annunzio the Duce of Italian literature, with the same upwards curve, the same mastery of the baser public mood; destined to end rightfully with a similar abandonment?

CHAPTER 14

The End of the Nineteenth Century

IF it was d'Annunzio who may be thought of as a literary Mussolini, with the same vulgar triumph and the same downfall, it was another who has been labelled as precursor. This is Alfredo Oriani (1852–1909), who in his time went largely disregarded, and who received in the 1920s posthumous consecration in an *Opera Omnia*. For the distaste with which he was received Oriani was himself responsible. His early novels incorporated the débris of late romanticism, and won him an uneviable reputation as pagan, voluptuary, immoralist. He seemed obsessed with the obscene and horrible, and his writing was turgid and formless. This is the Oriani of *Memorie Inutili* (1876) or *Al di là* (1877), leaving an impression of charlatanry and extravagance which turned attention from the later, more balanced, work. Besides, by the violence of his attitudes and his distrust of others' motives, he aroused hostility. Yet from these unpromising beginnings he came to balanced writing and systematic ideas, based on conservative-reactionary sympathies, and with a strong tinge of moral austerity. Above all, in the age of Crispi (the representative of *africanismo*, the policy of colonial expansion), Oriani stands for that concept of action which is later to fascinate many in this century.

In *Matrimonio e Divorzio* (1884), in answer to the campaign of Dumas Fils for divorce, Oriani showed his new colours, with the family at the centre of all cultures, dependent in its turn upon monogamy, with monogamy involving indissolubility of union. This was followed by his *magnum opus*, *La Lotta Politica in Italia* (1890), a re-examination of Italian history in the light of, or tending to, the struggle of the present. This is Gioberti's *Primato* written in a different key.

This vast attempt to synthesize the series of civil wars and revolutions into a single whole and show the new generation how out of the old fragments the unitarian Italy had been formed tries to be above partisanship, and obviously could not avoid some errors in detail or emphasis. But compared with later statements Oriani's claim remains a moderate one: in spite of the Triple Alliance the unchanging enemy is Austria, and the sea which can, and must, be Italy's own is only the Adriatic. Oriani ends, where he wished to begin afresh: 'And now let us examine the conditions of the political struggle of the present day.' But since his book fell on stony ground this was destined to be omitted. But his bitterness against the current hour was expressed, firstly in *Fino a Dogali* (1889). Dogali had been an ambush and a massacre of a small Italian force in Abyssinia, the prelude to Adowa: and Oriani affirms the rightness of conquest of Africa, the replacement of darkness by the light of civilization, even at the price of disappearance for populations which cannot make the grade. Here we have his creed, a profound sense of the value of action, the necessity for faith. Needless to say, the record of Italy in Abyssinia, or at home in the Humbertine era, gave cause for abundant bitterness, expressed also in articles, collected as *Fuochi di Bivacco* (1914). As a counter he set out his turbulent ideas and ideals in *La Rivolta Ideale* (1908). The *Lotta Politica* had looked back to the history of Italy, and found in the accents of imperial or papal greatness the basis for the future. And now the word is spoken, the revolution is begun, the time at hand when no one will accept 'an unknown order or follow a nameless captain'. 'Light all the torches, for the march is begun in the night ... the dawn is near. Its redness may seem blood, but it is the smile of the purple, flashing from the mantle of the sun.' This is heady language, from a tumultuous book. Here imperialism becomes a right and a duty, and all the signals are set towards faith, action, and strength. Congresses and diplomacy are swept aside, 'because all great ideas grow, watered with blood'. That gives a savage twist to an idea expressed – in what different circumstances! – by Cavour;

and it shows plainly enough, what was clear with d'Annunzio, that the breeding-ground of Fascism is not limited to the period after the Great War.

Oriani is an isolated figure, and it is Antonio Fogazzaro (1842–1911) who has more right to stand with d'Annunzio, and was coupled with the latter by Croce: both seeming to represent a weakening of the rational processes pre-eminent with Carducci, an accentuation of sensuous elements. That does not imply any uniformity, for Fogazzaro, after alternation between religious doubts and consolations, moves towards faith. His first novel, *Malombra*, was written in 1881, when Zola and materialism dominated the novel, and while Verga was producing *I Malavoglia*, setting an inexorable current towards naturalism, as towards regionalism. In 1901 *Il Fuoco* was flaming, and for many there was no literary salvation outside d'Annunzio. Verga was the master of contemporary detail, in limited zones; d'Annunzio glorifies the past, and dreams of future greatness. And between them Fogazzaro finds a course of his own, with a general lyric tendency counterbalanced by comic and dramatic elements, and tempered by a hankering for philosophical discussion. Here is the clash of human passions, but out of it there is to come the ascension of the spirit towards the Ideal and towards God. Science (and Fogazzaro cannot help looking to the new toys, including spiritualism) and faith combine in the interests of Christian morality. This is a formula which recalls Manzoni, even if Manzoni belonged to a less complicated age; and Manzoni has been thought of as a pattern for Fogazzaro's best novel. But if *Piccolo Mondo Antico* (1895) can seem a worthy counterpart to the *Promessi Sposi* it is because there, exceptionally, Fogazzaro achieves an equilibrium only precariously established in the rest of his work. The irrational elements, which Croce saw as a tendency of the time, are dominant among his other books. They are presented as characteristics of Corrado Silla in the first one, *Malombra*: a mind not lucid, mystic by tendency ... with indefinite ideas, impractical; an ardent spiritualist, so given to considering in mankind the beginning and the end; fond of leaning even in small matters on some general principle ... obeying a philosophic concept. These are the characteristics of Fogazzaro and here we are at the mercy of the impulses of an artistic and poetic temperament. Nor is Fogazzaro for nothing a pupil of Zanella, who had made himself the apostle of the ascent to light through the combination of faith with science. In his life Fogazzaro made shift to temper his imaginative temperament by concern with practicalities; in his novels it is tempered, at their best (which is to say again, in *Piccolo Mondo Antico*), by a sharpness of comic observation which seems to presage a little the infusion of Pirandello into the solemnity of Verga's regionalism.

In Fogazzaro, then, there is a tension, a heightening of the colour, which carries him normally outside the sphere of Manzoni. Moreover, with the latter love was something to be distrusted, or at the least, to be held in check. In Fogazzaro it is instead accepted as the chief means to ascend from everyday reality, taking us out of our common life into a somewhat nebulous metaphysical world. For all Fogazzaro's *innamorati* love should be a passion of the mind more than the body, and they trust to a will of more than ordinary calibre (at its strongest in Daniele Cortis) to tame the rebellion of the flesh. The agitations of this passion are intended to lift man up: they are caused by, are proof of, the force by which we gravitate upwards. For all his lovers there is an ascending course, a growth in will and strength of mind. The first pair, Corrado and Marina (*Malombra*), fall by the way, and are unique in this; but even here, they stoop to death, and not to sin. With Marina, turning from a normal girl into a morbid recluse with the fixed idea that she is the reincarnation of another, Fogazzaro can indulge his dabbling in the occult world. And Corrado dies because he is unable to resist the fascination of Marina, and because he loves her with an earthly passion only. This strife of discordant elements, where sensuality should be overcome by what is higher than it, forms the staple of Fogazzaro's books; and it may be doubted whether the element that triumphs is the one he means, and states, as winning. And at times the atmosphere is heated to the point of morbidity. This we may feel in *Daniele Cortis* (1885), where the strife is sharper, the sacrifice more painful, and the renunciation of sensuality forms in itself one of the most sensuous episodes in the book. The attempted ascent is carried further with *Mistero del Poeta* (1888). Here Violet is doomed to death, after obtaining freedom from her fiancé (who was grossly material), and from the memory of her first faithless lover; and to death just when she seems to be in sight of mystic marriage with the poet. Even dead she remains a temptation; and Fogazzaro tries to pierce beyond the veil, to reduce the mystery of life to make it admit of an innocent reward.

It is a relief to turn to the most positive of all his novels, *Piccolo Mondo Antico* (1895). Perhaps it is the influence of Manzoni which is responsible for the background. For this also is a historical novel, though its period is nearer. The *little old world* lies on the other side the curtain, before the elimination of Austria from Lombardy, in the years 1852–9. Franco and Luisa are set to renew the contrast between hero and heroine, and this time there is intended a mutual victory. But behind this pair are all the varied sentiments and types of Lombard life: those who accept the foreign rulers, those who abhor them, and who yet behave in various ways. The social scale produces abject spies and noble patriots; priests fired by love of Italy, and contemptible bigots; there is rebellion in the air, and the fierce undercurrent of Lombard hatred against Austrian rule. In this there is a Manzonian sense of comic observation, and this solid substructure makes this seem the sanest of Fogazzaro's books. The interest in the occult is limited to Luisa's attempts to enter into touch with her child when she has been drowned; and her spiritualism is doomed to failure. Here Luisa's strength breaks down: she had been all active virtue, works without faith, thinking only of this world, while Franco, dreamy and unpractical, left her to make ends meet, or deal with the affairs of life. But after the death of their child Maria it is his reliance on faith which proves, for Fogazzaro, the dominant quality; and at last Luisa returns to him, and to a new maternity, in acceptance of life, and of his faith. So Luisa and Franco are reunited, in body and soul, for this world and the next.

We may deal briefly with the epilogue, which involves two novels, *Piccolo Mondo Moderno* (1901), and *Il Santo* (1905). These continue by their characters the web of *Piccolo Mondo Antico*, but lose its balanced presentation. Pietro Maironi, son of Franco and Luisa, carries renunciation further: his wife is mad, and he loves Jeanne Dessalle who resists him while his wife is alive, but would yield when she has died. But now it is he who flees, since faith calls him to the higher spiritual plane: in which he will be the protagonist of *Il Santo*, inspired with a mystic programme of social reform in a new theocracy. And in the patent abnormality of Pietro the doubts which Fogazzaro's work arouses come to a head. His characters are overcharged, and after Franco and Luisa there is no pair without a touch of neuroticism. Moreover, these eccentrics are remote from the minor characters, treated with a broad comicity. For these latter Fogazzaro has been thought of as an Italian Dickens; but the two treatments increase the lack of harmony in the general effect. And there is another contrast, between the lyric description of Nature and the naturalistic treatment of the social scene. Here Fogazzaro makes perhaps too liberal a use of dialect. But with all his habitual faults Fogazzaro wrote one of the three most significant novels of the Italian nineteenth century; and of course, in front of Verga and d'Annunzio he has one merit. We have seen the pessimism which fills the naturalistic novel, the aesthetic impurities of d'Annunzio: Fogazzaro stands, though cloudily, for human and social good; the light that shines may not be clear, but it is meant to carry a fervent message of hope and love.

With a similar lifespan, Giovanni Pascoli (1855–1912) moves into the irrational world in a different way, and comes for other reasons to a pessimism which brings him near to Verga. Though opposite in temperament to d'Annunzio he also takes the bones of structure out of poetry to make it the picture of a (melancholy) mood. His life is dominated by a personal tragedy. Born at San Mauro di Romagna, he was twelve when his father was shot at and killed by an undiscovered assassin as he was returning from market at Cesena. Pascoli's mother was unprovided for, with young children on her hands: she died not long after this, as did a sister and two brothers of his. This crisis left its indelible imprint on all Pascoli's work. His youth began with a surge of revolutionary sentiment, leading to imprisonment in 1879, and after languishing thus for some months he came to the melancholy meditation on the problem of evil which will dominate the rest of his life. Here the old view of Manzoni on the unhappiness of both the oppressor and the victim spreads like an oil-stain through his mind, and he resigns himself before the mystery which surrounds and conditions the whole life of man. Like the family faced with the mare that brings home his father's body, there is no option but to resign oneself; and here the mood of sadness may have been accentuated by the note of Slav melancholy then coming to western consciousness with translations of Tolstoy and Dostoyevski.

If we put Pascoli in balance against Leopardi (and some of the premisses inevitably remind us of the latter) it is to feel at once the robustness of fibre of all Leopardi's attitudes, and the rightness of a judgement which puts him, even if unexpectedly, amongst the great positives of poetry. For Pascoli there is left the gently contemplative cast of his temperament, the wide landscape of his native Romagna, where he listens to mysterious voices from the depth of an unknown world. Less than for Carducci does his career matter, though he finally succeeded to the Chair which Carducci held at Bologna. It is San Mauro and Castelvecchio which fix his eye. Brought up amidst the prevailing positivism, Pascoli shares in Fogazzaro's reaction towards a spiritualistic idealism. But since the unknown and the unknowable are the substance of his poetry, this tends inevitably towards imprecision of statement and of outline.

> Nella prona terra
> Troppo è il mistero.

In that there is implicit the fact that he stands apart from

Fogazzaro, without allegiance to Christianity. True, he has ethical aspirations which embrace all mankind: they are Christian in mood, but lead to no Christian affirmation. Even if he forgives, he cannot forget, and in the face of bafflement can only afford a gentle renunciation which softens all the outlines and gives his poetry the nature of a sigh. His *Myricae* come first in 1891, added to until their definitive edition (1905), and with the *Canti di Castelvecchio* (1903) they have seemed for many the essential Pascoli. Here he looks to the countryside, and finds in the silence of the fields, in a muted autumnal landscape, a feather fluttering in an empty nest, a bird singing in a silent wood, a plough forgotten in a field, or the wind over the wide and lonely countryside, the melancholy which he and Nature share. Like d'Annunzio he serves some apprenticeship to the author of the *Odi Barbare*; and like d'Annunzio he leaves Carducci behind him from the start. All the zest which characterizes Carducci's attitude to life has here evaporated. And as with d'Annunzio, the narrative basis on which Carducci so painstakingly depended for a start has melted to give place to the notation of an atmosphere. The one thing which is precise is the observed detail out of Nature's book, with an accuracy of naming unknown before in Italian poetry. A fault, perhaps, is the predilection for little things, with a consequent attempt to load a wide significance on to a simple, childlike, symbol (as in *I Due Cugini*).

In the *Poemetti Primi* and *Nuovi* (1897, 1909) and in the *Poemi Conviviali* (1904) Pascoli strives hard to elaborate and co-ordinate his thought; and the same process of elaboration brings his pictures of country life in the *Poemetti* to the level of *genre*. In *Sementa* we have the cottage, the fields, rural and domestic tasks ... and our nearest parallel is Tennyson in some of his more decadent moods. Here there is nothing of the old eclogue, or of the refreshing piquancy of Lorenzo's rusticity. And with this as a mannerism goes a care for onomatopoeia, a *scilp* of sparrows, a *vitt-vide-vitt* of swallows. At the same time he accentuates the erudite elements of his verse. In the *Poemi Conviviali* especially he contrives to speak

Greek with Italian words. What of the higher reaches of his thought? He erects an ethico-sociological theory, with Nature a sweet mother, conscious of what she does, loving her children, drawing good for them from evil. Life would be beautiful did men not spoil it. We must declare war on war, allow no fatal divisions, belong to no party, but subscribe only to the one party of humanity. It is charity, or philanthropy, rather than socialism or individualism that we should look to: but true socialism is an increase in kindness in the heart of men. And through this there breaks still the *Sehnsucht* which is the core of Pascoli's poetry, reminding us that in the essences of all his work – nature, death, goodness, piety, humility, and poetry – death and poetry are the most insistent beats. At first he was unwilling to write and publish, but overtaken by the success of *Myricae* he went on to write perhaps too much. In the preface to *Odi e Inni* (1906) he wishes that his poems were more in number, since they have not exhausted the feelings they set out to express: hence his constant return to the same themes, the classic instance being that of his father's death, which recurs over and over again. As for his state of mind Pascoli invented a supporting theory, so he drew an image of the poet as the *poverello* of humanity, a child who loves the little things (hence the diminutives within his poems), inspirer of good sentiments, of love, for country, family, mankind. But still, in the brief symbol of the book open on the lectern for man to read, with the wind turning the pages so that he cannot find his place in the volume of the world, Pascoli remains, in so far as it can give effectual poetry, the poet of the ineffectual.

Pascoli is regional only in his dependence on Romagna for his vision; but meanwhile it was obvious that the lead given by Verga and Capuana would be widely followed. Italy unites, but a literary dispersal attends the process, and if there is nowhere a writer of the calibre of Verga, yet there is a flowering of regionalist narrative with a high standard of competency. Amongst the best-known are two women writers, who add Naples and Sardinia to Sicily. Matilde Serao (1856–1927) brings to the observation of Neapolitan life all the fertility of meridional imagination, winning for her books the widest audience without sinking to the level of a mere best-seller. In a long list of works (*Il ventre di Napoli*, 1884; *Suor Giovanna della Croce*, 1901; *Evviva la vita!*, 1909) pride of place belongs to *Il Paese di Cuccagna* (1891), where all the passions of Naples are concentrated round the lottery, with its lure of winning numbers (dreamt of or symbolized or otherwise invented), and its train of misery, which involves Cesare Fragalà in spite of his prosperous business and the decayed noble house of Cavalcanti. Here is a dantesque *ridda* where everything is converted to this one currency of numbers, nor is the Ecce Homo in the Marchese's house, or San Gennaro, out of the orbit, or out of danger of the most violent revulsion of feeling. Sprouting from this fulcrum is all the crowded, hectic, life of Naples, with the Land of Cockayne a golden promise round the corner, and the inevitable promoter of a current misery.

From the multitudinous world of Naples we pass with Grazia Deledda (1871–1936) to the lonely spaces of Sardinia. Here the primitive background is different in all its details (with the *tanca*, or sheep-ranch, out on the far hillside, and months of isolation) from that of Sicily; but the note of tragedy returns inevitably: based on feelings, not on economic catastrophe. This is clearly instanced in her best book, *Elias Portolu* (1903), which is the tragedy of one who returns to Sardinia after a period in a mainland penitentiary with white face and white hands, to take his place alongside the rough animality of the rest of the household. The drama of the story, based on this misfit, is fired by the meeting of Elias with his brother's bride, Maddalena. He loves her, she him: but to what avail? Pietro would crush him if he knew, and Elias has his loyalty. His father has all the scorn of rough strength for the weakling ('Se stai male, curati o muori ...'), and Elias's refuge in the Church as priest – having been lent a book on the Passion when in prison – does not save him from sinning with Maddalena. It is only when their child has died and Maddalena belongs to another that Elias, purged of all human emotions, can find peace of mind 'davanti al Signore grande e misericordioso'. In the simplicity of its canvas, and the tension of its feelings, this is an impressive piece of work, and Grazia Deledda by this and other works (*Racconti Sardi,* 1894; *Il Vecchio della Montagna,* 1900; *Marianna Sirca,* 1915) brought the unfamiliar world of Sardinia to wide appreciation in Italy. Within the orbit of Verga and naturalism, this is nevertheless something original and independent, with at her best an individual poetry that cannot be found elsewhere in the range of Italian narrative.

Rather than the cloud of minor writers who form the regional chorus, it is natural to place alongside *Elias Portolu* an individual tragedy with a Milanese setting: *Demetrio Pianelli* (1890) by Emilio De Marchi (1851–1901). This book is just a little unhappy sometimes in its surface, as in the subtitle to the first section, *Lord Cosmetico,* which turns out to be the nickname for Cesarino Pianelli, the lucky half-brother of Demetrio. And it is when this first section, which recounts the burning out of this rapid fortune of Cesarino, with his suicide after debt and dishonesty, is out of the way that the novel gains in stature. On Demetrio, the clumsy peasant's son turned clerk, there falls the load of Cesarino's family, with a showy widow used to being spoiled and spent for and three children, all surrounded with debts which Beatrice cannot understand, while she despises and distrusts the only person – Demetrio – who can offer any help. His little savings, fruit of years of stinting, put by against the hardship of old age, go to stop the holes and bring some bread for the children. Luckily for Beatrice his cousin Paolino, a well-off farmer, is taken by her elegance, and offers marriage. Demetrio thinks of him as an angel in disguise, then looks to see what men can find in Beatrice, till now at loggerheads with him. He realizes the world of the senses, so far outside the hard realities of his working world; and is doomed to frustration as she passes to Paolino, and his sacrifices cease to have actuality or reward. This study of Demetrio, another *bourru bienfaisant,* though very different from Goldoni's, has a solidity and sensitivity which deserve for the book a wider recognition than it has had; though without quite bringing

De Marchi within challenging distance of the major novelists of the century.

It was Manzoni who decided that the historical novel was not viable, and pointed to the contemporary one; and from Verga to De Marchi we have been seeing the truth and consequences of Manzoni's conclusion. But naturally there is another trend, to some of whose representatives we must look briefly. And in looking thus over our shoulder we may find the first usage of *verismo* in a sphere which is not Verga's. This is by Pietro Cossa (1830–81) in his play *Nerone* of 1871, where the prologue appeals to a new conception of history. But it will not surprise that this appeal to realism is linked with a taste for times of dissolution, of orgies and of crime, the Rome of Nero, or of *Messalina* (1875), of the *Borgias* (1881), or *Cola di Rienzo* (1879). It has the advantages of a clear and quite unromantic tone in exposition, and Cossa has from his time a bias to the private life of characters, the small causes, the pathology of the case, as forming the truer side of history. In a way his fertility exhausts itself with *Nerone*, and the later plays tend to repeat, in spite of changed surroundings; noticeable too is the lack of that patriotic fervour – which we might have expected with Cola – on the pattern of *Arnaldo da Brescia*. Cossa rises to no great heights, nor falls to any depths, and may afford a pleasant introduction to a theme. The same can conspicuously not be said of Arrigo Boito (1842–1918), who is akin to Emilio Praga in his verse, linked with the *scapigliatura* of the mid-century. This shows strongly in *Il Re Orso* (1865), a vast and formless work into which has been thrown all the lumber of late romanticism, and over which Re Orso himself presides as the incarnation of evil. Here is a false Middle Ages, with a whole repertory of banquets, slaughter, funerals, tombs, and apparitions. As the collaborator with Verdi and Rossini Boito may have more importance than as a man of letters in his own right; but Croce found a good word to say for him, especially for his *Nerone* (1911), which naturally has none of the calm qualities of Cossa, but brings instead a vast gusto to all the disorders of imperial Rome.

From Boito it is a relief to turn to Paolo Ferrari (1822–89). He had begun, in the middle of the century, with historical plays, of which the best-known is *Goldoni e le sue Sedici Commedie Nuove* (1852). In this he has a moral programme, with the courage and loyalty of Goldoni, reformer of the stage, shown up against the interested parties who attack him; and a similar theme ensues with *La Satira e Parini* (of 1854–6), with a rough identification between the protagonists and Ferrari. From these he passed to plays with a thesis, but a thesis complicated by parallels and opposites. Thus with *Le Due Dame* (1877), where the thesis is that vice masquerading under penitence must not penetrate into *famiglie onorate*: which would be better shown if the theme of Rosalia versus Emma were not obscured by other superimposed elements. This is still true of the best, *Il Duello* (1868), written against a contemporary fashion, but characteristically involved in plot. What may be most interesting for us now is the anticipatory touch of pirandellianism in the dialogue: in the everyday colourlessness of some of the *battute*, and in the taking and abandoning of an attitude on the presentation of an opposing one, we have a distant suggestion of the scenes in Pirandello's *Ciascuno a suo modo* where all opinions dissolve in a general scepticism about opinions. But once again, Ferrari has not been content with the stupidity of duelling, but has complicated the plot with Sirchj's wife and Amari's daughter. ... We may add *Il Ridicolo* (1872), *Cause ed Effetti* (1871), with a touch of Ibsen in its theme of marriages socially desirable, but doomed to misery if between innocent youth and men morally and physically tainted; and *Il Suicidio* (1875), which might have remembered Leopardi's hint in the *Operette Morali* on the wrongness of killing oneself and leaving others to the consequences of one's errors: which is, after all, a lesson of *Demetrio Pianelli*.

By the side of Ferrari we have one who is less respectable (I do not mean in the social sense), and more successful: Giuseppe Giacosa (1847–1906), one whom Croce called a constant tamer of poetry – an amiable, but not a legitimate thing to do. Giacosa lacks a genuine content of his own, and is a follower of literary fashions, usually to his advantage, for working with decorous carefulness he finds himself in harmony with his public's mood. It was only late on, and following Ibsen, that he ran into some unpopularity. He was meant to be a lawyer, but wrote at twenty-four a pseudo-medieval idyll, the *Partita a Scacchi* (1871), whose success decided a change of career. The mechanism was from *Huon de Bordeaux*, but the medieval exuberance of the source has been converted to a romantic melancholy, in verse of over-facile fluency. Huon the page boasts of his prowess at chess, and is matched by the Lord of the castle against his daughter: a night and a hundred pounds if he wins, his head if he loses. In the original it was played in an animated way, in a castle full of barons; here it is empty and forlorn, with an old man and his loving daughter (waiting without knowing it for a husband). Into this gloom comes the old friend Oliviero Conte di Fombrone and his boastful young page Fernando. Fernando plays, would lose through gazing on Iolanda's eyes; but she is determined not to win, although she does not know the terms of the bet, and when he still hesitates to make the winning move she does it slyly for him:

M'offrivate uno sposo e lo scegliemmo in due,

and turning to Fernando she asks him why he gazes and says nothing. He answers, as he did before, bemused,

Io ti guardo negli occhi, che sono tanto belli.

Which is simple enough for any beginner in the language, and guaranteed bogus enough to please any appetite for idyllic sentiments in the blue bath of happiness. Giacosa continued with more ambitious efforts, first in the medieval vein, as the *Trionfo d'Amore* (1875), *Il Fratello d'Armi* (1878), and with the *Conte Rosso* (1880), or *La Signora di Challant* (1891, based on Bandello), he added historical drama with a note of blood; meanwhile with *Tristi Amori* (1888) and *Come le Foglie* (1900) he came to contemporary bourgeois themes, or in *I Diritti dell' Anima* (1894) played with those of Ibsen. *Tristi amori* has dated obviously, but with its simple triangle (the busy lawyer, neglecting wife and child, befriending the poor son of a decadent Conte, only for him to become inevitably a focus for the wife) it remains more convincing than *Come le Foglie.* This is tied more closely to the social conditions of 1900, and the air of international smart society seems more irksome than the homeliness of *Tristi Amori.* But Giacosa will be remembered mostly for his medieval idyll, and as a trifler with the name of literature.

To counteract any disagreeable impression, let us add one whose earnestness is above suspicion. Ada Negri (1870–1945) was an elementary teacher, daughter of a peasant mother who had sacrificed for her, living herself in poverty. Her early poetry reflects her environment, is autobiographical and melancholy, with an all-embracing pity for the *vinti* in life. Like a knife-blade in the side, or blood throbbing from a wound, is her feeling for the griefs of the poor, and all they ask is 'Pace! ... lavoro! ... pane!' That is the *Canto della Zappa* in her first volume of verse, *Fatalità* (1890), and it is close to Thomas Hood, *The Song of a Shirt* in spirit. Although the experience and inspiration of an elementary teacher is not likely to be very deep, or very wide, the best part of her poetry springs from her early life. By an ironical twist, *Fatalità* raised her status, and she found herself caught between happy motherhood and the necessity to persevere with the lugubrious strain which had brought her fame. She is driven towards repetition, and to a purely sociological type of verse in such later volumes as *Tempesta* (1896) or *Maternità* (1906). This is a distressing world, and Ada Negri's voice may be taken as the epitome of that last decade of the century, with the rise of a social conscience, and of socialist unrest. But as the parallel with Hood suggests, or the vicinity to De Amicis, the descent to bathos is easy. We began the nineteenth century with that revolution in literary fashion, captained by Rousseau and by Herder: instead of climbing the steep slopes of Parnassus the man of letters was to come down towards the popular and universal.

It was a policy which gave a tremendous impulse to the appeal of literature, and works like *Le Mie Prigioni* or *I Promessi Sposi* had a currency beyond anything that could be dreamed of for Parini. But to look always downwards is not an unmixed blessing.

CHAPTER 15

Pirandello and the Question-Mark of the Twentieth Century

THE nineteenth century had begun with a limited revulsion against the past, the twentieth starts with the proposal to obliterate the past *in toto*. We in England have adopted *futurism*, but have no equivalent to the term which it was intended to abase and to replace, *passatismo*.

> O lune triste, somnolente et passéiste,
> que veux-tu que je fasse de ces flaques du déluge?
> Je te biffe d'un trait, en allumant mon réflecteur
> dont l'énorme rayon électrique est plus neuf
> et plus blanc que le tien!

So wrote Marinetti, inventor of futurism, in a poem called *Le Monoplan du Pape*; and we see in the affinity to Paolo Tarsis, of d'Annunzio's contemporary novel *Forse che sì forse che no*, the limitations of this attitude. And we who live in the rush of the modern world may look back with detached interest on those who, like Papini, cursed the sluggishness, the tortoise quality of Italy (*Italia lumacosa ... tartarugaggine*), offering a general rebuke to the universe: Faster! Piú presto! Faster we go, and fiercer grow our machines, while Italy has been caught in the new tempo, torn between the desire of the northern intruders whom Papini hated for the sunshine and the historic past and that of her inhabitants for noise, speed, and new cement. And we, who are accustomed to angry young men, may look back with a sad amusement at those who took themselves so seriously, in so questionable a cause.

It was F. T. Marinetti (1878–1944) who launched in 1909 the futurist manifesto, and who is the protagonist of such activities as *vers libres* (*parole in libertà*). But he is overshadowed by more combative fellow-travellers. The chief of these, even if a late-comer, is Giovanni Papini (1881–1956): but it is typical of him that in announcing his conversion, in 1913, he claimed to have invented futurism himself anticipatorily, and stepped in as a leader, not a follower. 'From childhood tremendously alone and different' was Papini's definition of himself in his autobiography, *Un Uomo Finito* (1912): what the ladies called a 'shy child', what the common women called a 'toad'. Toads, like hoopoes, are quite different in life and literature; but of the latter, venomous, variety Papini is the choicest specimen. Rarely has so much venom been more forcefully squirted in so many directions. And, of course, what others lose Papini gains himself. *Aut Caesar, aut nihil:* 'I wanted to be really great, epic, colossal, I wanted to accomplish something gigantic, unheard of, that should change the heart of men and the face of the earth. Either that, or nothing.' Certainly, as founder of *Leonardo* (1903), editor of *La Voce* (1912) and finally *Lacerba* (1913), Papini made himself the leader of his generation in Florence. He initiated the revolt against positivism, pursuing it in *Il Crepuscolo dei Filosofi* (1906). The flaunted banner and the taunt for decadent opponents belongs to all his writing, and in *Un Uomo Finito* we have his restless search for truth, with vast literary projects feverishly pursued, then cast aside. For others he invents the *stroncatura*, the savage demolition of a writer (*Stroncature*, 1916; *Ventiquattro Cervelli*, 1912).

For Papini futurism meant liberation from the weight of all the *anticumi*. If Florence was the mecca of the northern tourist that was something to expiate, and to expunge. The whole of the city was a stifling museum (as it would be for Mr Kingsley Amis), from which one needs escape. His new adherence is of 1913, and was marked in the same December by a speech entitled, *Contro Firenze passatista*. It ends with the aspiration to see such a gust of futurism as would blow away the fourteenth century (on which Florence lived) and show 'that we are in the year 1913 and that the future is truer and greater than the past'. That denies an attitude that we have seen with

Carducci, and is the reverse of something we shall find with Pirandello. The past, said Mr Eliot, is what is already alive. For Papini it is what is already dead. The choice may be a personal one between these attitudes: but to reject in 1913 the *Primavera* and Brunelleschi's Dome (to sum Florence up), and take an open cheque upon the twentieth century, will seem poor prescience.

In the matter of movement we have seen a kinship between Papini and d'Annunzio, and this exists elsewhere in spite of the differences between the aesthete and the Florentine *becero*. In *Un Uomo Finito* Papini accepts the class struggle, and proclaims himself a socialist in reverse: here is the creed of nationalism. 'We thought of Africa, we wanted battleships, and sought to stir up the little bit of imperial spirit which could be left in Italy after the Abyssinian defeats.' He was not sure what was the mission of Italy in the world, but he embarked on a campaign to awaken the country to a messianic passion. This is not only on the way to Fascism, this mission needed, but not known, is symptomatic of Papini as writer. What he cared for was self-assertion. Others have given themselves (as Leopardi in the *Canti*): what Papini gives is the continual exhibition of himself. This artificiality, disguised with all the raciness of Florentine linguistic resources, appears in his creative writing; as in such volumes of short stories as *Parole e Sangue* (1912), where his revolt against photographic reality leads Papini to the type of story based on the smart trick.

Even within *Un Uomo Finito* the pretence of jettisoning the past rings hollow. There is a section in which Papini reviews the world's best literature, and counts his affinity with its noblest authors. And is not the stage of *bourgeois defence* and *spiritual nationalism* a preparation for other sorts of *right-minded* orthodoxy? Atheist by birth, and by conviction (his boast in *Un Uomo Finito* that he was a man 'for whom God had never existed'), Papini was converted to catholicism soon after the Great War, and marked the passage with his *Storia di Cristo* (1921). And alongside this new devotional strain (*Sant' Agostino, Pane e Vino*) there comes an academic one.

For Papini who had condemned Carducci for all the professorial elements of his poetry also succeeded to Carducci's Chair, and wrote his *History of Italian Literature*. And he who had cursed all the artistic heritage of Florence as a load of *anticumi* devoted one of his longest volumes to the life of Michelangelo (1949), ending in humility, 'held back by the shame of my own nothingness and the terror of that lonely grandeur' from kissing the furrowed brow which is his image of Michelangelo. The world of futurism, of dynamism, monoplanes and searchlights, racing motorcars or submarines is far away. But we cannot put the earlier Papini aside for this last incarnation; and perhaps there is some poetic justice in this inventor of the *stroncatura*, the brutal frontal assault on an unworthy literary practitioner, receiving a little criticism. Did not Perillus roar in his own brazen bull? Few authors in Italian literature invite more temptingly to a *stroncatura* than does the inventor of the term.

It was Papini and Pancrazi who put out in 1920 an anthology of *Poeti d'Oggi*, and from it I may content myself with the quotation already made from Marinetti's poem. Here, frequently enough, poetry has turned to prose-poetry, and prose-poetry turns out prose. Some of this galaxy of names (forty-six in all) remain familiar, and may have some claim upon a history of twentieth-century literature. But we may take from Papini's hands the touchstone of greatness, of Dante or of Leopardi (the staple of our narrative), and give short shrift to futurist poetry. It believed in dynamism, but had no dynamo. We might take its epitaph from the voluntary abnegation of Sergio Corazzini, who died young, 'Perché tu mi dici poeta?' And are not these futurists now irrevocably the past? and if *passatismo* is a heinous crime, then may not we shun it, and them? Let us be generous, and single one other from the throng, the one who was at Papini's right hand, and who links literature with the new bag of tricks in painting: Ardengo Soffici (*b.* 1879). He provides us with the revolutionary title *Bïf§ƶf + 18. Simultaneità. Chimismi lirici* (1915) meant to tease and to annoy. But in his *Giornale di Bordo* (1915) he also steered the course. Here, in a less aggressive form, we find

Papini's attitudes: the necessity of getting out of the old
literary and artistic formulas, the need to cultivate harshness,
discordance – 'il brutto e l'urtante'. The poetry of unpoetic
things, with Soffici's disgust at the 30,000 people who had
filed hat in hand in front of the Mona Lisa, 'that old crust',
on its replacement in the Louvre. Better a new lie than an old
truth: religion, patriotism, things to throw away ('Can I love
this fat and sweaty Tuscan broker, and fight against Apollinaire, or hate Picasso?') or to combat ('The greatest miracle
that God has worked is having made people talk of Him
without existing'). This sacrifice of the past is so complete
that even the voice of Leopardi, for all its sweetness, and for
all its own renunciation, meets the same rejection: for
Soffici to be himself, even against Leopardi, if necessary.

Au fond de l'inconnu pour trouver du nouveau!

It is in such a book as *Lemmonio Boreo* (1911) that we may
sample the product of this search; and Lemmonio's real name
is plainly Soffici. He has a healthy taste for the natural realities
of the Tuscan scene, and a healthy distaste for all the contemporary literature of Italy. Since actors and actions round
him are all abject he sets out to put his Tuscany to rights,
enlists first a strong arm to reinforce his own self-righteous-
ness, and then a knowing card (a variant of Panurge, or of
Cingar). Together they accomplish a series of exploits whose
purpose and morality grows increasingly dubious, ending in
rape and arson with the same healthy purpose of rectifying
wrong. And after this, they enter Florence smiling, just to end
the book. It is a warning that futurist literature, when its
present has evaporated, can smell as fusty, prove as stale and
uninspired, as any other segment from the *past*. From this
flurry we can turn with some relief to one who followed
quietly his own path, and found in his own time little encouragement. Italo Svevo (the pseudonym of Ettore Schmitz,
1861–1928) was born at Trieste, bringing into Italian literature the province furthest from Verga's Sicily. But belonging
to the generation of Verga Svevo partakes of his sobriety.
In the heady world of d'Annunzio's spectacular achievements

there was little room for appreciating Verga, and none for Svevo. His first works (*Una vita*, 1892; *Senilità*, 1898) met no response, and left him to a silence of a quarter of a century. Then when other than Italian eyes had sensed his value he produced his longest book, *La Coscienza di Zeno* (1923). For Svevo great claims have been made, and great names proposed as congeners, of which we may take Proust as an example. But his merits are of a lower order, and placed opposite Verga it is apparent that the heroic poetry which bathes Verga's Sicily is greater achievement than this bourgeois atmosphere of Trieste. With Soffici and Papini Svevo shares the modern disenchantment with life. In the *Giornale di bordo* there is the reflection: 'The ancient hero was one who confronted death, the modern hero is one who accepts life'. And in *La Coscienza di Zeno* Svevo adds, 'Unlike other illnesses life is always mortal. It admits of no cure.' And elsewhere Zeno denies pity to his brother-in-law, for once we admit pity for the unfortunate there would soon be no room for any other feeling. 'The natural law does not give right to happiness, rather it prescribes wretchedness and suffering. ... Nature does not make calculations, but experiments.' In this climate it is one's own interest which becomes important, and there are passages insisting on *il proprio interesse* which link *Senilità* with *Zeno*. Not only in tone, but even in the situation of the central pairs of characters these two novels, divided by thirty years, have a similarity which is not accidental. In a world without idealisms, and without purpose, Svevo sets out to illuminate the currents and cross-currents of an individual consciousness. This register of the unplanned and uncharted sands and quicksands of ordinary provincial life, something unforced to any preconceived pattern, ending not like Verga with catastrophe, forms the strength of Svevo's work; and adds an element of weakness too: for here there is no pulse of dominant ideas, nor is any character made compelling for us by its own intensity. Here life is analysed and dissolved into its purposelessness. That is to say that with Svevo we are on the threshold of Pirandellianism.

And, indeed, we have approached it in a different way with

the Futurists. Papini in *Un Uomo Finito*, amongst the other passages in praise of himself, has one on being without prejudices and blinkers, the only person capable 'of stripping everything, every idea, of the meretricious veils of habit and convention; of freeing humanity from all the opprobrious mental servitudes which shackle it'. The past as a mould set hard by the passage of time, until our new bones are forced to its old shape. ... Let us rid ourselves of the preconceived, the accepted notion, look at life as it is in its inconsequent fluency: from Svevo and Papini we pass naturally to the one who is for Italy with the incarnation of this attitude, the last major writer who may close, with his own question mark, this exploration into the twentieth century. It is apparent, I imagine, that we should here be entering a Waste Land. But it is the merit of Pirandello that beginning with the most strenuous of negatives he brings a positive contribution of his own, which is as welcome as it is unexpected.

Pirandello is primarily the great continuator of Verga: only now the sphere of observation is extended. Indeed, in Pirandello we shall find the statement of the same detachment which Verga posited in the face of the real world, only applied now to the inner world of the mind. The character appears, and Pirandello waits and watches, letting its movements and reactions follow from their own momentum. This is the *verismo* of Verga, operating under the skin, instead of looking at the face. And in this there is explicit the relationship to Svevo, who also explores in *Zeno* especially the inner world of feeling and consciousness. This exploration flowers in the *Maschere Nude*, and to this the earlier writing of Pirandello forms a long prelude. In two stories, of 1914–15, we may catch a hint of what is to come. In *L'Avemaria di Bobbio* there is the image of consciousness as like the little water at the neck of a bottomless well, of ourselves as we were still living under the surface of what we are. It is a formula which immediately suggests Proust, but Pirandello is not so much concerned with the *Recherche du temps perdu* as with the dissolution of the structure of the present, the suggestion of a limitless uncertainty under the known outlines. In *Nel Gorgo* there is a corollary to do this: we change our shirt daily, there are no holes in our socks. But what about our conscience? Are we sure that there is nothing dirty inside? And here Pirandello's answer is that we are all forced to discover 'that we are swine in some moment of lucid interval'. Not only what is past, and forgotten, but what is not avowed, is also an element in the present. But in this perplexing world there is this reassurance: as this passage shows, Pirandello thinks in terms of black and white, which means ultimately that his choice is white. That is different from Svevo, in whose work the undulant quality of life and consciousness does not admit so readily of moral categories. With Pirandello we may have to wait for the positive notes, but they are implicit, and will at last emerge.

Meanwhile there is before him a long career which does not win him overmuch attention. Luigi Pirandello (1867–1936) left his family environment to study at Palermo, Rome, and Bonn, and in the fervour of liberty for himself found the currents which derived from Leopardi and Carducci. His first verse, as *Mal giocondo* (1883–8), showed a predilection in form for *odi barbare*, in spirit a tinge of pessimism, but with the appeal to life against the mortifying claims of religion. Here there is even a dash of dannunzianism, with a fiercely antichristian note which might be paralleled in Carducci's imitator, Stecchetti. This has not any importance as poetry, it illustrates the disillusionments of his youth, his rebellion against mediocrity and incomprehension round him. And it is here that misfortunes marshal Pirandello the way that he was going: his father had not understood his mother, the one love of his youth had been left in Bonn, the marriage which (after a long engagement to a cousin) had been arranged for him by his father turned out a torment to him. At first it brought independence, the chance to live and write in Rome. But the sulphur-mine on which his wife's fortune depended was wrecked by a landslide; and she, soon after, developed paresis of the legs. Pirandello was forced to look to his pen for a living, supplementing this with teaching. The success of his novel *Il fu Mattia Pascal* (1904) meant acceptance for other

279

volumes of short stories (which had begun with *Amori senza Amore*, 1894, and the series *Beffe della Morte e della Vita*, 1902–3). Now these continue without interruption down to 1919, later to be subsumed and rearranged in the collection *Novelle per un Anno* (though its fifteen volumes did not get to 365 stories). Meanwhile worse was in store for his marriage, since his wife developed persecution-mania, shown in a furious jealousy of her husband. From 1904 life became a daily torment for him, and for the children. For long months Pirandello would be separated from his wife, who had fled to Sicily, taking the children with her; or he would take refuge in furnished rooms, where the children brought him news of his wife. The wife who peers at her husband in the café (*L'Uomo dal Fiore in Bocca*) can remind us how this personal ordeal sharpened Pirandello's perceptions, adding a concealed personal note to stories which may seem objective.

For Pirandello's conception of his art we have his long essay, *L'Umorismo* (1908). It is a process of decomposing reality (or better, the appearances which we call reality), instead of building up towards a stable pattern. Here each yes becomes a no, which in the end assumes the same value as the yes. And here the titles, from *Mal Giocondo*, *Amori senza Amore*, *Erma Bifronte* on, find their illumination. Life is a continual illusory construction, in which the mobility and uncertainty of outward objects is matched by the uncertainty of the inward ego which has to meet their impact. In art (a statue, let us say, or a tragedy by Racine) all is composed and clear; but Pirandello is forced relentlessly towards something which may seem supremely un-artistic, and un-literary: where there can be neither order nor coherency. The conclusion of this essay is a foregone one, clinched by a quotation out of Carlyle's *Sartor Resartus*, made only to be turned inside out. 'Man is a clothed animal, society has clothes as its basis.' But clothes also *compose*, compose and hide, and we have come to 'la vita nuda, la natura senz' ordine apparente, irta di contraddizioni'. Croce denied the poetry of structure, to insist only on *la poesia della poesia*; and Pirandello is going further and more purposefully, away from life and literature with a prepared surface. That might seem to be towards an anti-literature, and it is a paradox that Pirandello aroused little interest in his earlier phases as a writer, and it was not till he turned to the theatre, with the success of *Sei personaggi in Cerca d'Autore* (1921), that the vogue for Pirandello sets in in earnest. It continues through his theatre, that is, during the time when he exploited resolutely all the new depths announced in *L'Umorismo*.

Indeed, though the hints of a new world are in his earlier production, Pirandello remained for long content with a traditional presentation, and even the theme of his most successful novel, *Il fu Mattia Pascal*, turns out to be substantially unpirandellian. Mattia by two accidents becomes someone else, and starts life anew. But as these are external to him, so it is mere physical obstacles which prevent him going on. And obviously, if we can all, and must all, be a plurality of persons, Mattia Pascal's are only artificial difficulties. This conflict between an individual and society is well told, and still remains, perhaps, the most popular of Pirandello's novels. Certainly, it has great advantages over his ambitious attempt at a historico-social novel, *I Vecchi e i Giovani* (1913, but written 1906–8). This was to be a picture of Sicilian life in the last decade of the nineteenth century: that sad period of repression for the socialist *fasci* in the Sicilian countryside, with scandals in Rome (as that of the Banca Romana), disastrous colonial campaigns, and as culmination, the assassination of Humbert I. When all Italy had slipped downhill from the idealism of the Risorgimento it was to be expected that Sicily, neglected since 1860 by successive governments, should have a poor balance-sheet. It was a fine setting for a canvas that should have taken its place alongside *Mastro Don Gesualdo*, but Pirandello did not prove at home in the historical novel, and it is the heaviest reading of all his work. Nor are the other novels of exceptional interest. There is a contrast between the bitter first tale, *L'Esclusa* (1893, published 1901), and its successor *Il Turno* (1895, published 1902). In the latter the theme of waiting for Stellina's old husband to die, only to find the lawyer stepping in and taking her

himself, so that poor Pepé is left to wait his turn, is optimistically and ironically treated. *L'Esclusa* has a harsher touch. The
men of the Pentagora family have always been betrayed by
their wives, and have always turned them out of doors.
Rocco Pentagora is so sure of this that he acts when he
discovers a letter to his wife, neither invited, nor answered.
He does what society demands. And calamities follow for the
wife, until she is driven at last to become – what she would
never have been otherwise – the mistress of the letter-writer.
It is a first Pirandellian thesis on the damage which conventions may do to the morality which they are intended to safe-
guard.

It is perhaps in *Uno, Nessuno e Centomila* (1925–6, but begun
in 1913) that Pirandello is most himself, though it is somewhat slight as a novel. For here Vitangelo Moscardi makes the
discovery (or, what is more cruel, his wife makes it for him)
that his nose is lop-sided. It is a proof that he is other than
what he has always thought himself to be, and from this
discovery a whole set of shifts can stem. This way madness
lies. It is an extension of Grandville's proverb, *Le bossu ne
voit point sa bosse; mais il voit celle de son confrère.* Before we
realize our defects, others see and laugh at them, while we
console ourselves by laughing at these others. And on both
sides we strive to stabilize the flux of life to suit ourselves;
and yet are carried at the mercy of external and internal
incertitudes which we cannot chart. Nothing but what is
past is certain, said Seneca despondently. The world of
Pirandello sets the mirror to such a present. Nothing in it
suggests or allows the comfort of accepted ideas, or of
accepted situations. Yet as I have suggested, nothing before
the plays really makes use of the new formulas, and this is still
true of the *Novelle per un Anno* (where the chronology of the
stories is upset). Here Pirandello still takes time and personality in a more straightforward way than we should have
expected. True, the satire of social conventions is a theme
frequently employed, and there is a bitter tinge to the whole
collection (the stories with a happy ending can be counted on
one's fingers); but in spite of this we can sense the derivation

from Verga, even though Pirandello adds to the milieu of Agrigento the bourgeois side of Rome (something very different from d'Annunzio). This is the raw material of pirandellianism, as we may see from *Il Professor Terremoto*:

> Life, alas, is not made of these rare moments. Ordinary everyday life, you know well what it is: where it is not squalid in its poverty, always bristling with little obstacles – innumerable and often unsurmountable – tormented by continual material needs, pressed on by often petty cares, regulated by mediocre duties.

Since ordinary life is unsatisfactory Racine built a world of literature without its petty obstacles. But Pirandello looks the other way, exploring with endless energy the unexpected creases which lie beneath the surface. It is because here the possibilities are so limitless that his invention is so fertile.

Many of his plays are adaptations of short stories – but the plays remain in a separate category, and represent the full flowering of his genius. We may take the cue for the added dynamic of Pirandello's theatre from the discussion in *Six Characters* of the reality of the character (in literature as well as on the stage). Mere men are born and die, and even in the process of living they may be nobody at all. But Sancho Panza? or Don Abbondio? They are always somebody, and the samebody, hooked to a situation which may be cruel, but remains intense. The Father in *Six Characters* protests against being identified with one (shameful) moment in his life, as much as Professor Terremoto did against being hooked to one (heroic) moment in his own: that is not all him, there are all the other moments when he was something else, and something better. The whole pulse of the play depends on this conception of the *character* as having a vitality *per se*, as being 'piú vero e piú reale' than the Capocomico, who is only flesh and blood, and does not know particularly his own position today, or what 'reality' will be tomorrow. For the ordinary individual life is an unpredictable fluid: for the six characters (and for the character in general) it is something which exists once and for all. This is why they can impose themselves on the aimless comedians. And here is the affinity with the next most celebrated of Pirandello's plays, *Enrico IV*. In this process of stabilizing, for the benefit of our tranquillity, the flux of life, some may be stronger than others, may in fact impose their own terms on life. They are the ones who win in the social struggle. And beyond them are those who in some way contract out, stabilize themselves in a world of their own, where all may be tragic, perchance, but has the merit of remaining constant. In one way this is achieved by the principal characters in *Così è (se vi pare)*, by 'creating for themselves a phantom which has the same consistency as reality, in which they live now in perfect harmony'. Indeed, if what we call reality is only haphazard and illusory, the substitute we make for it from within ourselves may be much more satisfactory, and quite as 'real'. And here *Enrico IV* has gone further, but in the same way, with the main protagonist fixed in the delusion that he is the German Emperor whose part he played in a tragic masquerade. For long years he remains with his fixation, gradually returning to the consciousness of his predicament. This is brought to a crisis by the visit of those principally concerned, brought by the report that he is near to sanity. Among them is the Marchesa, loved twenty years before, along with her present lover, and her daughter – who looks now what the mother was then. Faced with these reminders, what should Henry choose? to step out of his sanctuary into the 'real' world, where he could not escape the pointed finger, and which has changed irrevocably since he was in it? or stay put in his madness, in the tragic struggle between Pope and Emperor, where each move has been discounted, because it has been already made, and exists (like the tragedy of the Six Characters) unchanged in its entirety? The choice which Henry makes is a sane one, though it is nominally the choice of madness. It is the choice of Don Quixote, who took refuge in an ideal world because the real one was insufficient for him. Live in the present, you will never know whether you are putting your foot on solid ground, and the effects of causes will always seem capricious. It is only the past which can seem logical, where you can know your way about; and even among the horrors of Thebes, or in the fall of Ilium, this may be sufficient compensation, and we be willing to live with a stable temperature. As Enrico IV put it, 'Il piacere, il piacere della storia, insomma, che è cosí grande!' And on the other side there is Henry's terrible accusation against his attendants, who think they live their own life, and on whom there weighs, unconsciously, all the network of habits and traditions, for which the past is responsible, and in which they are inescapably imprisoned. 'The day breaks. Time is in front of you. Dawn. – This day that is before us, you say, we will make it! – Yes? – You? And what of all the traditions? What of all the customs? Start to speak! You will repeat all the words that have been always said! You think you are living? You are chewing over the life of the dead.'

We are back, where futurism started, in the rejection of all *passatismo*. And here, for Pirandello, the letter killeth, while the spirit might go better free. The lesson of *L'Esclusa* is repeated in the plays, as with *Pensaci Giacomino*, where the labels of conventional morality lead to a devilish conclusion, and the kind solution (so also the moral one) is based on what seems immorality. Here, once again, the negatives of Pirandello are based upon a positive. With this we have a variant on the theme of *Enrico IV* in *La Vita che ti diedi*: life changes those we love, and we may preserve them better in our imagination, even when they happen to be dead, than in 'real' life, where they pass inexorably up the moving stair which takes them out of our reach. This will reach its climax in *Come tu mi vuoi*, with its dilemma of the wife disappeared in the tide of invasion, and found, apparently, in peace long afterwards. Cia, the Unknown, who comes back to play this part, and who may be (how not?) the wife, can cast herself exactly as husband and relatives knew her, years before. It is, of course, her success in this which proves she is not really what she so completely seems. For (like Henry IV) she is playing a part in the consciousness of doing so, and so can succeed more completely in it, than someone in life, who may not realize with any clarity the role which events have assigned to him. Or cognate to this matter of the role which falls to us, we have the near-tragedy of poor Martino Lori in *Tutto per bene*, who has played for years a part that everybody else assumes a fiction, so winning general contempt. For since we cannot see others as they see themselves, so others do not see us as we see ourselves. Martino Lori's long faithfulness to his dead wife's memory (she having betrayed him in circumstances all think he knows) is palpably overdone: for all, except himself. It is by chance that he makes the great discovery that his life has been based on a lie, and that his role is one he never knew of. *Tutto per bene*, in its richly comic opening, is one of the most succulent of Pirandello's comedies; and in its grave and tragic close it reaches a level near that of his most tragic plays.

In the later plays, too, Pirandello proved himself capable of a tragic intensity, notably in *Questa Sera si recita a soggetto*, where the theme of southern, primitive, jealousy, has an epic quality which rivals Verga in *Cavalleria rusticana*. And sometimes, as in *L'Amica delle Mogli*, the pursuit of an idea under the skin has an almost diabolic momentum. Here it is what we have seen touched on, the thoughts we think we have not thought, and which instead we have thought, for the simple reason that they were there to think. It is another way that madness lies; as perhaps it does in that dissolving mirror which Pirandello called *Ciascuno a suo Modo*. After the first act we come to the commentaries:

THE THIN YOUNG MAN: But what do you think of it?

THE OLD MAN: What I think! (*Pause*) I don't know. (*Pause*) What do the others say?

THIN YOUNG MAN: According to what you say, nobody could have any [*opinions*]!

OLD MAN: And don't you think that is an opinion?

THIN YOUNG MAN: Yes, but negative!

OLD MAN: Better than nothing, eh! better than nothing, my friend!

Here we might well look back through Leopardi to Bayle, the first assertor in modern Europe of the incapacity of the human mind to hit on truth, with reason a negative instrument only.

Ciascuno a suo Modo proclaims, quite as much as *Così è*, the inconsistency of the world we live in. The best that we can do is to touch the *corda civile*, putting a social face on to mask the blows we take from fate, and from our fellows (who harm us, as we harm them, casually, by mere existence – *Il Giuoco delle Parti*). When this process can no longer be endured, we can find relief in the *corda pazza*.

It's easy enough to appear mad, believe me! I'll teach you how to do it. It's enough for you to start blurting out the truth in people's faces. Nobody believes it, and everybody takes you for mad! (*Il Berretto a Sonagli*)

It may seem that the further we progress into the disconcerting world of Pirandello the further we have gone from any firm ground; that we shall be lost, like his own characters, in a trackless labyrinth. In *La Nuova Colonia* (1928) Pirandello appears as a moralist with a scale of healthy values, to be attained in a simple environment, away from the degeneracy of urban life. It is the last echo of Rousseau's optimism about the primitive past: something akin to the Leopardi of *Alla Primavera* or the *Inno ai Patriarchi*. And this recurs triumphantly in *Lazzaro* (1929), which is in some ways the summit of his achievement as dramatist. Here he has returned, it seems, towards a quasi-religious view of life, but it is a religion which is concerned supremely with the now, not with the after-now. And Sara makes appeal – the usual Pirandellian appeal against conventions – to her rustic lover, who has taught her the purity of Nature, with the real joys of human life, away from the *città maledetta*, and from the obsession of her husband, Diego, with the next world which is so obstinately out of our ken. So we are led by Lucio to the conclusion of the play, that our business is in this world, which also is God's world, to live, and let live, *working and suffering and enjoying as do all men*. It is a simple creed, maybe a limited one; but after the maze into which we had been led it is a welcome note. Nor is it limited in its implication to this one play, or to one phase, of Pirandello's thought. Behind the bewildering variety of his work there breathes the warmth of a human heart, with a sense of human values, and of human charity. That is not an unencouraging thing; but the labyrinth into which we have advanced may afford some reasonable excuse for not adventuring into that other labyrinth, of recent and unsorted literature. *Nothing but what is past is certain*: but is that quite sure itself? Who can be quite sure of the outlines of the Baroque, the Gothic, or the Classic work of art or literature? Is not the past at the same mercy of the individual vision, and Pirandellianism to be extended in a whole new sphere? At this point it may be best to leave the reader to do, what he will do in any case: to use his judgement as he will.

CHAPTER 16

The Fascist Era and Beyond

THERE are two 'labyrinths' in modern Italian literature. The more intricate is the poetic revolution broadly classifiable as hermeticism; easier to explain is the post-war reform which tried to narrow the cultural divide between literature and the masses and which introduced greater realism and 'popularity' into narrative prose. This essay intentionally concentrates on the more complex question, but its main importance lies in tracing Italy's literary development after 1922 in those two fields, to the inevitable exclusion of intriguing but secondary trends, such as post-Pirandellian drama.

The history of Italian literature, up to the advent of Ugo Foscolo, lent itself to classification under fairly clear-cut headings, corresponding to genres and movements which tended to derive, each from its precursor, without any jarring reaction to preceding traditions. Social, political and religious pressure helped to maintain conformity, by brute force if necessary. The Romantic protests and the patriotic aspirations of the nineteenth century led to the literary and political clashes with which the reader is familiar – the *classicoromanticomachia*, the exhaustion of the so-called *secondo romanticismo* and the austere and pagan reaction of Carducci and his *amici pedanti* which effectively interrupted the 'natural' development of Romanticism in Italy. With the less austere but more influential rebellion of d'Annunzio and the quieter revolution of Pascoli (and their far-reaching consequences for the language of poetry), the nineteenth century was brought to a close in a ferment of experimentation and innovation. Since the death of Pascoli the century has hardly witnessed two consecutive years without the creation of some new literary movement, formalized or otherwise, the publication of new cultural journals or the growth of affiliations of littérateurs loosely classifiable in 'schools'. Interaction and reaction between groupings have been speeded up by catalysts such as Giovanni Papini and Antonio Gramsci, and, in the first quarter of the century at least, were further accelerated by revolutionary groups of all political complexions, still free at that time to express their views.

It would be foolhardy to make any dogmatic assertions about such a period of literary ferment. Further complications spring to mind when we consider the effects of the censorship imposed by the fascist regime, a repressive tendency which began in 1922 and reached a peak after 1929. Progressive thinkers and writers had to conceal their views, on pain of imprisonment, exile or worse; many, indeed, went into voluntary exile. One effect of such repression was artificially to prolong until well into the 'forties conservative cultural influences reminiscent rather of nineteenth-century than of twentieth-century values. The fashionable names tolerated by the fascist hierarchy for their blandness or their right-wing views included the influential Papini and his contemporary Emilio Cecchi. Riccardo Bacchelli continued to produce his gargantuan historical novels. Instalments of d'Annunzio's *Opera omnia* appeared at regular intervals in their *Edizione nazionale*. Ironically, too, Pirandello's fame, particularly because of his international successes, reached a peak after the consolidation of the fascist dictatorship in 1929, and Pirandello, despite his universal warnings about the relativity of truth and although justifiably regarded as the father of modern experimental theatre, is essentially a writer whose roots lie in the final years of the nineteenth century. The contradictions do not stop here. Conversely, at the same time, Italo Svevo, whose major works express in semi-prophetic vein the uncertainty and perplexity of the period *after* his death, received true recognition only later and became increasingly popular only after 1930. And that splendid circle of (largely) ironic sceptics which made up the *Crepuscular* group were, understandably, regarded by the establishment as a cul-de-sac of literature, despite the fact that their realistic view of life and their sceptical approach to traditional values (and particularly to heroic vainglory) were attitudes which characterize many post-1945 writers, though *their* ironic laughter died in 1916.

There are other paradoxes which make for further complications. Fascist censorship was usually effective. Yet at no time in its history had Italy been so imbued with influences from abroad. Superficially Mussolini's xenophobic policies seemed to work, but even that most conservative writer, Emilio Cecchi (1884–1966), was an expert critic of Anglo-Saxon literature and an international traveller and lecturer. The leading poet of the 'twenties, Giuseppe Ungaretti (1888–1970), unconsciously the creator of the new poetic movement, *ermetismo*, was born in Egypt, educated at the Sorbonne and would later spend many years abroad, six of them as Professor of Italian in Brazil. Translations from foreign literature, particularly of American authors, abounded. It is true that the fascist censor often intervened, sometimes with bizarre results, such as the anglicizing of proper names in Cesare Pavese's rendering of John Dos Passos' novel *The Big Money* (translated in 1937). Some volumes were confiscated, notably the first edition of Elio Vittorini's anthology *Americana* in 1941, which contained translations from fifteen American authors. Yet most major contemporary novelists were translated into Italian, a growing preference being shown for American authors; in *their* work the young intelligentsia saw moral, civic and stylistic ideals of absolute liberty which compared favourably with the conditional liberties available to them under fascism. The inflow of those new ideas, their absorption by the most progressive intellectuals and the simultaneous prohibition on native Italians freely to express like thoughts could lead, after the Liberation, in only one direction. When the pressure was taken off in 1945 the explosive mixture which had been latent for over a decade erupted in new and revolutionary directions. The criterion for art and life would then be *impegno*, 'commitment', and significantly it would be left-wing writers and thinkers who would most influence the new trends.

Indeed, if there is one thread which leads through the next literary labyrinth – the post-war period – it must be political commitment. Since the end of World War II that preoccupation has at times become obsessive, often to the detriment of literary work. It was natural for a reaction to arise against the suppression of free speech and equally natural for the reaction to come from the Left. The symbol and catalyst for the new development was Antonio Gramsci (1891–1937). His ten years in fascist prisons, a period which ended in illness and death, gave him added time to meditate on the inequity of Italian society and, outside the traditional and bourgeois groups, the cultural alienation of the Italian nation. The publication of his *Quaderni del carcere* after 1948 came as an added boost and inspiration to his disciples. His ideas had been shared by dynamic young contemporaries of his, notably Elio Vittorini (1908–66), all equally anxious to oppose totalitarianism and involve the nation as a whole in many kinds of cultural and political activity. Vittorini and others fought intellectually, then physically against nazism, and he and his fellow partisans were, after the war, handed the means to put their cultural ideas into practice.

To understand the new attitudes fully we need to refer briefly to the political situation of the 1920's. Supporters of Mussolini's fascist regime attempted from the outset to attack and possibly suppress not only liberal and left-wing movements, but also lively and stimulating ideas from other quarters. Contributors to the more reactionary journal *La Ronda*, for instance, which was published 1919–23, attacked the earlier and livelier *La Voce* (1908–1916), whose political supplement urged political involvement. They also conducted campaigns against the degeneracy in Italian letters brought about, they thought, by Futurism; one of their number, Vilfredo Pareto (1848–1923), defended the violence he saw inherent in fascism; other articles attacked even the innocuous linguistic innovations of Giovanni Pascoli. Perhaps their most typical attitude is expressed by Vincenzo Cardarelli (1887–1959), who preferred to act and write 'prudently', to concentrate on beauty of form and on uncontroversial rather than provocative content, considering and stressing those aspects of the Italian classics which might have contemporary significance for society; Cardarelli laid particular emphasis in this last respect on the work of Leopardi. Manzoni and Leopardi were upheld by him as major stylistic exemplars: he even regretted that the *H* had fallen from the spelling of *umanità*, thus blurring the essential 'humanity' of those studies. The programme, as outlined by Cardarelli, and the vast majority of its articles were at best complacent and often defended right-wing points of view. For some years such opinions were effectively opposed in liberal and left-wing publications, such as the socialist *Ordine nuovo*, edited by Antonio Gramsci, or the liberal reviews of Piero Gobetti (1901–26), *Rivoluzione liberale* and *Il Baretti*. But by 1928 the regime itself was intervening more and more to prevent freedom of expression, literary or otherwise. By then the mild *Baretti* had been suppressed, Antonio Gramsci had been imprisoned, despite parliamentary immunity (he was communist Member for Venice), and the courageous Gobetti, severely beaten on three separate occasions by fascist *squadristi*, had died, his physique weakened by the attacks, in a Paris hospital. He was just twenty-five years old; there were worse outrages.

Subsequently the regime would treat with increasing harshness its literary as well as its specifically political opponents. Some were banished to distant villages or islands (and they included first-rank writers like Carlo Levi Cesare Pavese and Emilio Lussu), others were thrown into prison (and Antonio Gramsci, Leone Ginzburg, Alfonso Gatto and Giorgio Bassani were among the many), still others were driven into exile (Ignazio Silone and Franco Fortini are instances of *letterati* who escaped persecution in this way). Other writers left Italy as foreign correspondents or academics, on long periods of virtually self-imposed exile.

The political corruption at the head of the state coincided with bizarre symptoms in its leading literary members. The hermeticists, with a fair contempt for anyone outside their narrow intellectual circle, expressed themselves in increasingly esoteric and, even for cultured Italians, largely incomprehensible verse. Italo Svevo's preoccupation with psychological abnormalities was accompanied and followed by Pirandello's scenic portrayals of schizophrenia. The dying embers of Futurism cast a mad light on that group's final attempts to demonstrate their originality. Italy's most popular novelist, Alberto Moravia, made his name with *Gli indifferenti* (1929), a study of the breakdown of human relationships, the sheer boredom of participating in bourgeois family life. Cesare Pavese (1908–50) summed up the lonely desolation of the sensitive but disillusioned intellectual with an increasing output of prose and verse which verged on the maudlin in its repeated themes of introspection, alienation and disillusionment. The man who was potentially Italy's finest poet of the time, Dino Campana, died with his talent not fully expressed, after a lifetime spent in and out of psychiatric clinics. And while it would be stupid to suggest that his madness had anything to do with the regime of the time (the first onset of his illness was in 1900), he was, paradoxically, a clear-sighted madman who saw through the vacuity of many literary contemporaries, argued logically with those who commiserated with him (*he* had obtained tranquillity, he claimed) and saw the emptiness, for him at least, of the Italian cultural scene. He admitted his madness, but wondered: 'Chissa chi, fra tutti, sia il pazzo?' His words might serve as an epigram on the inter-war years.

The poetic production of three important writers usefully

bridges the gap between the rise of fascism and the present day. Giuseppe Ungaretti (1888–1970), Eugenio Montale (b. 1896) and Salvatore Quasimodo (1901–68) are the best known and most influential Italian poets of the past half-century, the last two being recipients of the Nobel prize for literature in 1975 and 1959 respectively. It was Quasimodo who declared that during the period 1939–40 the three of them were considered to be the leaders of the so-called hermeticists. *La poesia ermetica* had been the title of a collection of essays published in 1936 by the influential critic Francesco Flora. He took his title from a reference to Hermes Trismegistus, the Graeco-Egyptian god, whose mystical and magical influence was said to have inspired some of the more obscurantist views of Neoplatonist philosophers in the fourth century. Flora evidently wished to allude, with his own form of limpid clarity, to what he considered the obscurity of these poems. Like other literary and artistic insults, *ermetismo* was taken and woven into a banner around which has rallied a generation of poets and poetasters.

The innovations introduced by the hermeticists came as a private social reaction to the bombast of fascism and, more importantly, as a rejection of the academic tradition which had made Carducci the *poeta-vates* of the Risorgimento, and, after his death, had led d'Annunzio and Pascoli to aspire in their different ways to his role. Blows had already been dealt to that pompous ideal by the *Crepuscolari*, the loosely knit group of ironic and unheroic poets whose most notable representatives were Guido Gozzano (1883–1916) and Sergio Corazzini (1887–1907). Gozzano can forgive God for his lack of help when he considers in the poem *L'altro*:

> . . . che avresti anche potuto,
> invece che farmi gozzano
> un po' scimunito, ma greggio,
> farmi gabrieldannunziano:
> sarebbe stato ben peggio!

And he pretends, for irony's sake, to have no illusions about his more modest style of poetry:

> Buon Dio, e puro conserva
> questo mio stile che pare
> lo stile d'uno scolare
> corretto un po' da una serva.

The futurists had launched more boisterous attacks on the academic tradition, and their noisy, if often vacuous and ephemeral, revolution, allied to the linguistic innovations introduced by Pascoli and d'Annunzio, meant that by 1920 it was no longer possible to gain a poetic reputation in Italy through the literary style which, for its highly academic aspects, had for centuries characterized Italian. Marinetti's *parole in libertà* had broken with the previous logic of language; Italy, he declared in his preface to *Revolverate* of G. P. Lucini (1867–1914), was the country of intellectual and moral tyrannies against which it was a sacred duty to fight with the arm of Poetry, 'di una poesia libera, emancipata da tutti i vincoli tradizionali, ritmata alla sinfonia dei comizi, delle officine, delle automobili, degli aeroplani volanti'. His attacks on the past in *Guerra sola igiene del mondo* reject the 'sentimentalismo balbuziente e botanico di Pascoli', the 'stomachevole caffè e latte di sacristia del nostro deplorevole Fogazzaro' and above all d'Annunzio's Romantic sentimentality, his morbid nostalgia, his obsession with sex, his mania for academic reminiscences and his relish for collecting the physical and moral bric-à-brac of history. Those criticisms are worth recalling. Marinetti expressed well the kind of judgement on *passatismo* which would be repeated more or less openly for the next thirty years and would surface again in the post-1945 period, generalized and politicized then to refer to 'bourgeois' literature. More immediately the *ermetici* seemed to have similar kinds of objections to the past, but tacitly they also objected to the illogicality of the futurists. And whereas the futurist revolt was to lead into a literary backwater, choked in its débris of unconnected logic and ungrammatical language, the *ermetici* reacted more austerely. On *their* verse they imposed a rigid linguistic discipline, preferring, to the formulaic monsters and mechanical noises of the futurist machine-guns and factories, a more human dimension; preferring, too, to restore to the *logos* its proper logic and so avoiding those devices of d'Annunzio which so obsessed *him* that often he allowed a plethora of them to swamp a lovely poetic idea. Their poetry, while expressing the basic essentials of their artistic message, also contains the germs of many more imaginative and symbolic statements.

The evocation of so many ideas in such precise and abbreviated expressions gave rise to poems like the famous tercet of Quasimodo, *Ed è subito sera*, where the poet compresses into three lines so many imaginative ideas – loneliness, nature's warmth and man's origins, the light of reason and of hope, the pitiless glare of the day, the transience of life and ambition and the advent of evening and death. That concision, particularly in the poetry of Ungaretti, stemmed from techniques learned from the French decadents and symbolists. As we shall see, one of Ungaretti's merits was to transplant into Italian poetry many unprecedented innovations from France. The contrast between the new 'provincial' atmosphere which the fascist regime encouraged, and the international (and particularly French) flavour of Ungaretti's poems made their comprehension as well as their reception difficult. Yet, with one of those paradoxes which characterize the inter-war years, it was Mussolini who wrote the preface to Ungaretti's edition of *Il porto sepolto* when it came out in 1923. The *ermetici* were not to achieve widespread recognition until the publication of Quasimodo's collection *Ed è subito sera*, in 1942. By then, however, the poetic mood was changing fast and *ermetismo* was worked out; indeed, just three years later, by the end of the war, some would say that poetry of any kind had to take second place to prose.

Before meeting the *ermetici* proper, a word must be added

about the life and work of Umberto Saba (1883–1957) and
Dino Campana (1885–1932), both of whom provide a
primary reaction against the futurists, Saba with his per-
sistent vein of gentle autobiographical (essentially pacifist)
poetry, Campana with open declarations against what he
called 'their colourless and unharmonic improvisations',
their 'false poetry'. Saba, the provincial poet from a still
Austro–Hungarian Trieste, secured for many years, despite
an inferiority complex, a certain physical serenity, until the
racial laws of the nazi-fascists drove him from his quiet
bookshop in 1944 to seek refuge in Florence and Rome.
His *Canzoniere* and the defensive, well written *Storia e
cronistoria del Canzoniere* trace his life from humble Jewish
origins in Trieste, through two periods of military service
(1908 and again 1915–18), the relative tranquillity of inter-
war Trieste, the frightening chaos of the last years of the
war and a final return to Trieste, a disappointed man but
still advocating ideals of human friendship. The two periods
of military service provided him with much original material,
particularly for his *Versi militari* (1908) and *Poesie scritte
durante la guerra* (1918). The first are unusual for their combination of simple vocabulary (reflecting the humble
soldiers who are there portrayed) and more formal syntax, a
technical combination which was to characterize most of
Saba's poetic production. The 'humanity' of the experiences
described contrasts with contemporary exaltation of war as
the great prophylaxis (d'Annunzio's and Marinetti's outbursts were typical of that attitude). His later participation
in the 1914–18 struggle was largely comforted by the thought
that he was helping to free Trieste from Austrian rule. His
verse is again anti-heroic, full of small human incident; the
wounded *Zaccaria*, for instance, recalls childhood, home,
mother and family, and writes his own epitaph: *Io sono | un
quore che con quista molti quori*. Never far away in Saba's verse
is his love of animals and affection for the countryside,
themes which crop up in many autobiographical poems
similar in mood to Pascoli's. This is especially so after 1945;

in his earlier work the mood associated with those themes is different. There is often found a transference to human figures of some of the animal characteristics most loved by the poet. Here perhaps we see a weakness – indiscrimination. It is one thing to describe soldiers scrapping light-heartedly as 'young puppies', but it is in doubtful taste, since he intended the poem in no uncomplimentary way, to ascribe to his wife (in *A mia moglie*) the characteristics of a pregnant heifer or a long bitch. Those similes are surrounded by other, perhaps more tasteful descriptions – she is 'like a young white pullet . . . a frightened rabbit . . . a returning swallow . . . a provident ant.' The poem, he wrote later, 'caused merriment and laughter' and, while he expected 'thanks and praise' from his wife, 'she took it badly, very badly'. He was to defend the poem for thirty years.

Although Dino Campana declared himself irritated by the 'vacuity' of the futurists, their fragmented and staccato world may seem often mirrored in his own wandering thoughts; other poems and prose poems of *Canti orfici* have reminiscences of d'Annunzio about them. But there are differences which, given time, might have made Campana into the Arthur Rimbaud of Italy. D'Annunzio had seen, beneath the phenomena of nature, an unknown magic which it was the poet's duty to examine – the deepest shadow in a wood might contain mysteries of nature which only the poetic imagination could evoke and describe. The revelation or examination of the unknown – Arthur Rimbaud's *inconnu* – went beyond mere natural description: d'Annunzio revivified myths which folklore had hallowed, many others he created from his fertile imagination and his close observation of nature. But, by comparison with Campana's new approach, d'Annunzio's most imaginative explanations of nature's hidden secrets seem transparent, his concepts logical and obvious.

Labyrinthine indeed are the thoughts of Campana, and space here permits only a brief (but, I hope, enthusiastic) mention. D'Annunzio called himself at one time 'the sighted blind-man'; Campana could well be called 'the wise mad-man'. D'Annunzio seems to have gone slowly mad towards the end of his life, Campana's first onset of madness came early, in 1900, and the final fifteen years of his life he passed in a mental hospital. Of the remaining thirty-three years, many were spent in more or less aimless wandering – through Italy, Europe, South America – engaged in an incredible number and variety of unskilled employments. Critics and gossip columnists created equally incredible myths about his life. His poetic output was small but infinitely varied. The *Canti orfici* (first edition 1914) were largely written before his worst bouts of illness. As their individual titles make clear, most of the poems describe autobiographical experiences: a night in Faenza, his native Marradi, visits to brothels, a trip to Montevideo, the contemplation of a Palazzeschi painting, the streets and buildings of Florence, a hike to La Verna. Reality, often sordid reality, is present here, but reality is of secondary importance; this is a new 'Orphism', concerned with the mysteries which underlie phenomena, and with the equally mysterious evocative and creative power of poetry. For Campana those mysteries did not lend themselves to rational explanation or description. Instead, if they *are* to be represented, they require some irrational or sub-rational means of expression. A flickering candle in a wayside shrine at Marradi (*L'invetriata*) becomes for the poet a symbol of uncertainty, of his unknown future and, hence, of anxiety and doubt. Contrasts in colours, in light and shade, visual echoes of the burning candle in a distant lamp on a river terrace, disquieting scents of putrefaction, the distance of the stars – 'mother-of-pearl buttons on an evening dressed in velvet' – the tremulous appearance of the evening and the red wound opened in its heart which corresponds to the paradoxical red seal of doubt in the poet's own heart – all are aspects adding to the uncertainty of the unknown hand which first lit the candle. The grammar here is traditional, but suggestion, intuition and impression are generally more important to Campana than logical, grammatical progression (just as those qualities became more important to Picasso than photographic representation). Yet even such paraphrases are over-dogmatic. The reader should feel free to interpret Campana as he wishes, and if he does not wish to do so, if this poetry is too obscure, Campana can make the classic reply that the public is free not to read it. Ardengo Soffici reports authoritatively how Campana deliberately forced people *not* to read it if he thought them intellectually incapable of appreciating it, how, during a period when he *had* to sell his works in the piazzas and cafés of Florence, he had recourse to the simple expedient of tearing out those more difficult poems which he thought his customers would find incomprehensible.

Campana's power is not exhausted here, however. It ranges from poetry of suggestion to more traditional and lyrical description, as in the sublimity of the fragment *Bastimento in viaggio*, where rhythm and language combine to evoke colour and chiaroscuro (again), unbounded space and narrow limits, sinuosity and angularity, silence and plashing water. And from this open-air lyric he can range to the experience in *Poesia fetida* of being thrown out of a brothel, too drunk to stay awake (and literally incapable), or the description of the *bassi fondi* of Florence in *Notturno teppista*. Unlike the experimenter Rimbaud, Campana indulged in these multifarious activities spontaneously rather than deliberately. It is worth recalling, finally, that Campana was a most erudite man, fluent in several languages and widely read. The title of the collection implies his Classical knowledge; the poems themselves are crammed with evocative allusions from past literatures. He may have been mad, but we should not regard him as an ignorant madman or as a charlatan, as so many contemporary journalists and patronizing critics alleged.

Interest in Campana's poetry increased after his death. His work seemed to foreshadow many of the innovations associated with *ermetismo*; his disregard for tradition, as well as his novel imaginings, certainly influenced his successors. Yet the new tendencies were not to every-one's taste. One of Saba's greatest disappointmentes was the acclaim accorded to his hermeticist contemporaries during the long winters of his own unfashionability. In 1946 his prose collection *Scorciatoie e raccontini* defines '*short-cuts*' as 'shorter but very difficult ways for getting from one place to another'. Their difficulty, he thought, produced 'a nostalgia for long, straight, provincial roads' (unfortunate that the *strada provinciale* now has undertones of 'secondary road'). The allusion was clear to him; more bitterly he can criticize the new poetics and the 'obscurity' of Montale in particular, defining *Ermetismo* in the same work as 'Crossword puzzles; plus (in the case of Montale) Montalian poetry'.

But Saba was swimming against the current, as were those critics generally favourable to him (Pietro Pancrazi and Francesco Flora, for instance) who preferred to ignore or scorn the new mood. The fact that, before 1945, Ungaretti, Montale and then Quasimodo wrote in an esoteric and difficult manner encouraged critics to classify them to-gether and Flora gave them their title – the hermeticists, *gli ermetici*. But the three major exponents of *ermetismo*, despite certain common (and superficial) features, are very different in style and mood.

Giuseppe Ungaretti spent his first twenty-four years in Egypt. He was educated at a Swiss lycée in Alexandria and from an early age was as familiar with French and French literature as he was with Italian. Two years at the Sorbonne (1912–14) and a friendship with Guillaume Apollinaire confirmed that familiarity; his second book of verse, *La guerre*, published in 1919, was in French; he married Jeanne Dupoix in Paris in the same year. Not surprisingly, then, when his poetry began to appear it had more French than Italian tradition behind it. Perhaps the most important feature common to all the *ermetici* was their willingness to accept, and exploit in their poetry, non-Italian literary tendencies. For traditional critics (such as Flora) it was slightly unnerving to find that Italy was participating in a European cultural movement and to discover (as did Cecchi and Cardarelli) that their ideals of classical Italian models were being ignored.

Ungaretti's experiences as a front-line soldier during the First World War find expression in his first collection, *Il porto sepolto* (1916). Many of his strongest themes are already present: the dreams of an expatriate (who, sadly, *never* has a true *patria*); alienation; a longing for 'brotherhood' with his fellows; *ennui*; the desire for a self-effacement verging on despair; at the same time a feeling for survival, as when he sits alongside a slaughtered companion and writes 'letters full of love', musing that he has never felt so attached to life (*La veglia*). The best poems in this group are *In memoria* and *I fiumi*, both of which treat of exile from one's native land, alienation and isolation from one's fellows. Like everything else he would write, this is autobiographical and very personal poetry; significantly, the Mondadori selection of 1966 is entitled *Vita d'un uomo*. Even the *Porto sepolto* is an obscure autobiographical allusion to an ancient harbour, buried in the sand, discovered by his fathers' friends in Alexandria. The melancholy tone of these and other poems will acquire a film of consolation when Ungaretti becomes a Catholic convert in 1928, and his religion later helps him to bear greater sorrows (particularly the death of his nine-year-old son, Antonio, in 1939). That consolation is his 'universal message' for his reader. The increasing conviction that man is a fallen creature becomes obsessive in the poems (1937–46) collected under the title *Il dolore* in 1947. *Mio fiume anche tu* is an extreme example – a prayer to Christ, ending in eight lines which echo the Catholic *Sanctus*. The mood rarely changes throughout the main stream of his poetry, and injections of remembered grief prolong it. *Gridasti: Soffoco*, published as late as 1952, is a harrowing description of his son's dying moments, its tone almost Pascolian (the Pascoli of *Il giorno dei morti*). Some, less subjective, work gets away from the doleful mood – *Mono-loghetto* is a long poem which describes a February journey through Corsica, carnival time and the countryside of Brazil, though even here the author's glance seems disapproving.

Ungaretti's initial importance lay in his revolutionary use of language, particularly in the early compositions. In his *Commiato* of 1916 he notes his receptivity to words appropriate to his purpose and implies the 'depth' of meaning and association which each word holds for him:

> Quando trovo
> in questo mio silenzio
> una parola
> scavata è nella mia vita
> come un abisso

He replaced the inarticulate formulae of the futurists and the luxuriant language of d'Annunzio with verses pared to the minimum limit. Not for him the traditional lyric to describe, for instance, rosy-fingered dawn (his *Rosso e azzurro* in *Sentimento del tempo* is a very unreal dawn indeed). His most striking poem of the 'essential' type is probably *Mattina* (1917), which consists of the two lines (some would say two words):

> M'illumino
> d'immenso.

It could reasonably be argued that without a title those lines would have little meaning; yet title, light and immensity, taken together, have an undeniable evocative power. This skeletal form may be a deliberate exaggeration of his reaction to the old Romantic rhetorical devices and to the futurists' onomatopoeic and formulaic noises, but the attitude will influence his linguistic notions in much longer poems. Ellipsis rather than elaboration will be the key to his meaning, and if his verses seem to have more than one interpretation, this is a proof of the incredible power of words, with their countless evocative possibilities, with their magic ability to translate into intelligibility the mysteries underlying life.

Ungaretti's experiences were international; his translations from other literatures are impressive. Yet he is essentially concerned with language, poetry and imagination, and, by contrast with Montale, never seems to get beyond a narrow personal and Italian limit in his moral for posterity. If Ungaretti's early direction was largely French and his later production largely personal and Italian, Montale, despite his massive allegiance to the Italian poetic tradition, was a European, his philosophy, from the outset, universal and cosmopolitan. Ungaretti continued to elaborate what had become a provincial movement, while Montale's quasi-Leopardian solution to the dilemma of man's existence anticipated existentialism and is international in scope. If Ungaretti was limited by his preference for French poetic sensitivity, Montale had no such limits; on the contrary, he had a finer feeling for the Italian tradition – particularly the work of Leopardi, the techniques of Pascoli and d'Annunzio and possibly the reaction of Campana. The main message which emanates from Montale's poetry is a paradoxical one – apparent hope in his early poems for his other, more naive fellows and an ironically wry view for the sceptic like himself. In his later poems the themes develop, hope passes to the poet. Men may be stupid and life ridiculous, but the very bloom of absurdity which surrounds the whole may make life seem worth living. Not all of Montale's readers will find hope in all this.

Ossi di seppia, Montale's first collection of poems (which go back to 1916), set the standard for his moral attitude and for his 'poetic'. They are essentially Leopardian, though Montale has a toughness which makes him seem at times more ironic, at times more positive than his great predecessor. Typical and illustrative of his attitude are the poems of *Meriggi e Ombre* entitled *Agave sullo scoglio*. 'ora son io / l'agave', says the 'humble' poet who had already declared in his introductory poems (*In limine* and *I limoni*) that he wished to help his fellow man and did *not* wish to use a high-falutin' style. He chooses objects from everyday life – particularly in *Ossi* from life on the Riviera di Levante – but to them he gives a universal appeal. The sea becomes for him the symbol of eternity, the cosmos, a father figure, a paradoxical entity, ever-present (and so eternal) but at the same time ever-moving, ever in flux. Why the poet should identify with the *Agave* is not immediately clear. This ridiculous botanical giant can survive a hundred years; it blossoms once, gives out its seeds, dies and rots away. Man's purpose may seem no stronger. When Montale says that he is now the agave, he is making of his own and of mankind's situation a much more absurd predicament than did Leopardi, who saw men as yielding genista bushes. Yet the agave clings on to the sheerest cliffs, loving its own survival techniques, even during the severest gale; it languishes in the tormented immobility of the hottest scirocco; in the days of warm and boring lassitude the possibility of the unknown, something beyond the horizon (*più in là*), stimulates to survive and hope for the best. Hope may be too strong a word for the mood of these poems; one remove from hope, they imply the need to hold on, to continue in the expectation that hope may come.

One important poetic theme (and imaginative device) for Montale is that of memory. *Le occasioni* (1939) as the title implies, are 'occasions' or 'chance happenings' which offer poetic opportunities, however tenuous, to recall past events, memory-triggers of a Proustian kind. The occasion may be a vision of some trivial reality – the amulet of Dora Markus, the flash of a mirror, the reflection of the sea. Many of the memories touched off are personal to the poet and may not always seem logical to his readers, but there is always some kind of thread. The darkest poems of *Ossi di seppia* had already contained apocalyptic thoughts on an after-life, where the dead (in *I morti* especially) have found not a peace beyond all understanding but an uncomfortable reality, more absurd than life. There are apocalyptic visions in *Le occasioni*, too. But, as in *Ossi* there were gleams of expectation to keep irrational hopes alive, so in *Occasioni* a figure re-appears (an anonymous *tu*, generally accepted as a feminine image) to add some consolation to life and particularly in the love poems, *Mottetti*, where Montale is looking into some hard problems concerned with love, sex and know-ledge. The poems are very difficult and Montale is disin-genuous (and may seem to us nowadays a little arrogant) in a prefatory note to his exiguous explanations of 'the few rare places where an excessive familiarity (*confidenza*) with my material may have induced me to be less than trans-parent'. Either the explanations are unnecessary or his comments unkind (he gives 'his simpler readers (*lettori più semplici*) some geographical indications'). The remarks lack the justification which made Bertrand Russell append similar barbs to his *Unpopular Essays*. Yet Montale must have been irritated by the incomprehension of the contemporary establishment and the ineptitude of the fascist hierarchy which was leading Italy to a grim destiny. In 1938 he had been dismissed from his comfortable post as Director of the Vieusseux Institute in Florence, having refused to enrol in the fascist party. *Il colpevole* in the prose collection *La farfalla di Dinard* (1956–1969) is an evocation of his experiences and of the atmosphere of the time; one of the *Occasioni, Notizie dall'Amiata*, shows the splendid isolation of the poet.

The underlying preoccupation of the collection *Finisterre* (1943), later included in *La bufera e altro* of 1956, is World War II.

Les princes n'ont point d'yeux pour voir ces grand's
merveilles;
Leurs mains ne servent plus qu'à nous persécuter.

Agrippa d'Aubigné's lines serve as an introduction for *La bufera,* and the allusion to contemporary political masters is clear. Some critics wrote about Montale's isolation as though it were something he regretted. There is no doubt that he felt it a good thing to steer clear of the lunacies perpetrated around him. These poems are also concerned with the consolation which, for the poet at least, may be obtained from what may often appear to be trivial reality. The feminine presence of earlier collections is more in evidence, more consolatory. Again the poems are very personal and difficult, both for their esotericism and for the many oblique echoes of other literatures and languages. *Bedlington*, for instance (in *Madrigali fiorentini*), was misinterpreted as a type of aeroplane until Montale explained that it was a breed of dog; *bovindo* (in the prose piece *Dov'era il tennis*) is another barely comprehensible word (except for graduates in architecture) until recognised as an Italianisation of 'bow window'. Irony and sarcasm are never far away in the poems of *La bufera e altro,* but consolatory notes are also present, particularly for the poet, in the final poems *Piccolo testamento* and, most importantly, *Sogno del prigioniero*. There the grim atmosphere of one of Stalin's (?) purges is mitigated by the prisoner-poet's dream – his imagination can change the mattress straw to gold and his dream can continue.

The collection of Montale's critical and other prose, *Auto da fé,* which came out in 1966, allows us to see something of the development of his thought. His isolation becomes clear; his opposition to all forms of dictatorship, popular or otherwise, is sustained in the name of art and culture; the intellectual's task is to hand on to future generations the best elements of the past, to open the eyes of his fellow men to the dangers of losing individuality. As we shall see, these are ideas which the political Left were simultaneously trying to combat. The ivory tower of the intellectual becomes a favourite target of theirs and the hermeticists seemed to encapsulate that concept more than most.

Satura (1971) contains his most ironic (and sometimes comic) productions. The first part of the book, however, *Xenia,* forms a series of colloquies – magnificently moving, some of them – with his dead wife; she appears as the consolatory feminine figure of so many other poems, evoked by the poet's memory or recalled by the presence of familiar old objects, trivial realities, an old daguerreotype, a tin shoe-horn, a family photograph in its oval frame. But *Satura* itself, as the name implies, is a collection or miscellany of often piquant, sometimes bitter pieces. *Botta e risposta* looks ironically at his own life and sees the Italy of fascism as Augean stables, its corridors deep in excrement; yet the fall of the regime seemed to bring no change for the better, the liberators seem no more than ants and the safety rafts swirling on the waters of the new Alpheus are solidified turds. Self-mockery is never far away, either; he can quote his own verse and make fun of it; he is simply more of a clown than his fellows. Without the ironic humour this poetry could be bitter indeed.

The same year saw the publication of his *Diario del* '71, published along with *Diario del* '72 in 1973. The new collection contained a variety of poems which continue many of the early themes, seen now through older eyes and perhaps with more than the usual disappointment. *La mia musa* ironically traces the parabola of his poetry while other poems imply that his purpose, such as it was, is no longer valid – indeed, that there is no purpose anyway. The only certainty is that someone else's backside will slide into the seat of the *Principe della festa*.

Montale was an excellent translator, his criticism is acute and penetrating – he was the first Italian to recognize and publicize the qualities of Svevo's novels. The prose of *La farfalla di Dinard* (more especially) and of *Auto da fé* and *Fuori di casa* is as stimulating as some of his poetry. Here, better than in the abstractions of his critics, the reader who finds his poetry difficult may find many clues to his meaning. The symbol which gave Montale's first collection its title was the dried cuttlefish bone – and d'Annunzio had noted its incidental gleam on the seashore. For Montale it becomes the poetic detritus of the all-blessing sea (whereas, by contrast, earth-bound 'civilization' pours into the parental bosom washing-up liquid and waste paper). The dry bones of cuttlefish are used in aviaries as gentle whetstones to allow singing-birds to sharpen their bills. For the younger generation of poets, particularly during the 'thirties, Montale was the most influential poetic leader.

One man who did whet his early poetic skills on Montale and his predecessors was Salvatore Quasimodo. To him belongs the merit of making the breakthrough and popularizing the new poetics. The problem of new techniques had been resolved when Ungaretti brought into Italian the theories and examples of the French decadents. Montale also accepted and developed the new forms. Quasimodo continued the elaboration of the techniques of *ermetismo,* until, by 1945, according to his *Discorso sulla poesia,* it seemed to him that its season was past, the younger generation *engagé* and the need for 'social poetry' most pressing.

In 1926 a new literary review, *Solaria,* was launched in Florence. During its eight years of life (it was suppressed by the fascist censor for publishing (1934) Vittorini's *Garofano rosso*) it provided a focal point for the livelier mind open particularly to literary influence from outside Italy. Montale, for instance, who had in 1929 been appointed Director of the Gabinetto scientifico-letterario Vieusseux, was a member of the Florentine inner circle, and his poems, along with those of Ungaretti and the new French poets, became major topics of discussion and argument. Quasimodo was invited to Florence by Elio Vittorini, who had himself begun to write for *Solaria* in 1929 and had become its editorial secretary the following year. Both Vittorini and Quasimodo were born in eastern Sicily; Vittorini had married Quasimodo's sister, Rosina, and in 1929 it was he who encouraged the budding poet to publish three poems in *Solaria.* And in 1930 Salvatore Quasimodo's first collection, *Acque e terre,* was published on the *Solaria* presses. As yet Quasimodo was still artistically unformed. This becomes clear when we consider the Pascolian features of poems like *I morti* and *Specchio,* or the Dannunzianism of *Fresca marina* or even the

Christian melancholy of *Si china il giorno*, with its echoes of Corazzini's religiosity. His reliance on earlier poetic trends must have seemed obvious to him; in the final version of *Acque e terre* (1942) many poems will be rejected, re-written or abbreviated, as is the famous *Ed è subito sera*, originally the final tercet of a longer poem called *Solitudini*. Yet the themes of the earliest poems will recur until the outbreak of World War II, evoking a sense of solitude, sadness, despair, suffering, regrets at death and the passage of all things, a nostalgia for the past and for his roots, particularly in Sicily. And the Christian sentiments of *Si china il giorno* are never far from the surface during the rest of his life, though they never become intrusive or overpowering.

Two years after this collection another group, *Òboe sommerso*, was published. Beginning in 1936, he was to publish on average a collection every two years, with one or two unavoidable pauses during the war and during transfers to new posts (until 1938 he worked as a surveyor in various government enterprises). From the beginning Montale recognized in Quasimodo a fellow artist with similar aspirations to his own. Reviewing *Acque e terre* in 1931, he comments upon the *difficulty* of these poems, and notes, in words prophetically applicable to his own lyrics of the coming years, that this art is 'closed to the understanding and the affection of the multitude'. That 'obscurity' was to persist in Quasimodo until the outbreak of war. In the collection *Giorno dopo giorno* of 1947 his style, as we shall see, had changed to a more realistic and universally comprehensible mode, and by the time of his Nobel prize (1959) his acceptance speech, *Il poeta e il politico*, describes the poet or artist as a prime defender of political as well as cultural liberties. It is a theme which will recur in many of his post-war critical essays, notably his *Discorso sulla poesia* of 1954, where his aspirations come much nearer to those of his brother-in-law, Vittorini, and those intellectuals who were seeking to close the gap between public and artist. Although it is no longer fashionable to see Quasimodo's development in such a light, in a brief essay like the present it does help to compress an otherwise undogmatic poet into a formula of this kind. Certainly this is biographically an accurate view of his development, and one visible in the chronology of the ten collections which precede *Dare e avere* of 1966, edited (1960) in the Mondadori volume *Tutte le poesie* (and in the splendid *Meridiani* volume of 1973/77).

Sergio Solmi, introducing *Ed è subito sera*, saw in the new poetry a sense of conflict or splitting of personality, a nostalgia, perhaps, for some lost paradisiac existence; other critics have defined the tone as elegiac. Certainly thoughts of death (paradoxically awakening him to life) and illusions which are disappointed, a *mal di vita* and a Leopardian *noia* which becomes *inerzia* in some poems, are recurrent motifs. Critics are generally agreed that, to express those moods, Quasimodo's choice of vocabulary and its collocation in certain recognizable 'Quasimodo' combinations is a feature of his poetry. Antithesis, oxymoron and paradox, for instance, seem at times an obsession with him: 'smiles which sadden', 'suffering which makes me serene', 'I lose you in order to have you', 'faithful enemy' – these are typical of a technique which sometimes creates a tension, sometimes a chiaroscuro (and so elegiac) effect in his work. Later, in *Seguendo l'Alfeo* (*La terra impareggiabile*), his visit to Olympia will show him the 'absurdity of obscure contrasts', and, despite the harmony of nature visible in Greece, he is searching only for 'dissonances'. The use of antonyms is, expectedly, frequent in this hermeticist period. The effect of these contrasts may well be to show Quasimodo's own particular reaction to the new *mal du siècle*, which in Ungaretti had led to a more open Catholicism and in Montale to irony and scepticism. In terms of the new jargon, this was an indication of his particular existential state, the sign of an irreducible interior conflict.

The relatively traditional verse of the first collection becomes more opaque in *Òboe sommerso* (1932). These poems are a good warning to his reader that he intends to evoke atmosphere in new and startling ways. The opening poem, composed with almost medieval attention to symmetry in its arrangement of words, sees the poet identifying with natural objects (the sea and sky are and will be particular favourites); his hands are grassy (*erbose*); but he allows himself liberties with the natural world: 'evening falls . . . into me', 'the water sets' (instead of the expected 'sun'!). He is fond of using reflected objects: his trees may grow upside-down, his boats may sail upturned; the dawn can avalanche into his mind. Yet there are also moments of less esoteric beauty in poems like *Ora sale il giorno* or *Già la pioggia è con noi* (in *Ed è subito sera*), which have a lyrical beauty about them appreciable in any poetic climate.

Quasimodo 'hung up his lyre' for most of the war: 'How could we sing with the enemy's heel on our heart?' (*Alle fronde dei salici*). The gloomy forebodings present in much of the poetry before 1939 seemed confirmed by the holocaust of the war. Abstraction became translated into red, swollen corpses in *Milano, Agosto 1943* (in *Giorno dopo giorno*), and in *Il mio paese è l'Italia* apocalyptic visions are converted into the death-camps of Poland with their heaps of burning petrol-soaked bodies. Suddenly the poet comes down from his ivory tower and begins to write committed poetry. The *Lamento per il Sud*, which opens the collection significantly entitled *La vita non è sogno*, reflects the gravest social problem in Italian history, the division of the peninsula into rich and poor, north and south. *Quasi un madrigale* of the same collection begins with what seems an old theme of Quasimodo's – sunset, autumnal season, the death of day and of the year – yet the poem has a positive affirmation: the day and the sun are 'ours' and the sun's rays, however thin, are 'affectionate'; life is 'endless' and the poet no longer has memories, no longer wishes to remember.

The change in the poet's outlook is complete. To accompany his speech on *Il poeta e il politico* he wrote *Ancora dell'Inferno*, revealing an attitude to the poet-prisoner which is akin to that of Solzhenitsyn. He can be sardonically amusing in *A un poeta nemico* or ironic in *In questa città*. His lyrics *Dalla Grecia* combine history, myth, irony and lyricism in a new relaxed style as he describes the sites of ancient Greece. There are even echoes of d'Annunzio's myth-making: as Quasimodo stumbles on the temple steps at Delphi, twisting his ankle, he cannot resist the esoteric image of 'Phoebus Apollo, lifting his bow and shooting straight into my tendon'. The final collection, *Dare e avere* (1966), reflects the many and various journeys and experiences of the poet after the award of the Nobel prize. The mood is more contented, and though his Christian beliefs are often present here, as they had been in his previous poetry, they are never overwhelming. One of his last poems, written in hospital in 1965, shows his tranquillity as he meditates on 'the absurd difference between death and the illusion of our heart's beating' (*Ho fiori e di notte invito i pioppi*).

Like his two great contemporaries, Quasimodo was a prolific translator from other literatures; his translations range from Greek lyricists (with whom he, as a 'Sicilian Greek', felt a special affinity), to Ovid and Catullus, and Shakespeare, Pablo Neruda, E. E. Cummings, Paul Eluard and others. He was also renowned for his critical statements and is remembered for his work as a teacher at the Conservatorio Verdi in Milan (1940–67). Among his critical essays I have already noted his awareness of the literary revolution necessary after the war. Already by 1946 (in *Poesia contemporanea*) he had noted that it was the poet's new duty to 'remake' (*rifare*) man; this is his 'heavier commitment': the poet can no longer be considered 'extraneous to life', 'climbing his tower at night to speculate on the cosmos'. 'Il tempo delle speculazioni è finito. Rifare l'uomo, questo è l'impegno.' Contemporaneously with his brother-in-law, in the year preceding publication of that essay, Quasimodo enrolled in the communist party. It was to be the intellectuals grouped around Vittorini who would attempt to bring about a reform in narrative prose after the war. To that topic we must now briefly turn.

It is impertinent to dismiss in a few words the enormous output of prose fiction produced during the inter-war years, but if this essay is not to degenerate into a series of names, dates and titles I must become more summary and schematic in order to proceed as rapidly as possible to the important movement which tried to change the face of narrative prose after 1945. Generalizations *are* possible concerning the prose fiction published during the fascist era, because the censorship of the time, official or otherwise, ensured an atmosphere of conformity. Prose was usually much easier to read and understand than verse, especially the verse of the hermeticists. As such, it was also easier for the fascist censors to go to work. Exceptions prove the rule. Two striking examples of *active* writers who opposed the regime are provided by Emilo Lussu (1890–1975) and Ignazio Silone (1900–79) both of whom did publish good work – but in France and Switzerland respectively. Alberto Moravia (b. 1907) was able to publish his satire on dictatorship, *La mascherata,* in 1941, but had its second edition confiscated, presumably because its (not over-subtle) allegory was too complicated for the regime to understand the first time. Even authors who were able to write fiction during the inter-war years produced their better work only after the fall of the dictatorship. Yet there were many novelists earning a living in fascist Italy: the Nobel prize was won in 1926 by Grazia Deledda (1871–1936); Riccardo Bacchelli (b. 1891) wrote (writes) some of the longest novels produced outside Russia. Yet, again significantly, Deledda took the prize when Mussolini opposed its being given to the more peppery Matilde Serao (1857–1927), and Bacchelli is at his best when seeing history as romantic episodes, many of them shot through with Christian piety – exactly the sort of mild Manzonian escapism which the regime favoured. Even Bacchelli's best novel, the life story of the father of St Francis, *Non ti chiamerò più padre,* comes out as late as 1959. One of the most striking triumphs of that conservative tradition was the success, in 1958, of *Il Gattopardo,* the swan song of Giuseppe Tomasi di Lampedusa (1896–1957), a chronicle of change and decay in nineteenth-century Sicilian society, seen in microcosm through the fortunes of the noble Salina family. The novel was 'discovered' and publication secured by Giorgio Bassani (b. 1916), who would later pay personal tribute to the Manzonian tradition with the prefatory quotation from *I promessi sposi* which introduced his own widely acclaimed *Il giardino dei Finzi-Contini* in 1962; Manzonian linguistic preoccupations were already evident in the re-writing of so many of Bassani's early short stories. Understandably (inevitably!) more committed left-wing colleagues have accused Bassani of escapist writing, an unjust and shallow imputation.

To choose here between the many writers who deserve mention is bound to lead to an arbitrary list of names. Alberto Moravia, however, despite his many limitations as a novelist, must be included for his unconscious anticipation as early as 1929 of the new prose, in his novel *Gli indifferenti.* His youthful contempt for the traditional literary style was at once apparent (he said, for instance, that he added the punctuation to the book only after it was written); he also had the nerve to write openly on topics not normally broached in polite society; he satirized fascism in *I sogni del pigro* and *La mascherata* and got away with only minor inconvenience as a result (though after 1935 he spent much time away from Italy travelling); he was seen to anticipate Sartre's notions of existentialism. All these qualities helped to keep him popular (or hated) but, above all, he was able to tell a story, as the new American novelists seemed to do, without traditional Italian preoccupations with elaborating his literary style. It was the popularity of his name (projected, literally, before an enormous public on the cinema screen) that helped prepare the way for the realism of the post-war novelists and short-story writers. The sometimes sordid reality of his own short stories, their attention to metropolitan low life (especially of Rome) led on naturally to a host of similar compositions. Lack of sentimentality was another feature which from the beginning also endeared him to the young intellectuals – sentimentality seemed to be part of the despised bourgeois system. Further, his novels seemed to treat of recent or contemporary reality almost as if they were reportage: *La Romana* and *La Ciociara* reinforced that idea. His critical essays are important reflections of the periods in which they were written, *L'uomo come fine* being a particular fine collection. Some of Moravia's work is undoubtedly repetitive; he stopped writing *Racconti romani* when, having written so many, he found them indistinguishable one from the other. His nonconformity, his pugnacious scepticism, his refusal to belong to a group and, at the same time, his ability to keep up with fashion while maintaining his independence are his most admirable features.

Grazia Deledda had consolidated her reputation with the novels and stories set in her native Sardinia, notably *Elias Portolu* and *Canne al vento*. That 'provincial' tradition had become popular after the wider publicity given to Giovanni Verga's work long after the composition of his Sicilian tales. Deledda denied that she had been influenced by Verga, but a group of younger writers, also interested in regional culture, and, especially after 1936, more than ever opposed to fascism, looked upon Verga as a potential model. *I Malavoglia* seemed to be an exaltation of the poor and humble – the very antithesis of fascist vainglory and bombast. Coincidentally, then, several young writers, at about the time of Italy's aid to Franco's forces in the Spanish civil war, look to their regional, and often popular origins for their inspiration, Vasco Pratolini (b. 1913) to Florence, Elio Vittorini and Vitaliano Brancati (1907–54) to Sicily, Cesare Pavese (1908–50) to the *langhe* of Piedmont, Francesco Jovine (1902–50) to the Molise. The list could include a host of other names. Interest in regional features often deliberately brought into sharper focus differences between 'bourgeoisie' and 'working class' or peasant, between north and south, between language and dialect, between metropolis and countryside. During the final stages of the war many intellectuals joined in partisan brigades actively to oppose the nazi-fascists. They included Vittorini, Lussu, Italo Calvino (b. 1924), Beppe Fenoglio (1922–63), Carlo Levi (1902–75), Carlo Cassola (b. 1917) and many others. These future authors were brought into close contact with people of all classes – teachers, lawyers, shepherds, factory hands, peasants, professors, road-menders – under circumstances which virtually constrained them to live in harmony, if not friendship, if they were to survive against a temporarily more powerful enemy. It was to be the preoccupation with the realities of life, as opposed to what the young writers saw as the former escapism of 'bourgeois' life (tired word), that led to the tendency loosely classifiable as *neorealismo* (a blanket term which also covered the new cinema of De Sica, Rossellini and Zavattini). The harmony of their life as 'comrades' was also to call into question the deep divisions in Italian culture and society which had always existed.

In 1967 Italo Calvino published his own version of Ariosto's *Orlando furioso,* much abridged and 'linked' by racy, popular prose which owed little or nothing to the literary and linguistic tradition still dominant in Italy before the outbreak of the Second World War. At the same time, on records purchasable with his handbook, his readers could listen to the great epic. Calvino's attempt to render popular what he considered one of the world's greatest poems was followed by Alfredo Giuliani's anthology of Tasso's *Gerusalemme liberata* (1970), an undertaking with similar popularizing aims. Both publications are symptoms of the great divide of incomprehensibility which lies between the academic, 'aulic' tradition of Italian letters and the great majority of Italians. The two anthologies were also an indication of the need felt by socially responsible intellectuals in the post-war period to make available worthwhile reading material to an audience whose main reading, from elementary school onwards, had too often been limited to picture magazines, the *Gazzetta dello Sport* and illustrated comics, the *'fumetti'*. For the first time in the history of Italian literature, a concerted attempt was being made by groups of the country's most gifted and cultured individuals to write and work for a popular audience, to create a literature which Gramsci had defined as *nazional-popolare*, to 'involve' a nation divided more unhealthily than most by cultural and linguistic barriers.

The process was one which had begun in the final years of the war. The anti-fascist struggle had brought home to the popular masses their own importance in any future government. It had also demonstrated the inadequacy of the old ruling classes, symbolically rejected, perhaps, in the referendum which abolished the monarchy in 1946. Previous revolutions in taste had never concerned the popular masses; earlier cultural innovations had usually been of a purely formal kind. For years international power politics, as well as internal squabbles between socialists and communists in the peninsula, combined to keep the Left politically helpless at a national level, but culturally they were at work preparing radical changes in literary form and content. The experiences of writers exiled or imprisoned for expressing even mildly anti-fascist sentiments seemed to indicate that, for the foreseeable future, politics and literature would be indivisible. The avant-garde, then, took up an aggressive stance vis-à-vis the past. It substituted new content which seemed less remote from the popular masses, more 'relevant', to use another tired word, to contemporary society. Now, Manzoni had been the first European writer to choose his hero from the working classes; Verga had made the grinding poverty of the Sicilian fisherfolk into a great new epic. It is significant, then, that, in the new atmosphere, critics (notably Moravia and Vittorini) were quick to indicate the essentially bourgeois quality of the art in the *Promessi sposi* and even of *I Malavoglia*. They saw their authors as voyeurs, putting the poor on stage for the benefit of the only audience who could read about them, the traditional upper circle. Whether these views were critically valid or not, they do reveal a new outlook, a reappraisal of traditionally accepted artistic as well as social values.

Yet the reformers were probably, from the first, fighting a losing battle. The popular medium was bound to be the cinema and then television. The *Promessi sposi* has never been so popular as when it was televised, and Vasco Pratolini's most popular efforts on paper will never reach the audience that his screen version of *Metello* achieved. Attempts to write of and for the 'people' were interesting but, artistically, almost by definition, rarely great. Techniques included the folkloristic appeal of Calvino's *Marcovaldo* stories, his humorous or grim accounts of recently past experiences of the partisans and above all his trilogy *I nostri antenati,* which seems to appeal to half-remembered folklore instincts or recall adventure stories of boyhood in order to capture the interest of a non-bourgeois audience wishing to be entertained by an exciting and, some say, morally instructive book. Pratolini's novels work in a different way. *Cronache di poveri amanti,* for example, are intriguing semi-autobiographical reminiscences, while *Il quartiere* beautifully reconstructs the early fascist period and indicts the social injustice of the time. Carlo Levi chronicled the experiences of his political exile in Lucania in the powerful and moving *Cristo si è fermato a Eboli*. Vittorini, after the success of the beautiful *Conversazione in Sicilia,* becomes simply harrowing in his (too obvious?) attacks on the viciousness of fascism in *Uomini e no,* and upon the viciousness of society in *Erica e i suoi fratelli*. One of their more prolific writers who deserves a mention here was Cesare Pavese, generally considered an opponent of the fascists – he was imprisoned briefly and later exiled (1935–6) for unspecified political activity. Yet it is difficult now to find much commitment in his work. He and his characters, even his partisans (including *Il compagno*), are so wrapped up in their own emotions that greater issues seem to pass them by. Pavese's suicide in 1950 probably came about for a combination of reasons – frustration in love, an obsessive preoccupation with his own cosmic depression and, one cannot help wondering, a general boredom with life and society. Carlo Bo viewed efforts at creating a 'new' literature as gropings in the dark (though, reviewing the authors of 1979, he chooses Calvino's most recent experiment in narrative prose as the outstanding literary achievement of the year). The greatness and the originality of the Italian mind lies in its independence and individuality, and here we must look for fresh genius. The man who bestrides the period we have been considering is Carlo Emilio Gadda (1893–1973). As his difficult style and language become more familiar his vast production will be seen as a new peak in Italian literary achievement.

Short Bibliography

(This list is intended only as a pointer to further study)

GENERAL WORKS

Enciclopedia Italiana Treccani – for articles on separate authors, with bibliography.

Dizionario Enciclopedico Italiano. Vol. VI: Umberto Bosco, 'Profilo storico della letteratura italiana'.

HISTORIES OF ITALIAN LITERATURE

Storia Letteraria d'Italia ('Le Origini', 'Il Duecento', 'Dante', 'Il Trecento', 'Il Quattrocento', 'Il Cinquecento', 'Il Seicento', 'Il Settecento', 'L'Ottocento', 'Il Novecento'). Milan (Vallardi). 10 vols. The latest collaborators in this fundamental series are: M. APOLLONIO, A. BELLONI, G. BERTONI, A. GALLETTI, G. MAZZONI, G. NATALI, V. ROSSI, N. SAPEGNO, G. TOFFANIN, and A. VISCARDI.

FLORA, FRANCESCO. *Storia della letteratura italiana*. Milan (Mondadori), 1947. 5 vols. (Also school edition in 3 vols.)

RUSSO, LUIGI. *Storia della letteratura italiana*, Vol. I. Florence, 1957.

MOMIGLIANO, A. *Storia della letteratura italiana*. 1935–6. 3 vols.

DE SANCTIS, FRANCESCO. *Storia della letteratura italiana* (ed. by B. Croce). Bari, 1954. 2 vols.

SANSONE, MARIO. *La letteratura italiana*. Bari, 1956–7. 3 vols.

CROCE, BENEDETTO. *La letteratura della Nuova Italia*. Bari, 1949–56. 6 vols.

Other recent histories of Italian literature are by G. ZONTA, N. SAPEGNO, G. PAPINI, and V. ROSSI.

ANTHOLOGIES

DIONISOTTI, CARLO (ed.). *Oxford Book of Italian Verse*. New edition. 1952.

KAY, GEORGE (ed.). *The Penguin Book of Italian Verse*. 1958.

PERIODICALS

Italian Studies. Published for the Society for Italian Studies by W. Heffer & Sons, Cambridge. An annual review edited by E. R. VINCENT, R. WEISS, J. H. WHITFIELD, and E. K. WATER-HOUSE. Vol. XIV, 1959.
Giornale Storico della Letteratura Italiana.
Lettere Italiane.
La Rassegna.
Nuova Antologia.
Delta. Etc.

TEXTS

Cheap editions are published by the Biblioteca Universale Rizzoli and (recent authors) the Biblioteca Moderna Mondadori.

Other editions are: Classici Mondadori, Classici Rizzoli, Classici italiani Sansoni (a new series). The Scrittori d'Italia, Bari (Laterza), are an unannotated series of over 200 vols., but have authoritative texts. La Letteratura italiana – Storia e testi, Milan (Ricciardi), is at present in course of completion; a series of large well-printed volumes which cover all the works of major authors, or anthologize a century.

Divina Commedia. DANTE. It is important to use the edition of the Società Dantesca of 1921, or later editions which reprint this critical text. There is a variety of adequate Italian commentaries in print, but no satisfactory one in English. There are useful translations by L. BINYON, J. D. SINCLAIR, and DOROTHY L. SAYERS (Penguin Classics).

LITERARY CRITICISM

BINNI, W. *I Classici italiani nella storia della critica.* Florence, 1954–5. 2 vols.
APOLLONIO, M. *Uomini e forme nella cultura italiana delle origini.* Florence, 1934.
SAPEGNO, N. *Frate Jacopone.* Turin, 1926.
FIGURELLI, F. *Il dolce stil novo.* Naples, 1933.
MAGGINI, F. *Introduzione allo studio di Dante.* Bari, 1936.
BARBI, M. *Dante, vita, opere, e fortuna.* Florence, 1933.
COSMO, U. *Vita di Dante.* Bari, 1930.

Short Bibliography

COSMO, U. *A Handbook to Dante Studies*. Oxford, 1950.

GILSON, E. *Dante the Philosopher*. London, 1948.

WHITFIELD, J. H. *Dante and Virgil*. Oxford, 1949.

WHITFIELD, J. H. *Petrarch and the Renascence*. Oxford, 1943.

BOSCO, U. *Petrarca*. 1946.

BRANCA, V. *Boccaccio Medievale*. 1956.

BRANCA, V. *Boccaccio*. 1957.

BARON, H. *The Crisis of the Early Italian Renaissance*. London, 1955.

FERGUSON, W. K. *The Renaissance in Historical Thought*. Boston, 1948.

GARIN, E. *Il Rinascimento italiano*. Florence 1941.

GARIN, E. *Medioevo e Rinascimento*. Bari, 1954.

PALMAROCCHI, R. *Lorenzo de' Medici*. Turin, 1941.

BIGI, E. *La Poesia del Boiardo*. Florence, 1941.

CARRARA, E. *I due Orlandi*. Turin, 1935.

HAUVETTE, H. *L'Arioste et la poésie chevaleresque à Ferrare*. Paris, 1927.

RIDOLFI, R. *Vita di Niccolò Machiavelli*. Rome, 1954.

WHITFIELD, J. H. *Machiavelli*. Oxford, 1947.

DONADONI, E. *Torquato Tasso*. Florence, 1936.

CROCE, B. *Storia dell' Età Barocca in Italia*. Bari, 1929.

GETTO, G. *Paolo Sarpi*. Pisa, 1941.

RUSSO, L. *Metastasio*. Bari, 1945.

CHATFIELD-TAYLOR, H. C. *Goldoni*. Bari, 1927.

CAPRIN, G. *Carlo Goldoni*. Milan, 1907.

FUBINI, M. *Vittorio Alfieri*. Florence, 1937.

VINCENT, E. R. *Ugo Foscolo: An Italian in Regency England*. Cambridge, 1953.

TONELLI, L. *Manzoni*. Milan, 1928.

COLQUHOUN, A. *Manzoni and his Times*. London, 1954.

ORIGO, IRIS. *Leopardi: A Biography*. Oxford, 1935. New ed. London, 1953.

WHITFIELD, J. H. *Giacomo Leopardi*. Oxford, 1954.

NARDI, P. *Antonio Fogazzaro*. Milan, 1938.

CAPPELLANI, N. *La Vita e le opere di Giovanni Verga*. Florence, 1940, 2 vols.

SAPONARO, M. *Carducci*. Milan, 1940.

LO VECCHIO MUSTI, M. *L'opera di Luigi Pirandello*. Turin, 1938.

WHITFIELD, J. H. 'Pirandello and T. S. Eliot: An Essay in Counterpoint.' *English Miscellany* 9, ed. Mario Praz. Rome, 1958.

Short Bibliography

Italian works available in translation in the Penguin Classics series are:

ALIGHIERI, DANTE. *The Divine Comedy* I and II. Trans. Dorothy L. Sayers. 1949 and 1955.

CELLINI, BENVENUTO. *Autobiography.* Trans. George Bull. 1956.

DELLA CASA, GIOVANNI. *Galateo.* Trans. R.S. Pine-Coffin. 1958.

For an extended bibliography see volumes of the *Storia della letteratura italiana*, published by Garzanti in the 1960s under the general editorship of Emilio Cecchi and Natalino Sapegno. Eight vols: I, *Le origini e il Duecento*; II, *Il Trecento*; III, *Il Quattrocento e l'Ariosto*; IV, *Il Cinquecento*; V, *Il Seicento*; VI, *Il Settecento*; VII, *L'Ottocento*; VIII, *Il Novecento* (from 1965).

Index